COLLECTOR'S GUIDE TO
VICTORIANA

Wallace-Homestead Collector's Guide™ Series

Harry L. Rinker, Series Editor

Collector's Guide to Autographs, by Helen Sanders, George Sanders, Ralph Roberts
Collector's Guide to Baseball Cards, by Troy Kirk
Collector's Guide to Comic Books, by John Hegenberger
Collector's Guide to Early Photographs, by O. Henry Mace
Collector's Guide to Quilts, by Suzy McLennan Anderson
Collector's Guide to Toy Trains, by Al and Susan Bagdade

COLLECTOR'S GUIDE TO
VICTORIANA

O. HENRY MACE

Wallace-Homestead Collector's Guide™ Series

Wallace-Homestead Book Company

Radnor, Pennsylvania

Designed by Anthony Jacobson
Cover photo of front parlor of General Phineas Banning Residence Museum, Los Angeles, California.
All photographs by the author.
Manufactured in the United States of America

Library of Congress Cataloging in Publication Data
Mace, O. Henry.
    Collector's guide to Victoriana / O. Henry Mace.
      p.   cm.—(Wallace-Homestead collector's guide series)
    Includes index.
    ISBN 0-87069-600-9 (hc)—ISBN 0-87069-576-2 (pb)
      1. Antiques, Victorian—Catalogs.   2. Decorative arts—Catalogs.
  I. Title.   II. Series.
  NK1378.M3   1991
  745.1′09′034075—dc20   91-7638
                                                                CIP

1 2 3 4 5 6 7 8 9 0   0 9 8 7 6 5 4 3 2 1

For Kathryn,
a reincarnated Victorian

Contents

less-formal homes the kitchen was the center of the household, where mother taught her daughters homemaking skills.

5. The Back Parlor 75

The back parlor served as the music room, den, library, or family room depending on the whims of the homeowner. Regardless of its designation, it was the center of family life, where each family member brought his or her favorite pastime to enjoy in the presence of others.

6. The Sewing Room 89

The sewing room belonged solely to madam, and served as her refuge to read, rest, write, gossip, enjoy her hobbies, and even, on occasion, sew.

7. The Library 103

The master's domain, the library was a place where cherished books and important papers were kept, friends were entertained, and family business was conducted.

8. Her Bedroom 122

The bedroom was madam's sanctuary, where she shared intimacy with her spouse; dressed and primped herself for visitors; conceived, bore, and nursed her children; and eventually died.

9. His Bedroom 150

Although the master spent as little time as possible in his bedroom, it still revealed his influence and contained the accoutrements of a hardworking businessman who had time only to sleep, wash, and dress there.

10. The Children's Room 164

The boy's bedroom was cluttered with pictures of horses and dogs, fishing rods, books, frogs and spiders in jars, and a sled under the bed. The girl's bedroom was a castle of laces and frills, dolls, and puzzles.

11. Miscellaneous Victorian Collectibles 179

Cameras; Civil War artifacts; architectural pieces; advertising giveaways; coin-operated machines; firefighting, police, and railroad relics and other antiques share the history and flavor of the Victorian era.

12. Guide to Restoration, Preservation, and Storage   198

Whether made of wood, metal, or other materials, collectibles from the Victorian era need special care. Methods of cleaning, restoring, refinishing and storing valuable pieces are clearly described.

Appendix   204

Index   211

Preface

The term "Victorian" has been, and will continue to be, misused and abused by a variety of writers, publishers, architects, historians, antiques collectors, and others. Since Webster lived in Victorian times, let's take a look at how his namesake dictionary describes the term.

> Vic-to′ri-an, **a.** 1. of or characteristic of the time when Victoria was queen of England (1837–1901). 2. showing the middle-class respectability, prudery, bigotry, etc. generally attributed to the Victorians. 3. designating or of a style of furniture of the 19th century, characterized by ornate, flowery carving and patterned upholstery.
> **n.** a person, especially a writer, who lived in the reign of Queen Victorian.[1]

Ah! There's the rub: "of or characteristic of." This allows anyone to use the term "Victorian" to describe anything that looks like anything that was produced from 1837 to 1901. What's worse, the term "Victoriana" isn't even listed, giving rise to a variety of books with "Victoriana" in their titles whose contents are as varied as their writers. Upon examining these numerous volumes, one might conclude that Victoriana means any group of items from the Victorian period that

[1] *Webster's New Universal Unabridged Dictionary.* New York: Simon and Schuster, 1979.

appeals to a particular person. But if Victorian means "of the time of Victoria," then Victoriana must relate to every item produced during that time. Therefore, this book is a guide for collectors of items produced during the years 1837 to 1901.

Like most writers I have fallen prey to the restrictions of time and space, which creates the challenge of what to put in and what to leave out. Since we are talking about every object or device produced during a period of sixty-four years, there was much that had to be left out. To help make those decisions, I traveled to antiques shops and Victorian museums across the United States. I perused countless volumes of *Harper's, Godey's,* the *Art Journal,* and other magazines and catalogs of the period. In the end I was able to visualize each room of the average Victorian home and picture the variety of objects found therein. These are the items that touched the daily lives of the average Victorian—the true Victoriana.

As you read this book, you'll visit that average Victorian home in your mind's eye. You'll find out what each room looked like, how it was used, and what objects were found there. Then we'll examine each of the objects in the room, learn how they were manufactured and used, and find out how and why those objects are collected today. You'll learn what to watch for and avoid and find out how much collectors are paying for certain pieces.

When buying Victoriana, remember that value, like beauty, is in the eye of the beholder. Each item in this book has been given a price range based on current values for similar objects in good condition. In cases where the range is especially wide (usually due to regional supply and demand factors or an abundant variety of styles), an average price is given. Gather as much information on the field as you can, then use these figures as a guide and pay what the item is worth to you. Occasionally you will discover that you have paid too much for a particular piece. However, just as often, you'll come across a wonderful bargain.

The Suggested Reading list at the end of each section notes a book or books containing information more specific to the particular subject. Wherever possible, the most recent and obtainable volumes are listed. Unfortunately, many subjects have not been written about in many years, and the books listed are now out of print. These often can be found at your local library or can be obtained for purchase at used book stores.

A Word About Victorian Furniture

The terms and designations that are used to describe antique furniture are seemingly endless—and ultimately confusing and vague. Styles are named for their designers (such as Chippendale and Eastlake), for the rulers of countries (such as Louis XV and Queen Anne), and for period influences (such as Greek Revival and Renaissance Revival). There is also Georgian, Baroque, Chinese, Rococo, Spool, Gothic, Jacobean, Cottage, Mission, Windsor, Art Nouveau, Federal, and others. To add to the confusion, many pieces of furniture combine elements of two or more of these styles together.

For the purposes of this book, I have chosen to include mostly common, factory-made furniture of the type typically associated with manufacturers in the city of Grand Rapids, Michigan, from the 1850s until the turn of the century. This was the inexpensive, mass-produced furniture found in the average middle-class Victorian home and is the type of Victorian furniture that is most accessible to today's collector. This furniture was generally produced in French Revival (including Rococo, Louis XIV, Louis XV, Louis XVI), Renaissance Revival, and Eastlake styles (see the Introduction for descriptions). Where research shows that a particular piece of furniture was especially popular in a style other than those just noted, I have included that style as well or instead of the other style.

A Word from the Wise

People collect Victoriana for a wide variety of reasons. Some collect it for the beauty, some for the history, and some for the investment. Regardless of your reasons for collecting, you will achieve the greatest degree of enjoyment and satisfaction from your efforts through a thorough and continuous education. Read every book and magazine you can find on the subject. Join a collector's club or clubs. Talk to experts whenever and wherever you get the chance.

There are many old adages that are appropriately applied to the field of antique collecting, but probably the most important is "Never buy a pig in a poke." In other words, before you pay good money and take it home, make sure you know what you're buying. About ten years ago my wife and I came across a wonderful Victorian-style clock with a hand-painted face and rich walnut frame. The seller said the clock didn't run, but that it could be repaired easily for very little money. After a bit of dickering, we took the clock home for the bargain price of $140 ("Never look a gift horse in the mouth"). I proudly wiped away the dust from its flawless frame and rushed down to the local clock repair shop, only to return an hour later with my newly purchased albatross in tow. The repairer called it "one of the finest Victorian reproductions ever made," circa 1960. The mechanical works, frozen by exposure to saltwater, were worthless. His estimation of the value of the face and frame was $40 ("Never judge a book by its cover").

Today, my library contains at least three good books covering every type of object I collect and many more on objects I might someday want to buy. My investment in books has been returned many times as they have helped me recognize bargains and avoid rip-offs. And yes, even though I am not a clock collector, I have five books on clocks ("Better late than never").

Acknowledgments

I owe a great debt of gratitude to the many antiques shop owners nationwide who extended their hospitality and provided important regional information for this book. A special thanks goes to those in my home state (California) who graciously allowed me to photograph items from their stock, including Jensen's Antiques, Amador City; Leepers Fantastic Antiques, Orange; Georgia Fox, Foxes Den, Sutter Creek; and William's Antiques, Ione.

For their cooperation and assistance in the photography of both interiors and artifacts, my thanks go to the following museums and their administrators: General Phineas Banning Residence Museum, Los Angeles, Ms. Zoe Bergquist; McHenry Mansion, Modesto, Mr. Wayne Mathes; Bernhard Museum Complex, Placer County Parks and Museums, Auburn, Ms. Doris Parker-Coons; and Amador County Museum, Jackson, Mr. Cedric Clute.

Finally, thanks go to Kathryn, my researcher, gaffer, spellchecker, gofer, filekeeper, receptionist, and wife.

COLLECTOR'S GUIDE TO
VICTORIANA

Introduction

When she was born on May 24, 1819, no one expected that the little princess, christened Alexandrina Victoria, ever would become Queen of England. She was far down on the list of accession. But following a series of events that can only be attributed to destiny, the eighteen-year-old Victoria became queen upon the death of her uncle, King William IV. On June 20, 1837, the Victorian era was born.

During the sixty-four years of Victoria's reign, the photograph, telegraph, telephone, electric light, and phonograph were introduced and the radio and automobile were conceived. Emily Brontë wrote *Wuthering Heights,* Poe wrote "The Raven," and Dickens wrote *A Christmas Carol.* Men's hats progressed from top hats to derbies to panamas; and ladies wore crinolines, bustles, and, finally, trousers. Abner Doubleday invented baseball, P. D. Armour opened a meat-packing plant in Chicago, and the United States celebrated its one-hundredth year with the Centennial Exhibition. Those six-and-one-half decades were, without question, the most active and productive period the world had known.

The people of the Victorian era had an insatiable thirst for living. Rich or poor, they looked upon possessions as a sign of achievement. They always bought the best they could afford. Among the middle and upper classes, this included a wide variety of luxuries: art, sculpture, decorative glass and ceramics, and souvenirs. Inventive minds provided an endless supply of gadgets and mechanical devices ranging from the absurd to the indispensable. The Victorians were—like you—collectors.

Style was important to the Victorians, and much of the established thought in this area came from Victoria's own England. Henry Cole organized the Royal Society for the Encouragement of Arts, Manufacturers, and Commerce Exhibition in 1847. Prince Albert's brainchild, the Great Exhibition of 1851, did much to establish trends in style. Unfortunately, at the time, the styles it established were not considered in the best of taste. In the 1870s and 1880s, Britons Charles Eastlake and William Morris helped set the latest trends.

Changes in Victorian taste and style are best seen in the development of furniture designs throughout the period. When Victoria took the throne in 1837, the then-current furniture style was Empire, represented by heavy wooden frames with classical, curving silhouettes. Representative of this style are the scroll-end sofa and the sleigh bed. This style was supplanted by the Gothic and French Revival styles of the 1840s.

Gothic furniture is characterized by "tracery" (interlocking carved arches and cutouts) and other Gothic carvings. Much more popular was the French Revival style called Rococo because of its elaborate, high-relief carved trimwork. Ornamentation in the form of seashells, leaves, grapes, and flowers; and curving "cabriole" legs are characteristic of the Louis XIV, Louis XV, and Rococo French Revival styles. Recognizable examples include the balloon-back chair and the tête-à-tête sofa.

To add confusion to an already complicated subject, one French Revival style, Louis XVI, bears little or no resemblance to its earlier cousins. With round or oval backs and seats, Gothic-style framework, and turned spool legs that later were "borrowed" by Renaissance Revival designers, Louis XVI furniture looks much like it was put together from parts left over from all the other Victorian styles.

Renaissance Revival furniture (from 1850) often is confused with French Revival because it, too, is characterized by elaborately carved ornamentation. However, Renaissance furniture lacks the distinguishing curve of its French-inspired predecessors and incorporates a variety of architectural elements (arches, pediments, columns, and so forth). Its front legs are always round and straight, in the "turned" style of Louis XVI. With the introduction of the Eastlake style in the 1870s, many furniture manufacturers began to combine elements of the two styles. These usually lean toward one style and are said to be influenced by the other.

Charles Eastlake was a British architect and lecturer who in 1868 published an influential book on design called *Hints on Household Taste.* It is interesting that the style that became known as Eastlake violates many of the rules that its originator set down. Eastlake furniture is characterized by sharp, rectilinear shapes with "turned" ornamentation, geometric trimwork, mother-of-pearl inlays, and "incised" decorations. Legs are turned or square-cut. Even though Eastlake, the Briton, advocated a return to the quality handmade furniture of bygone eras, most Eastlake furniture was machine-made in the industrialized United States.

In addition to these recognized "styles," a variety of common and "patent" furniture was produced as well. Because pine and maple furniture commonly was used in country homes, these basic early pieces have been referred to as Country or Cottage furniture. Even in wealthier households, Cottage furniture saw use in the kitchen and servant's quarters. Cottage furniture often incorporated elements of design from established earlier styles such as William and Mary or Queen Anne. Patent furniture refers primarily to mechanical pieces that folded, rocked, or converted into another form. Examples of patent furniture include the platform rocker, the convertible high chair (which changed into a carriage), and the Wooton desk (which opened to reveal an entire office in one unit).

For anyone who has seen a contemporary photograph of a typical Victorian parlor, one thing becomes immediately obvious: The Victorians liked clutter. The walls are covered with floral wallpapers in busy patterns. Curtains are tassled and lined with ornate lace. Lace also adorns every table, and lace or crocheted protectors cover chair backs and arms. Tables are covered with decorative cups, plates, vases, and urns. Sitting among these are framed photographs and souvenirs from trips to Europe, Asia, Africa, or maybe an American beach or mountain resort. Magazine racks are overstuffed with copies of *Harper's, Godey's, Peterson's, Leslie's,* and various catalogs touting miracle cures and the latest mechanical kitchen devices.

The average Victorian home had at least ten rooms. These would include a front parlor; dining room; kitchen; back parlor or sitting room; a

I-1 Floor plan for a three-bedroom, two-story home, as shown in an 1889 architectural guide.

study or library; a sewing room; one bed chamber for the master of the house and one for the madam; and two additional chambers that may have been children's rooms, guest rooms, or rooms with other purposes.

Wealthier homes also may have had a reception room, servant's quarters, a number of additional bedrooms, and perhaps even a ballroom. Downstairs rooms usually were interconnected via large doorways with sliding doors. A large entry hall served as a centralized access to the front exterior of the house, the main stairway to the second floor, and often to other connecting rooms on the lower level. Upstairs rooms were linked by a central hallway that often was quite large and handsomely decorated. The estimated building cost of a typical ten-room Victorian in 1888 was $3750. It could be completely furnished for around one thousand dollars.

The oldest Victorian-period antiques are now over 150 years old, the youngest are at least ninety. Soon, the last of the true "Victorians"—those with vivid memories of the pre-1901 period—will have passed into history. But the Victoriana, those fascinating items that were a part of their everyday life, will survive for centuries to come.

CHAPTER 1

The Entry Hall

The entry hall of a Victorian home was not really a hall as we know it, but a room with a specific function. It was the first room you entered when you passed through the front door, and therefore its primary purpose was as a place of greeting. In wealthier homes the visitor was met by a butler with a silver tray or *calling card receiver* upon which you would place your calling card, or *carte de visite,* so that it could be taken to the master or madam of the house. If you were to be received, the butler would return to take your hat and wrap and, after placing them on a *hall tree,* direct you to the front parlor where you would wait for your host.

The hall tree (or hall stand) was a tall piece of furniture placed flush against one wall. In addition to hooks for items of clothing, the hall tree also contained a mirror so that the visitor could check his or her appearance while waiting. It also had an *umbrella stand* to store dripping umbrellas. Some hall stands included a storage box for overshoes and a drawer for gloves.

If a hall stand was absent, one might expect to find a number of individual pieces of furniture that served the same functions: a *hall table,* a *pier mirror* above the table, an umbrella stand, and possibly an accordion-style *hatrack.* If the visitor was a stranger, or if there was some doubt as to whether he might be received, he might be asked to wait in the entry hall. *Side chairs* were provided for this purpose (see Side Chairs in Chapter 3, The Dining Room), or, in large entry halls, a *settee* was used.

The decor of the entry hall was kept simple yet classy. It had to be impressive without overshadowing the front parlor. The floors of many entry halls were made of marble or ceramic tile placed in decorative patterns. The lower half of the wall often was covered in fine wood panels or embossed tin. If expense was a problem, the walls might be covered with paper or painted to give the appearance of marble or wood grain. Unlike other rooms, the upper walls and ceiling of the entry hall usually were painted in solid colors, although occasionally patterned wall coverings were used. The ceiling may have been covered with embossed tin tiles if not simply painted a solid color. At the point where the wall and ceiling met, decorative carved wood or a painted paper divider almost always was used (see *Cornice* and *Frieze* in Chapter 2, The Front Parlor introduction). In the center of the ceiling was a molded rosette from which hung a fine *chandelier.*

In entry halls where space and design permitted, a *tall case clock* (now called a grandfather clock) often was displayed. The only other small

4

items to be found in this room were *doorstops, boot scrapers,* and some decorative items such as framed prints, statuary, and vases (see Chapter 2, The Front Parlor). In homes where live greenery was kept, the entry hall usually contained one or more large urns that held tall, leafy plants.

From the entry hall one might proceed to the connecting front parlor and up the stairway to the upper hall; or down the main hall to the dining room, kitchen, or back parlor.

Boot or Foot Scrapers

Throughout the nineteenth century, the United States was the destination of millions of immigrants heading for the United States, "where the streets are paved with gold." Not only were the streets not paved with gold, but in most places they weren't paved at all. In both small towns and major cities, it was not unusual to see wagons and buggies buried to their axles in mud during the winter months. While this condition was the cause of much annoyance, the gentlemen who were bound by chivalry to carry ladies from the carriage to the door seldom complained.

Upon reaching the entry hall, the young Sir Walter could remove the mud from his boots with the aid of a boot scraper. Usually this item was made of heavy, decorative cast iron and sat on the floor, often atop last week's copy of *Harper's Weekly.* A tree of metal, with a flat area along the top for scraping, rose up about six inches from a wide plate that acted as the base and (theoretically) captured the falling mud. As with most decorative Victorian ironwork, the designs usually were ornate Rococo patterns, although some patriotic and character pieces were produced. Boot scrapers also were manufactured with marble bases, in brass, and in wood.

The collector is cautioned that boot scrapers have been produced from time to time throughout the twentieth century as decorative novelties. Careful consideration should be given before paying a high price (occasionally as much as $1000)

for a Victorian boot scraper. Study nineteenth-century cast iron and decorative metalwork techniques as thoroughly as possible.

Prices of Victorian boot scrapers are affected by materials used, complexity of design, identification of manufacturer (if any), and condition of the piece.

Price Range

Boot scrapers: $75 (wood) to $1200. Average: $125 (with high-quality decorative ironwork).

Suggested Reading

McNerney, Kathryn. *Antique Iron.* Paducah, Ky.: Collector Books, 1984.

Schiffer, Peter, *et al. Antique Iron: A Survey of American and English Forms, 15th through 19th Centuries.* West Chester, Pa.: Schiffer Publishing, 1979.

Calling Cards

Although the practice of carrying calling (or visiting) cards with one's name imprinted on them had been in vogue for several centuries, it was during the Victorian era that the custom became widely accepted. Usually the cards were carried in the gentleman's coat pocket or lady's purse in a calling card case (see Chapter 8, Her Bedroom). The cards were freely passed out to friends and business acquaintances and were required by the butler who greeted you at visitations (see also Calling Card Receivers and Cartes de Visite). Although the occurrence of dueling was considerably less frequent than during the previous century, the exchange of cards was an important part of preduel etiquette, usually preceded by the stinging slap of leather gloves across the face.

Calling cards were seldom printed with more than the person's name, although cards including the individual's occupation are not uncommon. Any additional information required (addresses, appointments, and so forth) could be written on the back in pen or pencil.

1-1 A selection of visiting cards.

Although most cards carried by "persons of breeding" were very plain with classic imprints, both men's and ladies' cards often had colorful emboss-printed chromolithographic overlays, glued at one end so that they could be lifted to reveal the name. (These overlays, as well as other larger chromolithographic pieces, were called "scrap" and were collected in albums by Victorian ladies and children.) During the latter part of the century, visiting cards were cut into unusual shapes with clever, elaborate overlays or printed designs.

Today, Victorian calling cards are collected by a large and ever-growing group that specializes in nineteenth-century printed paper ephemera. Since the average calling card in good, clean condition with a nice overlay usually sells for around $3, they are a wonderfully inexpensive way to own a small, romantic piece of the Victorian era. Cards with information handwritten in the flowing Spencerian style of the period are highly prized by collectors, as are those with unusual shapes or elaborate overlays.

Price Range

Visiting cards: 50¢ (ordinary cards without overlays) to $25 (cards with imprints of famous people).

Suggested Reading

Hart, Grossman, and Dunhill. *Victorian Scrapbook.* New York: Workman Publishing, 1989.

Calling Card Receivers

The elegant custom of leaving ones' visiting card required an equally elegant device to use as part of this ritual. The calling card receiver varied from a simple silver tray to elaborate decorative pieces in silver and glass. The receiver usually sat on the hall table where it was easily accessible to the butler, and where visitors who had not yet left their card might do so. In many cases the highly ornate receiver served a function more decorative than service oriented. One style, often used in illustrations, was produced in silver plate by Meriden Silver Plate Company of Meriden, Connecticut. It consisted of a silver cherub riding a blue

1-2 Silver-plated visiting card receiver. (Courtesy Georgia Fox, Foxes Den)

glass cornucopia vase attached to a two-wheeled, shell-shaped chariot on an ornate platform (approximate value: $350). Cards were placed on the gilded surface of the shell.

Receivers are not always recognizable as such and often appear to be some sort of serving tray. Sometimes these are only identified by comparison with illustrations in Victorian catalogs and other reference materials. Since most receivers are made—at least in part—with silver, several styles are usually shown in books on Victorian silver and in antique silver price guides.

Prices of Victorian card receivers are based on size and complexity of design, materials used, and condition.

Price Ranges

Card receivers (glass and porcelain): $25 to $150.
Card receivers (silver plate, alone or in combination with other materials): $75 to $500+ (depending on complexity of design).

Suggested Reading

Davidson, Marshall B. *American Heritage History of Antiques from the Civil War to World War I*. New York: American Heritage, 1969.
Feild, Rachel. *McDonald Guide to Buying Antique Silver and Plate*. Philadelphia: Trans-Atlantic Publications, 1988.
Fennimore, Donald L. *Silver and Pewter*. New York: Alfred A. Knopf, 1984.

Cartes de Visite

In 1854 a French photographer named André-Adolphe-Eugène Disdéri devised a way of taking

1-3 Carte de visite, circa 1880s.

eight individual photographic portraits on a single negative. When printed, these separate images were cut apart and glued to calling-card-sized mounts to be used as visiting cards (*carte de visite* in French). These were used in much the same manner as the calling card, but received wider use and often were collected in albums designed specifically for the purpose.

The *carte de visite* was extremely popular in America, especially during the Civil War (1861–65). Later, commercially made cartes depicted famous celebrities, landmarks, inventions, and historical events in both the United States and Europe. These are highly prized by collectors, as are images produced by well-known photographers of the period such as Mathew Brady, Nadar, Napoleon Sarony, André-Adolphe-Eugéne Disdéri, Julia Cameron, Oscar Gustave Rejlander, Henry Peach Robinson, Lewis Carroll, and others. In the past some of these have brought in excess of $1000 at auction.

Nice, clean *carte* portraits of interesting subjects usually sell for around $1 to $2. Prices are affected by subject, photographer, condition, and supply and demand.

Price Range

Cartes de visite: 25¢ to $100 Some rare *cartes* are more expensive. Average: $2.50.

Suggested Reading

Darrah, William C. *Cartes de Visite in Nineteenth-Century Photography.* Self-published, 1981.

Mace, O. Henry. *Collector's Guide to Early Photographs.* Radnor, Pa.: Wallace-Homestead Book Company, 1989.

Chandeliers

It is quite possible that Victorian architects designed the typically high ceilings of nineteenth-century homes specifically to provide space for elaborate chandeliers. There is no doubt that these ornate iron, brass, and crystal ceiling lights

1-4 Brass chandelier set up for gas (upper) and electric (lower) lighting. (Courtesy Georgia Fox, Foxes Den)

became a strong status symbol, much like our automobiles of today. In an era when the average income seldom topped $10 a week, quality chandeliers sometimes cost in excess of $1000.

While the best examples (of the type produced in crystal by Tiffany and Company) usually were reserved for the front parlor, it was necessary to have a fine chandelier in the entry hall for that all-important first impression. Often the base and arms of the fixture were ornate brass with a multitude of glass "fingers" dangling from them. Surrounding each flame (or bulb) was a fancy cut-glass globe.

New lighting methods and devices constantly were being invented as the century progressed. At the end of the 1700s, whale oil and beeswax candles were the primary light sources. During the 1840s and 1850s, central gas lighting and heating were introduced, and finally, in 1880, Thomas Edison introduced the electric light bulb. By 1900 a great number of existing light fixtures had been converted to electricity.

Most Victorian chandeliers found in today's market date from the turn of the century. Early examples are naturally quite valuable, especially if in good, original condition. Examples by Tiffany have brought in excess of $25,000 at auction. Because of the variety of styles and embellishments that were produced (the lighting fixture business was quite lucrative in the late nineteenth century), there are examples to fit nearly every taste or pocketbook.

Price Range

Chandeliers: $75 (simple chain and candle holder designs) to $10,000+ (elaborate brass and crystal by well-known manufacturers).

Suggested Reading

Thomas, Jo Ann. *Early Twentieth Century Lighting Fixtures.* Paducah, Ky.: Collector Books, 1980.

Doorstops

Around the time that our forebears shut the door on the British Empire and declared independence, a clever person invented a device that would automatically shut the doors on our homes. The new device was very handy—except when we wanted to keep our doors open. So another clever fellow invented the doorstop, a decorative piece made of heavy materials kept near the door for use as a prop.

Doorstops from the Victorian period often were appropriately elaborate and gaudy. They were produced in a variety of materials, including wood, cast iron, brass, bronze, lead, ceramic, and glass. These materials were molded, beaten, or carved into nearly every shape one could imagine—and especially celebrities and characters from fiction. Probably the best-known design was a likeness of the character Punch, based on the

1-5 Victorian lady wrought-iron doorstop with original paint. (Courtesy Jensen's Antiques)

drawings of Richard Doyle. Other popular subjects included dogs, cats, horses and jockeys, flowers (often in baskets or bowls), band members, cottages, circus performers, and a variety of common and exotic animals.

Once again we remind the collector that modern reproductions abound and this is especially true in this category. The average price for an original Victorian doorstop ranges from $100 to $300. Examples offered for substantially less may be reproductions. Prices are affected by material used, complexity of design, identification of manufacturer, and condition.

NOTE: Do not attempt to restore painted doorstops by repainting. Pieces in original condition bring the highest prices, even with missing paint.

Price Range

Victorian Doorstops: $50 to $500 (based on supply and demand; check the following references for prices on specific pieces).

Suggested Reading

Bertoia, Jeánne. *Doorstops: Identification and Values.* Paducah, Ky.: Collector Books, 1985.

Hamburger, Marilyn, and Beverly Lloyd. *Collecting Figural Doorstops.* San Diego: A.S. Barnes and Company, 1978.

Most comprehensive antique price guides have a substantial listing in this category.

Hall or Pier Tables

The Victorians relied heavily on terms from early Greek and Roman architecture (see Chapter 2, The Front Parlor). The term "pier" originally referred to the columns that supported the ends of an arch. In nineteenth-century architecture, the term was used to describe the part of a wall between two windows or other openings. Items intended for placement on that wall (pier tables, pier mirrors) were given the name as well.

The pier table is probably one of the least-recognizable pieces of Victorian furniture, mostly because nearly every type of table made during the period (game tables, work tables, parlor tables, and others) was used as a hall table at one time or another, and because pier tables often resemble many of these other pieces.

The most distinctive design feature of a pier table is one flat edge that is made to lie flush with the wall. Some pier tables incorporate a drawer in the front, and those of very basic design often are mistakenly identified simply as work tables or "side tables." Those with back galleries (a standing piece running along the back of the top) might be identified as dressing tables.

Many pier tables are easily identified by the "petticoat mirror" attached below and behind the table. With a pier mirror hanging above, this configuration allowed the Victorian lady a discreet yet complete view of the condition of her apparel.

Since contemporary nineteenth-century advertising and catalogs are the only sure way of identifying most pier tables, collectors must rely on the following, somewhat dubious method of resolving the dilemma. If a piece is identified by the seller as a pier table and the buyer sees no evidence to indicate that this is incorrect, it is then, for all intents and purposes, a pier table.

The average price of a simple Eastlake-designed pier table is about $325. Heavier, more ornate pieces with Renaissance influence average $450. Prices are affected by style, type of wood, complexity of design, and condition.

Price Ranges

American Eastlake pier table: $200 to $400.
French Revival Rococo pier table: $450 to $1000.
Grand Rapids Renaissance pier table: $300 to $800.

Suggested Reading

See Hall Stands, this chapter.

Hall Stands

Hall stands (also known as hall racks or hall trees) were made in a variety of shapes and sizes but almost always included a hat rack, a mirror, an umbrella stand, and a small table as part of their design. Some also included a glove drawer, a small seat, or a shoe storage compartment.

The term "hall tree" is derived from the shape of a particular style that has a somewhat wide base (roots), narrows at the middle (trunk), and spreads out at the top (branches). Victorian hall trees, which are lighter in weight and appearance, sell for considerably less (average $650) than full-sized Eastlake ($1150) or Renaissance ($1650) hall stands. Hall stand prices are influenced by

1-6 Renaissance Revival hall stand. (Courtesy McHenry Mansion)

McNerney, Kathryn. *Victorian Furniture.* Paducah, Ky.: Collector Books, 1988.

Swedberg, Robert W. and Harriett Swedberg. *Victorian Furniture Styles and Prices* vols. 1, 2, 3. Radnor, Pa.: Wallace-Homestead Book Company, 1983, 1984, 1985.

Hatracks

Victorian hatracks primarily were hung on walls, although standing bentwood racks were not uncommon in country estates. Many hat-

style, type of wood, size and complexity of design, and condition.

Price Ranges

Eastlake hall stands: $850 to $1600.

Hall stands: $1000 to $2500.

Hall trees: $200 to $1000, depending on size and embellishments.

Suggested Reading

Davidson, Marshall B. *American Heritage History of Antiques from the Civil War to World War I.* New York: American Heritage, 1969.

1-7 Bentwood standing hatrack.

racks closely resembled the upper portion of a hall tree, with branches spreading out from an oval mirror (with or without a small shelf beneath).

Accordion-style hatracks could be opened to hang horizontally or vertically as space permitted. They usually were produced in walnut with porcelain (or porcelain-tipped) hanging knobs.

Price Range

Bentwood hanging hatracks: $25 to $75.
Bentwood standing hatracks: $50 to $125.
Wall racks (ornate): $200 to $500. Average: $300.
Accordion-style hatracks: $50 to $100. Average: $75.

Suggested Reading

See Hall Stands, this chapter.

Pier Mirrors

The pier mirror was a long mirror with an elaborate frame that usually was hung on an entry hall wall either alone or in combination with a pier table. (For the origin of this name, see Hall or Pier Tables, this chapter.) Some pier mirrors incorporated a small table or shelf and/or a hatrack into their design. Pier mirrors often looked much like the upper portion of a hall stand, featuring a pediment or scrolled crest at the top.

The average price of an American Eastlake pier mirror with minimal embellishments is about $500, while a larger example with a shelf and drawer might bring $700. Heavier Renaissance versions sell for about $900. French Revival examples with a gold-leaf finish are prized by collectors.

Pier mirror prices are based on style, size, complexity of design, wood used, and condition.

Price Range

American Eastlake pier mirrors: $400 to $1000.
French Revival pier mirrors: $600 to $2500+. Average: $1200.
Renaissance Revival pier mirrors: $700 to $2000.
Prices in both categories increase with size and embellishments.

Suggested Reading

See Hall Stands, this chapter.

Settees

A settee is a long chair, like a loveseat, except that it may seat more than two persons. It is smaller than a sofa and may have some wood showing on the back while a sofa usually is fully upholstered. Settees were occasionally used in large entry halls instead of one or more side chairs. They provided a sitting place for the long good-byes of courting couples and last-minute gossip between visiting friends. They also were found in parlors and sitting rooms. (For additional information, see Loveseats and Sofas) in Chapter 2, The Front Parlor.)

The average price of an Eastlake settee is $600; for a more elaborate Renaissance settee, $750. Prices are based on style, complexity of design, wood and upholstery used, and condition.

Price Range

American Eastlake settee: $450 to $1250.
French Revival settee: $600 to $2000.
Renaissance Revival settee: $600 to $1500.

1-8 Renaissance Revival settee showing Eastlake influence. (Courtesy Bernhard House)

Prices are affected primarily by ornamentation and quality of artisanship.

Suggested Reading

See Hall Stands.

Side Chairs

See Chapter 3, Dining Room.

Tall Case Clocks

Many tall case clocks (also known as grandfather or grandmother clocks, or long case clocks) found in Victorian homes were produced in the seventeenth and eighteenth centuries by British manufacturers. These clocks often were the only "antique" in an otherwise modern furnished home and may have been passed down from previous generations (hence the terms "grandfather" clock for tall and "grandmother" clock for shorter pieces). Today, these early examples are still the most prized among collectors. However, tall case clocks were produced by American artisans throughout the nineteenth century, and Renaissance Revival or American Eastlake styles are not uncommon. These generally did not show the same attention to quality in artisanship (case and works) as those pieces manufactured during the first two decades of the nineteenth century. (For additional information see Wall and Shelf Clocks in Chapter 7, The Library.)

Prices of tall case clocks are affected by design, manufacturer, woods used, and condition.

Price Range

Tall case clocks: $800 to $10,000+. Average: $5000.

1-9 Brass umbrella stand as illustrated in a Victorian period catalog.

Suggested Reading

Guappone, Carmen. *Antique Clocks.* Self-published, 1978.

Miller, Robert W. *Clock Guide Identification with Prices:* Radnor, Pa.: Wallace-Homestead Book Company, 1978.

Roberts, Derek. *British Long Case Clocks.* West Chester, Pa: Schiffer Publishing Ltd., 1990.

Robinson, T. *The Longcase Clock.* Ithaca, N.Y.: Antique Collector's Club, 1981.

Swedberg, Robert and Harriet Swedberg. *American Clocks and Clockmakers.* Radnor, Pa.: Wallace-Homestead Book Company, 1989.

Umbrella Stands

Umbrella stands were made in a variety of styles from a variety of materials (primarily walnut, brass, and more commonly, cast iron). Walnut examples often resemble small hall trees, with a hook at the top on either side and an iron drip pan in the base. Cast-iron examples are more varied in design and often incorporate novelty figures like those seen on door stops or the ornate Rococo designs common on Victorian ironwork.

1-10 Elaborate tall case clock as illustrated in an 1880s catalog.

Original Victorian umbrella stands in brass are rare, and the collector is cautioned that many brass versions are reproductions.

Prices for Victorian umbrella stands are based on materials used, complexity of design, and condition. Old cast iron is nearly impossible to repair. Therefore, cracked or broken examples are worth considerably less.

Price Range

Umbrella stands: $75 (simple, unadorned cast iron) to $500 (more elaborate walnut or cast iron pieces). Average: $350. Most examples in brass are considerably more expensive.

Suggested Reading

See Hall Stands, this chapter.

CHAPTER 2
The Front Parlor

The largest and most impressive room in a Victorian home, the front parlor was seldom used by the residents alone. Containing only the finest furniture and accessories, this chamber was reserved for receiving and entertaining guests. Most of the time, it was closed off from the rest of the house so that it would be saved the wear and tear of regular use.

Usually, guests were greeted in the entry hall by the butler, who then seated them in the reception room or front parlor. The hosts would wait a few minutes to allow their guests to settle in before making their entrance. Prior to dinner, tea would be served in the parlor, accompanied by lively conversation. After dinner, the ladies would return to the front parlor while the gentlemen would retire to the library for smoking and after-dinner drinks. For this reason, most front parlors had appropriately feminine appointments and excessive *passementerie* (tassels, cords, fringes, and so forth). The front parlor, sewing room, and bedrooms were considered feminine rooms. All other rooms of the house were considered masculine, although there usually was a noticeably feminine influence in all but the library or study.

The front parlor was also a place for courting. The young lady of the house would receive her beau in this least-active room, where the couple was most likely to be safe from interruptions by a vigilant father or pesky younger sibling.

The floors of the front parlor were usually hardwood or parquet and covered with a large *carpet* or, in the latter part of the century, numerous carpets and rugs that often overlapped. Walls typically were covered in the best quality hand-painted cloth or paper coverings, often with large floral designs. (Wall coverings of this type were abhorred by Charles Eastlake in his 1878 edition of *Hints on Household Taste*. He suggested that only the most subtle of geometric patterns in pale colors be used.) In better homes, large, artistic tapestries could be found hanging on one or more parlor walls.

Ornamentations, found in nearly every room of every Victorian home, were based on ancient Greek and Roman architecture. While definitions of the various terms were somewhat changed from their original application to the pedestal and arch, the basic concept remained the same. These terms were an important part of Victorian home decoration; collectors should become familiar with the basic definitions.

Architrave—Ornamentation (wood or plaster) above and along the sides of a door or window.

Cornice—A decorative molding that runs horizontally around the room at the top of the wall.

Dado—The lower portion of the wall, decorated differently (paper or paint) from the upper portion, and often separated from it by a wooden molding or other decorative strip (called a "dado rail").

Frieze—A horizontal, decorative band (paper or paint) running around the upper wall, just below the cornice (if any).

Plinth—Molding or decoration (usually wood) at the juncture of the floor and wall.

Parlor furniture was usually varied and abundant, often placed to create various nooks or conversation corners. Depending on the size of the room, there would be at least one *sofa*, possibly with a matching *loveseat* and several matching *side chairs* (see Chapter 3, The Dining Room). At one or both ends of the sofa, there may have been a *sofa table* with a narrow oval top and a hidden drawer. Various other tables could be found throughout the room, including the *center table* (also called "parlor table"), which was used for a variety of purposes but primarily to hold large *lamps,* plants, statuary, or other decorative items; round-topped *pillar tables,* often called "lamp stands" or "plant stands" because this was their primary purpose (versions with larger square or rectangular tops are now often called "parlor stands"); a *teapoy table,* with a shelf beneath for holding a *silver tea service;* and possibly a *game table* (see Chapter 5, The Back Parlor).

With this proliferation of tables, it is hard to believe that an occasion would arise where another was needed, but one type of table was created for just such times. Called a *tilt-top table,* it has a hinged top that can be dropped to a vertical position to take up less space until needed. In this mode, it is purely decorative.

In the corners of the room, one might find *corner chairs,* designed specifically to fit in corners; or an *étagère,* a multishelved stand on which *decorative objects, souvenirs,* and other objects were displayed.

Souvenirs were very important to the Victorians and were often a large part of the omnipresent clutter seen in contemporary photos of nineteenth-century homes. Items of intrinsic worth were usually kept in the back parlor, while more impressive pieces were prominently displayed for visitors in the front parlor. Also, only the finest *framed art and photographs* were displayed here.

Most front parlors had a fireplace with a mantel on which a *mantel clock,* as well as *candlesticks* or *candelabra,* usually could be found. A popular pastime for Victorian ladies was creating tapestries for *fire screens.* These decorative wood-frame stands were used to reduce glare from the fireplace, and some were even adjustable so that they could be raised for use in front of windows. Other accessories for the fireplace included the *coal box* and various *fireplace tools.*

From the front parlor, you could proceed directly to the dining room (usually through large double doors) or depart through the entry hall. By using the central hall, servants and others could pass to other rooms of the house without disturbing the occupants of the front parlor.

Candelabra and Candlesticks

The term "candlestick" can be applied to any candle holder, but for the purpose of this description we will refer to all standing holders designed for more than one candle as candelabra, and those holding only one candle as candlesticks.

During the Victorian era candle holders were produced in wrought iron, brass, silver, pewter, wood, glass, porcelain, and other materials, in an endless array of designs and configurations. During the latter part of the century, they were displayed (with or without candles) on mantels, tables, and shelves. Their function was primarily decorative, since oil lamps (and later, gas and

2-1 Silver-plated candelabrum. (Courtesy McHenry Mansion)

electric lamps) provided most of the lighting. Then, as now, candlelight was usually reserved for romantic occasions, or anytime when the flickering glow of candles might provide the proper atmosphere—especially at the dining table.

Candle holders were among the favorite impromptu weapons of Victorian ladies, second only to the hatpin and the fireplace poker. Because they often were quite expensive and not really a necessity, silver candlesticks and candelabra were often the first items to be pawned or sold in hard times.

The basic candlestick of the Victorian period has a decorative shaft about ten inches long with a pedestal base and a wax-catching rim called a "bobeche" surrounding the candle cup. The distinctive knobs that give shape to the shaft are called "knops." Pear-shaped sections of the shaft are called "balusters." Throughout the centuries candle holders have been produced in similar form, based primarily on early Greek and Roman architecture.

Candelabra (usually made of silver or silver plate) also incorporate the knop and bobeche in their designs, often at the end of S-shaped arms radiating out from a central shaft. A candelabrum might have as few as two cups or more than a dozen. Short, individual candlesticks (under five inches) are called "chamber sticks." A favorite style of candlestick or candelabrum from the Victorian period was the "push-up," in which the entire candle, except for the tip, was enclosed. A spring or lever, or both, allowed the candle to be pushed up as the wick burned down. Many of these were topped with colorful glass shades.

The largest variety of Victorian candlesticks probably were produced in glass. These were pressed or blown (or a combination of both) into assorted shapes from a variety of colors and types of glass. (For more information on glass types, see Decorative Glass, this chapter.) One of the most distinctive candlesticks from this period featured a dolphin balancing a candle cup on its tail. These are extremely popular with collectors (average price: $300 a pair) and, of course, have been frequently reproduced. As with most decorative glass, opaque glass candlesticks are usually more valuable than transparent pieces.

Today prices for Victorian candle holders range from $25 for turned wood candlesticks to $10,000 and up for certain silver, cut-crystal, or gold candelabra. Prices are affected by materials, artisanship, elaborateness of design or decoration, and identification of manufacturer. Prices of candelabra are greatly affected by size and number of arms.

Price Ranges

Candlestick pairs

Brass: $50 for basic stemmed design to $1000+ for heavy or elaborate designs. Highest prices are paid for those with cut-glass or crystal embellishments.

Carved wood: $50 to $300 depending on intricacy of carving.

Glass: $60 to $2000+, depending on type of glass and the manufacturer. Wide variety.

Pewter: $50 to $250. Watch for hallmarks and beware of reproductions.

Porcelain: $125 to $1000+, depending on quality of work and the manufacturer.

Silver: $250 to $5000+.

Silver plate: $75 to $1000. Highest prices in both silver and silver plate are paid for quality hallmarked examples.

Turned wood: $25 to $75.

Candelabra

Brass: $75 to $2000, depending on complexity of design.

Glass: $75 to $300 for ordinary pieces; $250 to $10,-000+ for crystal. Identification of the manufacturer is very important.

Porcelain: $200 to $1000+, depending on quality of work and manufacturer.

Silver: $200 to $10,000+. Premium prices are paid for elaborate, artistic designs from well-known silver manufacturers.

Silver plate: $175 to $3000. Highest prices in both silver and silver plate are paid for high-quality, hallmarked pieces.

Suggested Reading

Archer, M. and D. Archer. *Collector's Encyclopedia of Glass Candlesticks.* Paducah, Ky.: Collector Books, 1983.

Wardle, Patricia, *Victorian Silver and Silverplate.* Nashville: Thomas Nelson and Sons, 1963.

Carpets and Rugs

By definition, a carpet covers all or a large portion of a floor, while a rug covers only a small area. In Victorian times they were used in combination, and sometimes there were far too many.

In the nineteenth century, as now, most fine carpets and rugs of artistic quality were manufactured in Asia and the Middle East. Until near the turn of the century, the colors were produced by the use of natural dyes, such as the juice from berries, nuts, and trees, or even from crushed snails. The proper "knotting" of a carpet was an artistic achievement, and even a moderate-sized rug could contain over one million knots. That many of these carpets, even from the early Victorian period, still exist in excellent condition today is a tribute to those early artisans.

Identifying rug types, dates, and countries of origin is quite difficult, and examples are often mislabeled under the popular term "Persian rug." In fact, many of these are probably of Turkish or even Oriental origin. Rug experts can often even identify the tribe or area that produced the rug by its pattern.

Small rugs were also produced by Victorian ladies, who made them as a hobby. These rugs were either hooked, knotted, or braided from scraps of material. They are especially popular with collectors today. However, buyers are cautioned that they have been produced throughout the twentieth century as well, and the specific dating of these rugs is most difficult. A certain amount of trust in the seller and any "provenance" that might accompany the item is required.

Prices for all types of rugs and carpets are based on size, condition, material, pattern, country of origin, and time period.

Price Range

Eastern knotted rugs (Persian type): $250 for small rug with basic design, to $8000+ for high-quality or large examples (carpets) with rare or unusual patterns. Average: $2000.

Hobby rugs: $100 for basic braided and rag rugs to $1000+ for large, high-quality hooked rugs with unusual patterns. Average: $500.

Suggested Reading

Hubal, Reinhard G., *The Book of Carpets*. North Pomfret, Va.: Barrie & Jenkins, 1971.

Kline, Linda, *Beginner's Guide to Oriental Rugs*. Berkeley, Calif.: Ross Books, 1980.

Von Rosenstiel, Helene, *American Rugs and Carpets*. New York: William Morrow & Company, 1978

Center Tables

The terms "center table" and "parlor table" originally were used to describe a multipurpose table kept in the middle of the room. In small homes, it was the dining table, work table, game table, and on some occasions, even an operating table. During the Victorian period it became a more general term applied to the largest and most obvious table in the room, especially in the parlor.

2-3 Large, oval Renaissance Revival parlor table. (Courtesy Jensen's Antiques)

2-2 Renaissance Revival parlor table featuring Eastlake influence. (Courtesy McHenry Mansion)

Center tables with French Revival or Renaissance influence may have been round or oval or with a "turtle top" (turtle shaped as seen from above), usually covered with marble. Legs on turtle-top tables are usually cabriole style, while those on oval or round versions are often massive footed pillars. Eastlake-style center tables were usually rectangular or square, with or without a marble top, and with angular legs. Many examples in both styles had casters so that they could be easily moved.

In Victorian homes, the primary purpose of the center table was to hold plants, lamps, and large decorative items. It might be placed along one wall, behind or at the ends of a sofa, or, traditionally, near the center of the room between two large chairs. In today's antiques market, center tables are nearly always referred to as parlor tables, although they were frequently found in other rooms of the house.

Most tables in the Victorian home were of approximately the same height—about thirty inches. Low tables of the type we today call "coffee tables" did not exist in the nineteenth century. Center tables have been cut down for use in this manner, but most antiques afficionados agree that this type of destructive conversion simply turns a valuable antique into an ordinary piece of furniture.

Prices for antique center tables are affected by shape, size, style, wood, condition, and quality of construction. Unbroken marble tops add considerably to the value of a piece. Small French Revival and Eastlake center tables with marble tops commonly sell for around $500, while the often heavier and more ornate Renaissance versions bring around $650. Larger tables average $950.

Price Ranges

American Eastlake center table (large): $550 to $1200.
French Revival (turtle top): $275 to $1000+.
Premium prices are paid for elaborately carved examples.
Renaissance Revival center table (small): $350 to $2000+. Heavy and elaborate pieces bring the highest prices.
Renaissance Revival center table (large): $650 to $2000+.

Suggested Reading

McNerney, Kathryn. *Victorian Furniture: Our American Heritage.* Paducah, Ky.: Collector Books, 1988.
Swedberg, Robert W. and Harriet Swedberg. *Victorian Furniture,* vols. 1–3. Radnor, Pa.: Wallace-Homestead Book Company, 1984–1985.

Coal Boxes and Wood Tenders

Victorian homes were heated primarily by fireplaces or cast-iron stoves and, in later years, by coal-burning furnaces. Wood and coal, the primary fuels used, were a messy addition to an ordinarily spotless Victorian room. To keep the mess in check, various devices were used to carry and store these materials.

In homes where the madam of the house permitted it, there was a large built-in wood box next to the fireplace. However, if this was considered unsightly, the wood would be brought in continuously throughout the day by the butler, who used a tender. Wood tenders were made of a variety of materials and in many configurations. However, the term has come to designate a shallow cast-iron "basket," in which small quantities of wood were stacked, carried in, and left next to the fireplace or stove.

While the use of coal for fuel was more widespread in England, many American homes relied on it as well. Coal was carried from an outdoor or basement coal bin in a coal scuttle, a bucket with a spout specifically designed for the purpose. It then was poured from the scuttle to the coal box, which sat next to the stove or fireplace. The coal box, like the wood tender, was made in a variety of materials and designs. The type commonly found in antiques shops today looks very much like a large cast-iron pot on legs. It usually has handles or rings on each end and a tall, heavy cover. Coal was taken from the box to the fire with long tongs (see Fireplace Tools, this chapter).

Coal box and wood tender prices are affected primarily by condition and complexity of design.

Price Ranges

Cast-iron coal box: $50 to $250. Average: $150.
Cast-iron wood tender: $35 to $100. Average: $75.
Toleware coal box: $250 to $1000.

Suggested Reading

Kaufman, Henry. *American Fireplace.* Nashville: Thomas Nelson Publishing, 1972.
———. *Early American Andirons and Other Fireplace Tools.* Nashville: Thomas Nelson Publishing, 1974.

Corner Chairs

Almost nothing fits in the corner of a room unless it specifically is made to go there. Victorian furniture designers devised several items, one of which was the corner chair, for exactly that purpose. A diamond-shaped chair, with three legs against the wall and one sticking out in front, it is likely the most recognizable (and most uncomfortable) piece of Victorian furniture.

Corner chairs were produced in nearly every design and substyle of the period, but not in large quantities. While they are not rare, the collector may have some difficulty locating a quality speci-

men in his or her favorite style (average price: $250).

Price Ranges

Corner chairs: $175 for basic Spool and American Eastlake examples to $650 for elaborate French Revival or Renaissance pieces. Average: $250 to $300.

Suggested Reading

See Center Tables, this chapter.

Decorative Objects

It cannot be overstated that Victorian interiors were overstated. The Victorians liked "things": gaudy things, big things, heavy things, flashy things, things made of plaster, papier-maché, marble, glass, ivory, coral, whalebone, wood, and shell. While most of these items had no function, they did have a purpose: to impress. They bought expensive things to show their wealth, artistic things to show their good taste and breeding, and

2-4 Eastlake corner chair with Egyptian Revival influence from a nineteenth-century photograph.

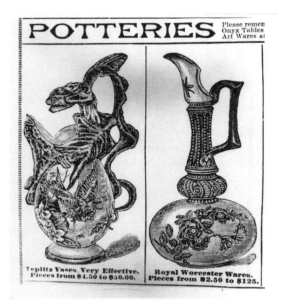

2-5 Decorative pottery as shown in a Victorian catalog.

foreign things to show that they were well traveled.

In a typical front parlor (and in the adjoining dining room) one might find several vases in various shapes and sizes, a decorative pitcher with matching goblets, one or two urns, several figurines, and a number of small decorative dishes. While all of these items were produced in an endless variety of styles and materials, they primarily were made of glass or ceramics. Ceramics (pottery, porcelain, and related materials) were also used to produce various statuary and other artistic display pieces found in the front parlor and throughout the house.

Glass

Hundreds of thousands of decorative glass pieces in a variety of styles were produced during the Victorian era. Glass items were pressed, free blown, mold blown, acid etched, cut, engraved, overlayed, flashed, tinted, colored, cameo carved, twisted, ribbed, treaded, bubbled, silvered, or gilded by the firms of Sowerby, New England Glass (later Libbey and Son), Wedgwood, Tiffany, Richardson, Blanchard and Company, Boston and Sandwich (Mary Gregory), Antonio Salviati, and many others.

Even though large quantities of British and foreign glass were imported to the United States, a hefty excise tax had been imposed until 1845. This allowed American manufacturers a foothold in the glass market, which blossomed into a major industry after the Civil War. The primary product of American factories was pressed glass, also called flint glass (a holdover from earlier days when flint was used in its production), pattern glass (because it was produced in patterns to resemble cut crystal), ruby glass (flashed or stained red), amber glass (flashed or stained yellow), and Sandwich glass (because large quantities were produced by the Boston and Sandwich glass works).

Blown glass had fallen out of favor with glass makers with the development of mechanically pressed glass around 1825. However, by the 1880s it was back in vogue, produced in a variety of shapes and colors and much of it intended to imitate fine porcelain. This decorative art glass was manufactured under a number of fanciful names. Among the most recognized were Amberina, a two-toned glass with a reddish tone gradually blending into amber; Agata, a gloss-finish glass with a mottled pattern giving the appearance of oil droplets on water; Burmese, an opaque, porcelainlike glass with soft yellow and pale pink swirls; Pomona, a frosted yellow glass with an amber band at the top; and the very popular Peachblow, made to resemble the Chinese porcelain from which it took its name. The toning of Peachblow glass varied with the manufacturer, but it traditionally was peach colored, blending to strawberry red.

The 1890s brought Art Nouveau and Louis C. Tiffany's iridescent Favrile glass. Produced by the careful and deliberate combination of various colored glasses during the molten stage, each piece of Tiffany glass contained a unique colorful pattern of flowers, feathers, or smokey swirls. In addition, Tiffany also produced numerous decorative items (photo frames, clocks, nut dishes, and so forth) that featured his Favrile glass inset or inlaid into bronze or silver.

Prices for decorative glass objects are based on size and type of item, type of glass used, method of manufacture, identification of manufacturer (if any), condition, and supply and demand.

Ivory and Whalebone

Ivory (elephant tusk) was used to produce boxes, fans, candlesticks, frames, masks, plaques, trays, figurines, and statuary. Both ivory and whalebone were used in the production of scrimshaw, a carving technique by which pictures were incised onto the surface. Whalebone and whale's teeth with scrimshaw designs can be found as boxes, footstools, hatracks, mirror and picture frames, desk items (see Chapter 7, The Library), ladies' items (see Chapter 8, Her Bedroom), and as handles for various tools and knives. Free-standing whole elephant tusks and whale's teeth with elaborate scrimshaw engravings were also quite popular.

Scrimshaw items were usually produced by sailors as a way of passing time on long voyages. The pieces were then sold to merchants in port or given to friends or relatives, from whom they often eventually made their way into the market. Much of the art work is comparable to, or even surpasses, the work of the best-known professional engravers of the period.

The Victorians loved exotic items like these. Unfortunately, they obtained them with little regard for the future. The unchecked slaughter of hundreds of thousands of elephants and whales during this period and into the twentieth century eventually resulted in the Endangered Species Act, which today severely limits trade in ivory and makes existing pieces in this country quite valuable.

This has also brought on the wide-scale production of fake ivory and scrimshaw. Many of these reproductions are so similar to the originals that extensive tests are required to validate a piece. Collectors are advised to exercise caution before paying a large amount for supposedly old scrimshaw or ivory.

Prices for decorative ivory, whalebone, and scrimshaw are based on size, bone quality, condition, complexity of design, and supply and demand.

Papier-Maché

Papier-maché was produced by mixing paper shavings with glue, chalk or fine sand, and other ingredients. The resulting mass was then shaped or molded under high pressure and baked until hard. Various finishes such as paint, enamel, or japan varnish were then applied. Snuff boxes, jewelry and photograph cases, masks, powder boxes, coasters, fans, and various toys and figures were all produced in papier-maché.

The most popular papier-maché items, how-ever, were trays and folding tables. Like many papier-maché items, these were usually inlaid with chips of mother-of-pearl incorporated into various painted motifs on a black japan varnish background. Inlaid papier-maché trays were popular gifts because of their simple beauty and low cost. They were used in the front parlor to serve tea or coffee, or as a base for vases or other decorative items.

The value of antique Victorian papier-maché is based on condition, rarity of design, and complexity of painting or inlays.

Porcelain

Most porcelain of the nineteenth century was composed of kaolin (a fine, white clay) and pulverized quartz and feldspar. This mixture was shaped, molded, or "thrown" to produce various functional or decorative items. These pieces were then glazed with a similar mixture and carefully baked to a hard finish.

Each of the many companies producing porcelain had its own secret formula and method that, each claimed, resulted in the best product. Accordingly, fine porcelain is recognized by the various manufacturers and places where the items were produced: Wedgwood, Coalport, Derby, Ridgeway, Limoges, Dale Hall, Haviland, Minton, Tucker, Chamberlain, Dresden, Staffordshire, Meissen, Copeland, and many others. Because imported porcelain was readily available and lower in price than American porcelain, large-scale production never really caught on in this country. Those few successful American manufacturers included Tucker and Hemphill, Ott and Brewer, Charles Cartlidge, Jersey, Union, and American Porcelain Manufacturing.

Compared to ordinary pottery, porcelain items were quite expensive and, therefore, purchases of decorative porcelain were made selectively. Those pieces were prominently displayed in the front parlor or dining room, where they could be seen by visitors and guests.

One of the more unusual ceramic items was the lithopane, a decorative panel on which the design was made to appear by varying amounts of light shown through the highly translucent porcelain. Thin areas of the panel let more light through and represented the highlights of the picture, while the thick areas held back light and created shadows. The process was also used to produce lamps, dishes, tea sets, and other objects.

Much of the statuary found in Victorian homes was produced in parian, a kaolin-based material introduced in England (1842) by Copeland and Garrett as a cheap replacement for marble. Other manufacturers followed suit and within a few years bowls, jugs, vases, and other items were being produced as parianware. In America, Vermont's U.S. Pottery turned out large quantities of parian up until the time of the Civil War. Several of the American porcelain manufacturers previously listed also produced excellent parianware.

Mention should also be given here to bisque—or biscuit—an unglazed porcelain used primarily in small statuary and china, which will be discussed thoroughly in the next chapter.

Prices of Victorian decorative glass and ceramics are based on a variety of factors including size, material, rarity of design, condition, and identification of manufacturer. Because registration marks are of primary importance in evaluating collectible pieces, serious collectors must invest in one or more of the books that describe and catalog these marks (see Suggested Reading).

Pottery

Pottery was created in clay and baked in ovens to produce two basic varieties: earthenware, fired at low temperatures and then glazed; or stoneware, fired at higher temperatures to create a nonporous finish that did not require glazing. Pottery should not be confused with its translucent ceramic cousins—porcelain, china, and parian—which, then and now, command a higher price.

2-6 Louwelsa Weller pot. (Courtesy Williams Antiques)

Much of the ordinary stoneware from the mid-nineteenth century was produced in studios by students. Designs were often copied or modified from early Greek and Roman art. One of the first British firms to manufacture stoneware in quantity was Doulton and Company, who employed promising young students to apply decorative colors and relief molding. Quality stoneware was also produced by Martin Brothers, William de Morgan, Della Robbia, and Pilkington in England; and Edmands, Wright and Son, and William Hare in the United States.

Probably the best-known type is called majolica (also called faience or delft, which designate the regions where the pieces were made). Popular with Victorians for its rustic patterns (and its low price), majolica pottery was produced in quantity, both in America and abroad. Themes from nature were prominent on decorative majolica plates, bowls, and vases. Colors were painted on soft clay and covered with a clear glaze before firing. Recognized manufacturers include Wedgwood, Smith and Hill, Griffin, Chesapeake, and Minton, among others.

The work of several pottery manufacturers is quite distinctive and easily recognized by collec-

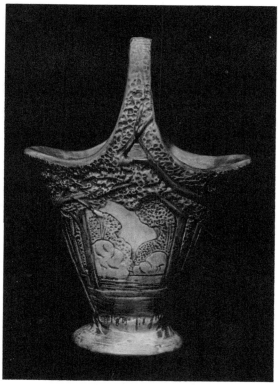

2-7 Weller vase with "Forest" pattern. (Courtesy Williams Antiques)

Manufactured items made from shell were also purchased for their beauty and novelty. Boxes and frames completely covered in mother-of-pearl or tortoise shell were quite popular. Whole tortoise shells were used as bowls, vases, and tea caddies. Both mother-of-pearl and tortoise shell were inlaid to make elaborate designs on trays, tables, and other furniture.

Small seashells were often arranged to form patterns or pictures, glued to cloth or cardboard, and attached to boxes or framed for display. These may have been purchased as souvenirs, but quite often they were produced as a hobby by Victorian ladies. This pastime was particularly common in the coastal resorts of lower New England and the Mid-Atlantic states just prior to the turn of the century.

Prices for antique Victorian shellwork are based primarily on rarity of design and condition.

Wood Items

Elaborately carved wood trimmings were an important part of Victorian home decorating. In addition to the architectural adornments previously mentioned, carved wood ornamentation was common over doorways and especially above and surrounding the fireplace. Many of these ornaments have been removed from homes set for demolition and are sought by collectors and interior designers.

Carved wooden figures and large busts were found in Victorian parlors. Quite often, these were souvenirs of a trip to Africa, South America, or the American West, where they were produced by natives.

An unusual and somewhat morbid decorative piece is the *tableau morte,* an arrangement of small stuffed animals in a wood and glass display case. Squirrels, mice, and even small kittens were treated by a taxidermist then placed in miniature furnished rooms or outdoor scenes. Many of these strange items still exist in good condition and are quite valuable to collectors with offbeat tastes.

tors who specialize in their wares. Among these is Weller, produced under the name Lonhuda in 1894, and Louwelsa Weller after 1895. Also popular is pottery produced in a variety of styles and glazes by Rookwood in Cincinnati. This company was still in business in 1960; however, modern pieces are clearly marked.

Shellwork

The Victorians brought back large conch shells and other seashells as souvenirs of visits to South Sea Islands and other such locales. These shells, as well as large turtle shells and bits of colorful coral, were displayed, like other souvenirs, to serve as conversation pieces.

The collector is advised that more modern copies have been made of Victorian decorative pieces than of any other antique items in existence. Prices of Victorian decorative items are based on design, function (if any), size, materials used, quality of artisanship, aesthetic appeal, manufacturer (if known), condition, and supply and demand.

Price Ranges

Agata: plate $500 to $750; vase $650 to $1500; depending on shape and size.

Amber glass vase: $40 to $175, depending on size and pattern.

Amberina: bowl $150 to $400; pitcher $125 to $350; vase $150 to $500; depending on pattern and embellishments.

Bisque: figurine $40 to $250+; plaque $50 to $500+; vase $75 to $300+. Higher prices paid for exceptional quality and identified pieces.

Burmese glass: bowl $245 to $1700; pitcher $150 to $500; vase $200 to $1500; figures $1500 to $2000.

Doulton pottery: figurines $100 (single) to $1500 (group); vase $75 to $450.

Ivory: figurine $100 to $5000+, depending on size and complexity of carving; carved or scrimshaw whole tusk $500 to $5000+; frame $50 to $150; fan $50 to $500+; vase $90 to $5000+.

Limoges porcelain: figurine $100 to $300; plaque $125 to $750; vase $45 to $1500+, depending on identification of manufacturer, patterns, colors.

Majolica: bowl $45 to $1000; pitcher $65 to $1000; plaque $250 to $500; plate $25 to $125; figurine $200 to $2000; urn $400 to $700; vase $40 to $275.

Papier-maché: mask $50 to $400; figures $75 to $1000+ (highest prices paid for realistic, life-size figures); tray $75 to $10,000+ (highest prices paid for ornate, painted, and inlaid examples).

Parianware: bust $45 to $1000+; figure $100 to $500; vase $50 to $500+; depending on size and identification of artist or manufacturer.

Pattern glass vase: $15 to $125; depending on size and pattern.

Peachblow: rose bowl $75 to $450; vase $25 to $2500; depending on manufacturer, size, and style. Highest prices paid for pieces by Wheeling and Mt. Washington Glass.

Pomona: water set (pitcher and tumblers) $800 to $1500; vase $100 to $350; depending on shape and size.

Porcelain: figurine $40 to $1500; jar $75 to $10,000+; plaque $250 to $800; urn $250 to $3500; vase $25 to $2000+.

Rookwood pottery (nineteenth century): jug $250 to $850; ewer $250 to $600; vase $250 to $7500; depending on pattern and artist.

Ruby glass vase: $45 to $200, depending on size and pattern.

Sandwich glass vase: $75 to $300, depending on size, pattern, and color.

Scrimshaw: whale's tooth $300 to $5000+, depending on size and complexity of carving; mirror and picture frames $100 to $1000; boxes $150 to $5000+, depending on size.

Shellwork: boxes and baskets $75 to $300, if positively identified as Victorian.

Stoneware: figurine $300 to $1200; pitcher $20 to $1000+; depending on quality and complexity of design.

Tableau morte: $250 to $5000+, depending on size, complexity, and condition.

Tiffany glass: bowl $275 to $3000; tile $100 to $150; vase $100 to $10,000+; depending on style.

Tiffany glass and bronze: frame $165 to $3000; hanging ornament $2700 to $3500; box $250 to $1000.

Tiffany silver: vase $1500 to $6500; picture frame $150 to $200; mint/nut dish $50 to $100.

Tortoise shell: whole shell bowls $75 to $250, depending on size and condition; inlaid boxes $250 to $3000+, depending on size and complexity of inlay pattern.

Wedgwood porcelain: bowl $150 to $3000; pitcher $50 to $500; vase $85 to $2500; depending on product line category (i.e., caneware, creamware, jasperware, and various "lusters").

Wood carving: figures $50 to $5000+; wall plaques $150 to $10,000+; depending on size and complexity of carving.

Suggested Reading

Bagdade, Susan and Al Bagdade. *Warman's English and Continental Pottery and Porcelain: An Illustrated Price Guide.* Radnor, Pa.: Wallace-Homestead Book Company, 1987.

Barlow, Raymond, and Joan E. Kaiser. *The Glass Industry in Sandwich,* vols. 2, 3, and 4. West Chester, Pa.: Schiffer Publishing (distributor), 1987, 1983.

Encyclopedia of Victorian Colored Pattern Glass. Marietta, Ohio: Antique Publications, 1981. There are several dozen books on glass by this publisher.

Feild, Rachel. *McDonald Guide to Buying Antique Pottery and Porcelain: Authenticity, Techniques, Dating, Reproduction.* Radnor, Pa.: Wallace-Homestead Book Company, 1987.

Flayderman, E. Norman. *Scrimshaw, Scrimshawers, Whales and Whalemen.* E. Norman Self-published, 1972.

Huxford, Bob, and Sharon Huxford. *The Collectors' Encyclopedia of Weller Pottery.* Paducah, Ky.: Collector Books, 1979.

Kock, Robert. *Louis C. Tiffany, Rebel in Glass.* New York: Crown Publishers, Inc., 1966.

McConnell, Kevin. *Majolica.* West Chester, Pa.: Schiffer Publishing, 1990.

Miles, Doris. *Price Guide to Pattern Glass.* Radnor, Pa.: Wallace-Homestead Book Company, 1986.

Peck, Herbert. *Second Book of Rookwood Pottery.* Self-published, 1985.

Rebert, M. Charles. *American Majolica 1850–1900.* Radnor, Pa.: Wallace-Homestead Book Company, 1981.

Shuman, John, III. *Collector's Encyclopedia of American Glass.* Paducah, Ky.: Collector Books, 1988.

Spillman, Jane. *American and European Pressed Glass.* Corning, N.Y.: Corning Museum of Glass, 1981.

2-8 Renaissance Revival étagère. (Courtesy McHenry House)

Étagères and Whatnots

With an endless array of small decorative items displayed in the front parlor, shelves were a necessity in the Victorian era. These came in the form of an étagère—a tall, sometimes elaborate stand that was placed against the wall or in a corner (corner étagère)—or the smaller whatnot—a system of shelves, usually connected with spindle supports, designed as a stand or to hang on the wall.

The étagère often looks at first glance much like a hall stand, with its large central mirror, tall crests or pediments above, and low marble shelf over a drawer. Shelves are also attached along the sides, getting smaller as they go higher. Closed étagères look much like a sideboard (see Chapter 3, Dining Room), except that the lower shelves have glass in the doors. Shelving on a closed étagère runs the full width of the piece below waist level and holds considerably more than a standard étagère.

Whatnots are very simple pieces of furniture and were used throughout the house where basic, attractive shelving was required. Made in a variety of sizes, they were designed to stand or hang on a flat wall or in a corner. More elaborate versions sometimes had carved fretwork along the back of the shelf, or possibly molded trimmings and a pediment at the top.

Both étagères and whatnots are found most commonly in the more ornate French Revival and Renaissance Revival styles. Pricing is based on size and complexity of design.

Price Ranges

Closed étagères: $1500 to $3000.
Corner étagères: $1500 to $3000.
Corner whatnots: $185 to $500 (higher prices paid for pieces with cupboard bases).
Hanging whatnots: $125 to $300.
Side étagères: $2000 to $3500.
Side whatnots: $225 to $500.

Suggested Reading

See Center Tables this chapter.

Fire Screens

The Victorian fire screen consisted of a standing frame into which a decorative insert was placed. The frames were made of a variety of materials, most often wood. The decorative inserts were made primarily of cloth, although other materials were used. The primary purpose of the screen was to protect an area of the room from the glare of the fire; however, its true purpose was more decorative than functional.

In a time when there was no radio, television, movies, or other similar forms of entertainment, hobbies were very important. One of the most common pastimes among Victorian ladies was the creation of decorative and functional textiles. They frequently made fire screen inserts to replace faded and soiled pieces or just as a change. Inserts may have a very basic woven design or an elaborate, artistic creation in needlepoint. Many of these have survived in excellent condition and are an important factor

2-9 Fire screen with hand-painted canvas in Eastlake frame. (Courtesy McHenry House)

in the price of a particular fire screen. On today's market, many antique screens are sold with modern reproduction inserts or without an insert.

Other factors that affect the price of fire screens includes style, size, condition, and wood used in the frame.

Price Range

Fire screens: $200 to $2500+.

Suggested Reading

Kaufman, Henry. *American Fireplace.* Nashville: Thomas Nelson Publishing, 1972.

Fireplace Tools

Until the introduction of central heating just prior to the turn of the century, the fireplace was the primary source of heat for the Victorian home. Even when warmth was not a primary need, the open fire presented a certain charm and comfort.

In the front parlor, the fireplace; with its elaborate carved wood frame, colorful tiles, or inlaid marble, was often the decorative focal point of the room. The various functional tools and accessories used at the fireplace often served an equally important decorative function.

Fireplace tools included the andiron (also called firedog or chenet), which sat on the floor of the fireplace and held the logs; bellows, used to blow air onto the fire to aid in starting it; short handled broom, to remove ash and clean in and around the fireplace; fender, which sat just in front of the fire to keep coals from rolling out; fireback, which protected the brickwork at the back of the fireplace from excessive heat; fireboard, a decorative door that closed off the fireplace when it was not in use; shovel, to remove ash; tongs, to place and adjust logs on the fire; and poker, to move burning logs or stir coals. Most items used in and around the fire were made of cast iron, although brass was occasionally used and the handles on some tools were wood or ceramic.

All of the tools mentioned here have been manufactured and used throughout the twentieth century as well; therefore, identifying Victorian period pieces is quite difficult. Andirons and fenders were generally quite ornate, with scroll or claw feet and balls, or animals or characters standing out in front. Bellows, which were made of wood, brass, or copper connected by leather folds, often have inlays in the style of the period or engraved names identifying nineteenth-century manufacturers. Victorian firebacks are decorative iron walls ranging in size from two feet long to as large as six feet square. These have been reproduced frequently and in large quantity.

Most tools that were in constant contact with heat and smoke have a thick layer of lead deposits and some amount of the dark rust that indicates age (recent rust is usually quite orange). Prices of antique fireplace tools are based on complexity of design, condition, and reliability of dating.

Price Ranges

Andirons and chenets: $100 to $2500+. Price is unaffected by material used. Higher prices are paid for identified manufacturers and designers.

Bellows: $50 to $1500, based on complexity of design and especially on condition.

Broom: $50 to $100. Dating is difficult to prove.

2-10 Wrought-iron fireplace tools, as shown in a Victorian period catalog.

Fender: $100 to $500+.

Fireback: $100 to $3500+. Highest prices are paid for elaborate, identified designs.

Fireboards: $250 to $2500+. Quality manufactured pieces are quite difficult to find.

Shovel and tong set: $350 to $2500, when date is certain.

Suggested Reading

See Coal Boxes and Wood Tenders, this chapter.

Framed Art and Photographs

Framed art of the Victorian period included paintings, lithographs, original drawings and etchings, and black-and-white or hand-tinted photographs. In addition, many framed craftwork items were produced as hobbies. These included beadwork, needlepoint, shell pictures, mosaics, and pictures done in a variety of unusual media, including butterfly wings, peacock and other feathers, leaves, and human hair.

From American primitive painting, born at about the same time as the Victorian era itself, to the wonderful etchings of naturalist John James Audubon and Currier and Ives, American history was rich in artistic endeavor. Never before or since has such an abundance of fine-quality art been available to so many people and at such comparatively low prices. The walls of Victorian homes and public buildings were so crowded with art work that all but the most important was simply taken for granted. Fortunately for us, much of this work still exists today and remains relatively inexpensive.

Many of the wonderful woodcuts of the period were produced for publication in a myriad of books and magazines such as *Godey's Lady's Book, Art Journal, Art Amateur, Harper's,* and many others. To produce these prints an engraver copied an original drawing in reverse by incising tiny lines into one or more wooden printing blocks. Large prints may have required a dozen

2-11 Victorian feather picture. (Courtesy Bernhard House)

or more blocks, each representing a section of the picture. These blocks were then locked together in a press and inked, and their images printed. Great skill was required to assure that the blocks matched perfectly so that the connections did not show on the finished print.

Among the most popular woodcuts were those based on Audubon's drawings of colorful birds. The earliest of these prints were produced in books from the 1820s to the 1850s. These are identifiable by their size (approximately twenty-six by thirty-nine inches or seven by eleven inches) and their artistic hand tinting. Many Audubon prints reproduced later in the nineteenth century were printed in color through the chromolithographic process. Beware of modern reproductions made to look old.

Other Victorian prints popular with collectors are those by Louis Prang, one of the first to produce color lithograph prints in quantity; Bishop Hopkins, who produced wonderful hand-colored prints of flowers in the 1840s; and Winslow Homer, staff artist for *Ballou's Pictorial* famous for his sketches of Civil War scenes and later for his paintings and watercolors of the sea.

31

The firm of Currier and Ives, the most recognized name in nineteenth-century lithographs, produced thousands of prints from 1857 to 1907. (Earlier prints, produced from 1835 to 1847, are marked "N. Currier.") Currier and Ives prints can sometimes be dated by changes in the street address printed on each picture. Because the prints have been reproduced in large quantities throughout the twentieth century, collectors should be certain that a Currier and Ives print is an original before paying large sums for it.

Current market pricing for Victorian prints is based on artist, subject, size, quality of artisanship, quality of coloring (if any), and condition. Signed and first-edition works bring the highest prices.

Photography was conceived in 1839 as a science and quickly became an industry. Early photographs on glass or metal were confined primarily to portraiture; the development and refinement of photographs on paper in the mid-1850s led to photography as an art.

Before the Civil War, the framed photographs hanging on the walls of Victorian homes were usually travel photos: images of pyramids, castles, and Greek or Roman ruins. After the war, allegorical photographers created artistic scenes using models and often employing unusual techniques, such as combination printing (using several negatives) or double exposure. British photographers Oscar Gustave Rejlander and Henry Peach Robinson were among the most famous of these early art photographers.

Westward expansion was documented by the camera throughout the Victorian era. American photographers Alexander Gardner, Timothy O'Sullivan, and George Grey Barnard, fresh from Civil War battlefields, set off to photograph the vast, unspoiled West. Other photographers famous for frontier views included William Henry Jackson, Carleton Watkins, and Eadweard Muybridge.

During the latter part of the nineteenth century, fine photographs were often mass produced as photogravures (high-quality mechanical prints) for inclusion in books or art journals. These frequently were cut out and framed for use as decorative art.

Prices for framed photographs from the Victorian era are based on subject, image quality, process used, size, and condition.

Prior to the invention of photography, likenesses were painted in miniature on various bases (wood, canvas, ivory, and so forth) or cut from dark paper in the form of a silhouette. Most Victorian silhouettes date from the early years of the period and are quite valuable, especially when identified or signed by the artist.

Much of the framed art found in Victorian homes was produced by family members as a hobby. Pencil-and-charcoal drawings were quite popular throughout the period, and many amateur artists produced excellent work. Pictures were also created in beadwork and needlework (see Sewing Room), and shellwork (see decorative objects this chapter). Unusual and sometimes quite beautiful artistic pieces were also produced by using colorful leaves, peacock feathers, or butterfly wings to create patterned mosaics or pictures.

One of the most distinctive media in nineteenth-century art and jewelry was human hair. It had been a custom for many years to keep a lock of a loved one's hair as a momento. It usually was placed in the family Bible or carried in a locket, but sometimes strands were woven together, placed under glass, and worn as a necklace (see Chapter 8, Her Bedroom). During the Civil War, soldiers' wives wove their hair into watch chains so that their husbands could take a remembrance of them into battle. After the war, the use of hair in jewelry and art became commonplace (see Chapter 8, Her Bedroom). Hair of different colors from family and friends was used to create pictures and mosaics under glass. One of the most popular creations (and the most fascinating to twentieth-century collectors) was the *hair tree,* a family tree woven with tufts of hair

2-12 Wedding portrait with wreath made from woven hair of husband and wife. (Courtesy Amador County Museum)

from each family member and arranged with dried flowers or other objects.

Today, prices for Victorian hobby art are based on size, novelty of design, quality of artisanship, and condition.

The Victorian period produced some wonderful and widely recognized painters and paintings. While it is beyond the scope of this book to advise in the field of investment art, it should be mentioned that the major painters of the period included Americans Thomas Doughty, Thomas Eakins, Louis Michel Eilshemius, Edward Henry, Edward Hicks (famous for his *Peaceable Kingdom*), Winslow Homer, George Inness, Joseph Pickett, Thomas Sully, and James Abbott McNeil Whistler (famous for the painting of his mother); Europeans Joseph Mallard William Turner, Jean-Baptiste-Camille Corot, Honoré Daumier, Jean-François Millet; impressionists

Eugène-Louis Boudin, Edgar Degas, Johan Barthold Jongkind, Edouard Manet, and Claude Monet. The Victorian era produced some of the most famous painters (with respect to those already mentioned above): Berthe Morisot, Camille Pissaro, Pierre August Renoir, Paul Cézanne, Paul Gauguin, Odilon Redon, Henri Rousseau, Georges Seurat, and Vincent Van Gogh. Even Pablo Picasso, commonly recognized as a twentieth-century painter, had his first exhibition during the reign of Victoria.

Two painters whose works are highly representative of the social as well as artistic changes that occurred during the latter part of the Victorian era were Frederick Remington in America and Henri de Toulouse-Lautrec in France. Probably the only thing these two artists had in common was that they both used paint and canvas. Yet both portrayed life in the nineteenth century as being lived to its fullest—Remington, through his realistic paintings of the working cowboy and the native American in the untamed West, and Toulouse-Lautrec, through his posters of cabaret dancers and Paris nightclubs.

The prices of paintings by these artists and others of the period are based on market trends, and it is highly recommended that those interested in this field obtain expert advice from an established art investment counselor.

Some wonderful decorative paintings were produced during the Victorian period by both professionals and hobbyists using a variety of bases, such as wood, cardboard, paper, ivory, porcelain, silk, velvet, tin, glass, and other materials. Many of these have survived to this day in excellent condition and are available at a wide range of prices. The value is based on quality of artisanship, materials used, size, and condition.

One fascinating style of painting was done in reverse on glass so that the image had the look of fine porcelain when lit from behind. By expert application of layers of paint, the finished product could also be made to resemble marble or tortoise shell, and this method was often used to produce decorative glass frames for etchings or photographs.

In many cases, the frames that contain Victorian art work are more valuable than the art itself. Ornately carved frames in fine woods with high-quality gilt or ebony trim often bring high prices on the antiques market. Beautiful frames were also produced in brass, pewter, silver, glass, and ceramics. Frame prices are based on size, complexity of design, type of wood or other material used, and condition.

Price Ranges

Audubon prints: $75 to $2500. Highest prices are paid for original early prints measuring approximately twenty-six by thirty-nine inches.

Butterfly wing pictures: $50 to $200.

Currier and Ives prints: (pre-1900) $75 (small prints with minimal detail) to $5000+ (certain large, elaborate prints).

Fashion prints: (*Harper's, Godey's, La Mode,* and others) $15 to $100. Highest prices are paid for well-tinted French plates in good frames.

Framed photographs: (pre-1900, art or travel themes) $15 (small prints by unknown photographers) to $5000+ (highly artistic prints by well-known photographers).

Hair pictures: $50 to $125.

Hair trees: $50 to $1000, depending on size and complexity of design.

Lithopanes: $75 to $1000. Highest prices are paid for elaborate designs on high-quality porcelain that are signed by the artist.

Needlework pictures: $25 to $75.

Paintings (on other than canvas): $20 to $2500+. Reverse glass paintings: $50 to $5000+, depending on size, complexity and artist identification.

Prang prints: $20 to $200. Highest prices are paid for prints marked Prang's American Lithograph Company.

Silhouettes: $25 to $250. Highest prices are paid for identified examples by well-known artists.

Winslow Homer prints: $30 (magazine illustrations) to $3500 (certain large lithograph prints).

Suggested Reading

Lithopane Collectors Club Bulletin. Toledo, Ohio: Lithopane Collectors Club (bimonthly).

Mace, O. Henry. *Collector's Guide to Early Photographs.* Radnor, Pa.: Wallace-Homestead Book Company, 1989.

McClain, Craig. *Currier and Ives: An Illustrated Value Guide.* Radnor, Pa.: Wallace-Homestead Book Company, 1987.

Pollard, Ruth M. *Official Price Guide to Collector Prints.* Orlando: House of Collectibles, 1986.

Rifken, Blume. *Silhouettes in America.* Burlington, Vt.: Paradigm Press, 1987.

Shorewood Staff. *Shorewood Collection Art Reference Guide;* Sandy Hook, Conn.: Shorewood *Fine Art Books,* 1966.

Lamps

During the nineteenth century, lighting evolved from candles and whale oil to gas and electric lamps. When the oil industry developed, starting in 1859, thousands of styles of kerosene lamps were designed in glass, ceramic, and metal in a myriad of shapes and sizes. Later, when gas was piped to wall and ceiling fixtures throughout the house, kerosene was still the fuel of choice for table-top and portable lighting.

In the 1880s electricity took the place of gas, making it easy to simply plug in a lamp wherever it was needed in the house. The mechanical simplicity of the electric lamp allowed manufacturers to concentrate more on design and beauty, and elaborate glass shades became the primary focus. During this period the most famous name in glass—Tiffany—also became the most famous name in lamps.

The lamp we have come to recognize as the kerosene lamp—a glass or metal bowl (font) sitting on a pedestal base, capped by a wick holder and a glass chimney, and often surrounded by a decorative glass shade—has been continuously

2-13 Silver-plated table lamp, as shown in an 1880s advertisement.

collectors, while variants from other manufacturers are also quite valuable. Glass lamps in opaque white, blue, or green are generally more desirable than the more common transparent yellow, purple, or clear examples.

Most major manufacturers of decorative glass and pottery—Mt. Washington Glass, New England Glass, Tiffany, Handel, and Rookwood Pottery—also produced lamps. The same methods and patterns used to produce vases and urns were used to produce lamps. Colorful shades were produced in leaded glass or painted by well-known artists.

2-14 Kerosene lamp with "coin spot" bowl and milk glass base. (Courtesy Williams Antiques)

produced in its original and variant forms for over 130 years. Many modern examples are identical to those produced in 1859 and are often passed off at flea markets as antique lamps. As always, collectors should exercise caution when purchasing often reproduced items of this type.

Kerosene lamps with elaborately pressed, cut, or engraved glass fonts are highly collectible, as are those with spiral twist stems. Atterbury lamps have an opaque pressed glass base connected by a brass stem to a variety of globe-shaped fonts. Those specifically identified as produced by Atterbury and Company of Pittsburgh are prized by

The lamp most definitive of the Victorian era is now called the *Gone with the Wind* lamp. Despite the fact that this style of lamp was not invented until the 1880s, it is the type seen most often in period films and television shows depicting the Civil War (1860s) and the Old West (typically 1870s). This lamp usually has a short pedestal base made of brass, a large teardrop or globe-shaped font, and a matching globe-shaped shade surrounding the chimney. Many of the lamps in this style are hung with faceted glass decorations or fringework. These lamps have been reproduced in large quantities.

During the second half of the nineteenth century, lamps were produced in nearly every type of metal, glass, and ceramic material, and they were being made by nearly every manufacturer who worked with these materials. There were floor lamps, table lamps, hanging lamps, desk lamps, boudoir lamps, wall lamps, and sconces. There were lamps in milk glass, amber glass, emerald glass, cut glass, frosted glass, Amberina, Agata, Burmese, Peachblow, and Pomona. There were bases of brass, bronze, silver, pewter, porcelain, china, and Parian.

From about 1880, parlor lamps were reproduced in detailed miniature for use as nightlights. These small lamps (2 to 12 inches high) were of the same quality as their larger counterparts and are now extremely popular with collectors, but beware of modern reproductions.

Lamp prices are based on the factors of age, style, manufacturer, materials used in construction, elaborateness of design or decoration, and size.

Price Ranges

Bradley and Hubbard: $100 to $750.
Gone with the Wind lamp: $350 to $1000, depending on complexity of design.
Handel: $300 to $10,000. Highest prices are paid for rare items in great demand.

2-15 Miniature lamp (approximately six inches) with silver base. (Courtesy Williams Antiques)

Kerosene lamps: $35 to $2500+, depending on complexity of design and decoration.
Miniature parlor lamps: $75 to $500+. Higher prices, sometimes exceeding $5000, are paid for miniatures in rare glass and pottery types.
Pairpoint: $300 to $2500. Highest prices are paid for elaborately painted shades.
Tiffany: $300 to $10,000. Highest prices are paid for rare items in great demand.

Suggested Reading

DeFalco, Robert, and John Hibel. *Handel Lamps: Painted Shades and Glassware.* Staten Island, N.Y.: H and D Press, 1986.

Maril, Nadja. *American Lighting: 1840–1940.* West Chester, Pa.: Schiffer Publishing, 1989.

McDonald, A.G. *Evolution of the Night Lamp.* Radnor, Pa.: Wallace-Homestead Book Company, 1979.

Smith, Frank and Ruth. *Miniature Lamps (vols. I & II).* West Chester, Pa.: Schiffer Publishing Ltd., 1982.

The Art Work of Louis C. Tiffany. Poughkeepsie, N.Y.: Apollo Books, 1987.

Thuro, Catherine. *Oil Lamps: The Kerosene Era in North America.* Radnor, Pa.: Wallace Homestead Book Company, 1976.

Thuro, Catherine. *Oil Lamps, No. II.* Paducah, Ky.: Collector Books, 1983.

Loveseats

A loveseat is a settee built for two. The origin of its name should be obvious to even the hopelessly unromantic. Loveseats were more popular than sofas among Victorians because they loved to talk, and the configuration of three or more people sitting in a row did not lend itself to easy conversation. The loveseat also fit well into the conversation nooks that were an important part of Victorian interior design.

Many styles of Victorian loveseats were not very comfortable. The back cushions of many Eastlake examples were often not very cushiony and were separated by ornamental wood. The back itself did not extend to the ends of the piece, so that if you were to lean on the arm, half your back had no support. It makes one suspect that some young Victorian lady's father had a hand in the design.

There were, of course, exceptions to this configuration. The double-medallion loveseat (French Revival and Renaissance Revival) looked much like two high-backed upholstered chairs connected together yet separated by a short, low ornamental back piece (father's touch again). Some Eastlake and French Revival versions have one-piece, fully upholstered backs,

but, oddly enough, these styles are not as common as the separated designs.

Price Range

All styles: $450 to $2500, with more ornate examples bringing the highest prices.

Mantel Clocks

If there was only one antique item to be found in a Victorian home, it would have been a clock. It wasn't that contemporary clocks weren't being made, but the best clocks were produced around 1800 or before. The definitive Victorian mantel clock was housed in an elaborate, gilded, cast-bronze Rococo casing. Leaves, flowers, shells,

2-16 *Elaborate French mantel clock as shown in a nineteenth-century catalog.*

2-17 Clock with matching mantel set, which includes candelabra and miniature urns. (Courtesy McHenry Mansion)

animals, cupids, and various other figures were featured in the curved, flowing, unsymmetrical motifs. The clocks were first produced in France and were often referred to simply as "French clocks" in catalogs of the period. French clocks produced during the second half of the eighteenth century were highly sought after by nineteenth-century Americans.

For those who could not locate or afford the original, French Revival clocks were produced by most major manufacturers in France and England and imported to the United States throughout the nineteenth century. Many of these were artistic and mechanical marvels, with rotating bases and figures that moved in various activities. The cases were carved from wood or molded in bronze or porcelain, and they were usually painted gold. The clock often was part of a mantel set with matching figures, vases, or decorative pillars.

As the turn of the century approached, many popular mantel clocks were produced in marble or black slate with designs incorporating Greek and Roman architectural elements. Mantel clocks are often similar to shelf clocks (see Chapter 7, The Library) except that they have a much lower profile and almost always have a footed or pedestal base that is wider than the rest of the clock. These clocks typically were made to operate for eight days when fully wound. They might strike every fifteen minutes, half-hour, or hour with the sound of a single gong or a melody of cathedral bells. Clocks that make elaborate striking sounds generally are more desirable.

In the United States, mantel clocks generally were not produced until the start of the Victorian era, when the introduction of the coil spring and balance wheel eliminated the need for a pendulum and weights to power the clock. This allowed for the production of shorter and more compact casings. Fine mantel clocks were produced by Brewster, Jonathan Brown (Forestville), William Gilbert, Birge and Fuller, Joseph Eves, Chauncy Boardman, Chauncy Jerome, Ansonia Clock, the American Clock Company, and the most famous name in nineteenth-century American clocks, Seth Thomas.

England was famous for its bracket clocks—so called because early versions were equipped with a top bracket or handle—which England had

2-18 Mantel clock with marble pillars. (Courtesy Williams Antiques)

been producing since the seventeenth century. By the 1800s there were a great many British clock manufacturers turning out not only fine bracket clocks but also some excellent reproductions of French-Rococo-cased clocks. Even the Royal Doulton company got involved, producing elaborate porcelain cases.

In addition to being famous for gilded Rococo mantel clocks, the French also produced a clock similar to the bracket clock called the carriage clock. Instead of the small bracket, it had a larger, more obvious handle attached to the top, and the face designs often included additional dials indicating seconds, moon phases, and spring tension. While the carriage clock was originally designed to be a portable traveling clock, it received wide use as a mantel clock during the Victorian period.

Prices of mantel clocks are based on style and complexity of design, manufacturer, condition of case and mechanism, and factors of supply and demand.

Price Ranges

Acorn clocks: $4000 to $10,000+.
American woodcase clocks: $175 to $2000.
French Rococo mantel clocks: $300 to $2500+. High-quality gilt bronze examples often sell much higher.

Nineteenth-century bracket clocks: $700 to $2000.
Nineteenth-century carriage clocks: $200 to $2000.
Ornate Ansonia mantel clocks: $100 to $2000.
Seth Thomas mantel clock: $200 to $1500.
Turn-of-the-century marble, slate, and onyx pillar clocks: $125 to $500+.

Suggested Reading

Guappone, Carmen. *Antique Clocks.* Self-published, 1978.
Miller, Robert W. *Clock Guide Identification with Prices.* Radnor, Pa.: Wallace-Homestead Book Company, 1978.
Swedberg, Robert and Harriett. *American Clocks and Clockmakers.* Radnor, Pa.: Wallace-Homestead Book Company, 1989.

Passementerie

Passementerie—textile trimmings and adornments such as cords and tassels—were a very important part of Victorian home decorating. Framed art and other wall hangings were frequently suspended by a golden braided cord with a tassel at the top and at each end. Draperies quite often were heavily fringed with tassels hanging from the valance, and no window treatment would be complete without heavy cord and tassel drawbacks. Table coverings in silk or lace were also trimmed with fringe or tassels. In fact, these accessories were so much a part of the Victorian home that the cord and tassel pattern was used on glassware, pottery, and other decorative pieces.

The French word *passement* means lace, and lace was found everywhere in Victorian homes: lace curtains, lace tablecloths, lace doilies under every vase or figurine, and lace protectors on the arms and backs of chairs and sofas. When these items were produced in silk or cotton, they were usually trimmed in lace.

Original Victorian cords, tassels, lace, and fringework are difficult to locate today in good condition. Those who wish to decorate in this style can easily locate high-quality modern reproductions. Prices of original items are based on size, quality of work, and condition.

Price Ranges

Braided silk cords: $15 to $200.
Lace coverlettes: $5 to $100.
Lace doilies: $5 to $50.
Lace Drawbacks: $15 to $75.
Lace table drapes: $50 to $500.
Tassels: $5 to $100.

Pillar Tables

In many Victorian homes, any space that was not filled with other furniture or needed for walking space was taken up by a pillar table, sometimes referred to as a lamp stand or a plant stand. These tall, thin tables were used to hold a single lamp, plant, vase, urn, statue, pair of candles, Bible, or other decorative item. In many current publications these stands are often named based

2-19 Eastlake pillar table sits to the right of a Louis XVI chair with Eastlake influence. (Courtesy of McHenry Mansion)

on the objects they held, for example, candle stand, Bible stand, and so forth.

Pillar tables frequently look like tall piano stools and many have marble or glass tops. They were produced in an extremely wide array of styles, many of which cannot be placed into the established Victorian style categories. Designs ranged from basic spool-turned pedestals to elaborately carved, four-legged stands with applied figures and other embellishments.

Prices are based on size, quality of artisanship, and complexity of design.

Price Range

Pillar tables or stands: $75 to $450.

Suggested Reading

See center tables this chapter.

Side Chairs

See The Dining Room.

Silver Tea Service

While the reader might assume that tea services would be more appropriate in the chapter covering the dining room, more tea actually was served in the parlor than in any other room of the house. Afternoon tea, and its use as an accompaniment to visits and social gatherings, was one of the few very British customs retained by Americans. In addition, the silver tea service was an important decorative item. Many examples from the period are works of art, and today certain nineteenth-century tea sets can bring in more than $10,000 at auction.

Like many items manufactured during the Victorian era, silver increasingly was machine produced after 1840. Silver plate (usually on a copper base), although introduced in the 1700s, became extremely popular during the middle to late 1800s and is commonly called Sheffield for the town in England where large quantities were pro-

2-20 An eleven-piece silver tea set, as shown in a nineteenth-century ad.

duced. (Silver pieces with the mark "EPNS" are plated silver; however, not all plated pieces are marked thus.) Tea sets were manufactured in both sterling silver and silver plate. Styles were often elaborate Rococo and Baroque designs, although some American manufacturers used scenes from nature or history. In some silver sets, colored glass or porcelain bowls are set into silver holders, or the item itself may be porcelain or gilt lined.

Prominent British manufacturers included Joseph Angell III, who continued a long line of family silversmiths; Barnard and Sons, one of London's largest and most prolific silversmiths; Garrard and Company, Britain's premier domestic silver manufacturer; Gibson and Langman; and the London firms whose names were variously combined as Storr and Mortimer, Mortimer and Hunt, and Hunt and Roskell.

In America, Samuel Kirk and Sons, Bailey and Kitchen, Reed and Barton, and Tiffany and Company were the major manufacturers of the nineteenth century, and all are still producing silver today.

The value of a Victorian silver tea service on today's market is determined by size, quality of artisanship, complexity of design, identification of manufacturer, and grade of silver or plate.

Investors in silver should obtain one of the many guides to silver hallmarks and beware of counterfeits.

> *NOTE:* For a more thorough discussion of silver collecting, see Chapter 3, The Dining Room.

Price Ranges

Plated tea service (hallmarked): $250 to $2500+.
Silver tea service (hallmarked): $1200 to $8500+.

Suggested Reading

Bradbury, Frederick. *Bradbury's Book of Hallmarks.* J W Northend England, 1987.

Feild, Rachel. *McDonald Guide to Buying Antique Silver and Plate.* Philadelphia: Trans-Atlantic Publications, 1988.

Sofas

The sofa was the largest piece of ordinary furniture designed for sitting. (Large circular ottomans were used in some large homes and in hotel lobbies.) The basic design is similar to the settee and loveseat mentioned earlier, except that it is larger and more fully upholstered, usually lacking the decorative wooden panels found in the center of many smaller pieces.

Although parlor furniture was often sold as a set, the purchaser was given a choice of loveseat, settee, or sofa. The decision was usually based on the size of the room, large parlors having a sofa and perhaps a loveseat as well. In the minds of many Victorian homeowners, quantity was more important than size, and many opted for a loveseat and a pair of armchairs instead of a single couch.

Sofas were produced in a large variety of styles, usually named for the design of the back: heart back, medallion back, oval back, round back, serpentine, mirror frame, double frame, and sleigh back. The most comfortable is a Louis XV substyle, which has a fully upholstered serpentine back, finger-roll trim, and a minimal amount of bare or protruding wood. The least comfortable is the Eastlake double-frame back, which is basically an ornate wooden bench with four thin cloth pads. However, one must remember that the Victorians were usually much more concerned with appearance than with comfort.

2-21 Elaborate Renaissance Revival sofa in the style of John Jelliff, a famous Victorian furniture maker who incorporated figures and medallions in his designs. (Courtesy of McHenry Mansion)

Elaborately trimmed examples with large amounts of festooned, carved, crested, cutout, and incised wood were the order of the day.

Victorian sofa prices are based on size, wood, condition, quality of artisanship, and complexity of design.

Price Ranges

American Eastlake sofa: $350 to $900+.
Louis XV sofas: $485 to $1200.
Renaissance Revival sofa: $750 to $1500+.

Suggested Reading

See center tables this chapter.

Sofa Tables

The coffee table as we know it today did not exist in Victorian times. However, various tables were kept next to or in front of the sofa, including center tables, teapoys, and even small pillar tables. There was a table designed specifically for the purpose, although if one were to find a sofa table today, the seller probably would not identify it as such.

Sofa tables are rectangular or long ovals, somewhat longer and narrower than a small center table and frequently contain a drawer with hidden finger grips instead of a handle. They are often identified mistakenly as game tables, work tables, sewing tables, or teapoys, and are priced accordingly.

Price Range

Sofa tables: $175 to $350. Highest prices are paid for elaborate designs, which are frequently in Renaissance Revival style.

Souvenirs

The Victorians were collectors—not so much that they put together an organized collection of objects in a particular category, but that everywhere they went they liked to bring something

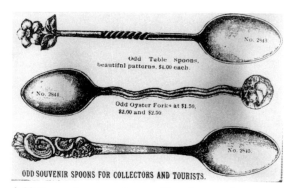

2-22 Souvenir spoons from a Victorian catalog.

back with them to remind them of a place or event and to impress their friends by showing where they had been. This tendency became increasingly widespread as the turn of the century approached, so that homes of the late Victorian period quite often literally overflowed with souvenirs, whatnots and étagères filled to capacity, tables crowded to their edges, and walls covered with plaques and framed papers.

After the Civil War, relic collecting became a widespread craze. Battlefields were stripped of all evidence of the major battles that had occurred there. Some overzealous collectors even resorted to grave robbing. Many war souvenirs were brought home by returning soldiers. Battle flags, guns, swords, buckles, and other spoils of war were prominently displayed in the homes of veterans throughout the country (see Chapter 7, The Library).

The various international exhibitions (world's fairs) held throughout the Victorian era were also wonderful sources for souvenirs. Among the most famous of these events were the Crystal Palace Exhibition of 1851 in London, the New York Crystal Palace Exhibition of 1853, the Paris Exhibition of 1867, the Centennial Exhibition of 1876 in Philadelphia, and the World's Columbian Exposition of 1893 in Chicago. Souvenirs from the exhibitions included silver spoons, postcards, lithographs, books, bronze and silver replicas of exhibition buildings, wall plaques, and many large items such as silver and ceramic pitchers, vases, and tea sets.

Many souvenirs came from other special events such as elections, centennials, openings, and local celebrations. Plates, mugs, spoons, buttons, and plaques were the most common items brought back from these events.

To be well traveled was to be highly respected in Victorian times. Therefore, the most prominently displayed souvenirs were those from foreign lands. Arrows, spears, shields, and items made from animal parts (elephant footstools were common) were brought from Africa; rugs and tapestries from the Middle East; swords, armor, and other medieval artifacts from Europe; and pottery and carvings from the Far East.

The Victorian souvenirs most collected today relate to specific events or depict people and places important to the period. Prices are based on condition, size, complexity of design, materials used, and factors of supply and demand.

Price Ranges

Postcards: $1.50 to $200+. Average: $5 to $9.
Souvenir plates: $35 to $350. Average: $120.
Souvenir Spoons: $20 to $250. Average: $40.

Suggested Reading

Megson, Frederic and Mary. *American Advertising Postcards—Set and Series: 1890–1920.* Self-published, 1985.

Rainwater, Dorothy T., and Donna H. Felger. *American Spoons: Souvenir and Historical.* West Chester, Pa.: Schiffer Publishing, 1990.

Ryan, Dorothy B. *Picture Postcards in the United States, 1893–1918.* New York: Clarkson N. Potter, 1982.

Smith, Jack H. *Postcard Companion: The Collectors Reference.* Radnor, Pa.: Wallace-Homestead Book Company, 1989.

Smith, Jack H. *Royal Postcards.* Radnor, Pa.: Wallace-Homestead Book Company, 1987.

Sterling Silver, Silverplate, and Souvenir Spoons with Prices. L-W Inc., 1988.

Teapoys

A Victorian host or hostess that did not offer a cup of tea to his or her guests was making a major breach of etiquette. As previously mentioned, this decidedly British tradition was continued almost religiously in the United States throughout the nineteenth and early twentieth centuries, especially in homes of high class and breeding.

The silver service (see Silver Tea Service, this chapter) often displayed in the parlor was not necessarily the one that would be used for serving tea. Often, a second less-ornate set was kept in the dining room or kitchen and brought out by the maid or butler on a table, called a teapoy, made specifically for the purpose. When not in use, the teapoy was often used as a display table for the tea service or other decorative pieces.

As is the case with many pieces of Victorian furniture, teapoys are often confused with other similar pieces or are simply identified as work tables. Part of the confusion stems from the name itself, which in Hindi means "three foot." The earliest teapoys, introduced in the eighteenth century, did have three legs. In addition, the top of the table had containers for various teas and a mixing bowl. In Victorian times the name was often used for any table used for serving tea; however, the definitive Victorian teapoy is a relatively small table (about twenty by thirty inches) with four spool-turned supports ending on two cross-feet with porcelain casters. There is usually a drawer beneath the table top for storing silverware and linens, and a shelf about halfway down to hold the tea caddy and other items while not in use.

The teapoy should not be confused with other tables such as drop-leafs, produced in early Chippendale and Federal styles, and Victorian tilt-top tables, which were commonly used for tea service and called tea tables by some dealers.

Prices of teapoys are affected by size, presence of drawer or shelf, wood used, and condition.

Price Range

Teapoys: $125 to $300.

Suggested Reading

Same as center tables this chapter.

Tilt-Top Tables

Various types of mechanical furniture have been around as long as furniture itself. Drop-leaf and extension tables were among the first and most functional mechanical designs. These tables took up a minimal amount of space until they were needed, which was also the primary purpose of the tilt-top table. The entire surface of this table dropped to a vertical position. A tilt-top occupied three feet of space when horizontal but only one foot or less when dropped.

Tilt-top tables were produced in a variety of styles, shapes, and sizes. Common functional styles were produced in walnut, with a round or oval top mounted on a tripod or pedestal base.

More elaborate pieces may have been octagonal or turtle shaped with molded edges. They were constructed of fine woods or papier-maché, inlaid with mother-of-pearl or painted with floral designs. Some tilt-tops were produced with glass overlays under which decorative needlework or art could be displayed. Serving both as decoration and as a quick source of additional table space, the tilt-top was an important piece of parlor furniture that was used in various rooms throughout the house.

Prices of tilt-top tables are based on size, wood or other materials used, complexity of design, and condition. Tilt-top tables tended to become slanted with years of use; therefore, pieces that maintain a level horizontal position are most in demand.

Price Ranges

Framed glass-top table: $500 to $1500+, depending on quality and originality of art or needlework displayed.
Papier-Maché tables with mother-of-pearl inlays: $300 to $1500.
Plain walnut oval or round tables: $300 to $500.

Suggested Reading

Same as center tables this chapter.

CHAPTER 3
The Dining Room

In Victorian homes, the dining room was almost always connected to the front parlor by a set of large sliding doors. When these doors were closed the dining room was a working room, that is, used by the family every day. When these doors were open, the dining room became a room for entertaining, almost an extension of the front parlor. The decor of the dining room reflected this connection.

The most obvious piece of furniture in the dining room was the large *dining table* in the center of the room, surrounded by a number of *side chairs*. When not in use, the dining table would be draped with an elegant decorative linen tablecloth. This cloth might be left in place for formal dinners, but for family meals it would be replaced by a more serviceable plain cotton cover. In small dining rooms the table may have been a *drop-leaf* or an *extension table,* which could be adjusted to accommodate the number of diners.

The only other large piece of furniture found in the dining room was the *sideboard.* This piece often was quite massive, with a towering pediment and a myriad of applied ornaments and moldings. On the upper half of the piece, several shelves would contain *glassware, china,* or numerous decorative items. The center drawers, containing *silverware* and linens, were just below

a large open shelf (often marble) from which meals were served. The large enclosed cabinets beneath held china, the *cruet set, silver serving dishes,* and other serving items.

Infants were fed, then as now, in a *highchair,* usually located near the mother's chair. When not in use, it would be stored against one wall or in the kitchen, where the child was fed by a servant during formal dinners.

In large dining rooms, there was a fireplace with a mantel holding a clock, candlesticks, or other decorative items. Game tables, center tables, and parlor stands were used to display decorative lamps and vases or provide additional serving space.

Mealtime was important to the Victorians. It brought the family together in one place to plan or review their daily activities. Dinner was the centerpiece of an evening's entertainment and provided the best configuration for social interaction. Everyone could see and hear everyone else and join in any discussion. In keeping with the Victorian penchant to impress, only the finest china, silver, and linens were used when guests were present.

From the dining room one could proceed to the front parlor or through the double doors at the other end of the room to the back parlor or music room. In many homes a smaller door used by servants connected the dining room to the central hallway and kitchen.

China

During the nineteenth century tin, wood, pewter, and various types of ceramics were used to produce dinner plates and serving dishes. However, in the proper Victorian dining room, only the best-quality fine china was used.

The term "china" always has been used somewhat loosely, but in this context it means the various cups, dishes, plates, and serving items made of high-quality ceramics (stoneware,

earthenware, and porcelain). This is not to be confused with the term "bone china," which is a specific type of porcelain containing bone ash. (For additional information about the history and production of ceramics, see Decorative Pottery in Chapter 2, The Front Parlor.)

The primary type of china used during the Victorian era was white earthenware, introduced in England by Josiah Wedgwood during the late eighteenth century. Prior to the mid-1900s, earthenware objects were "thrown," that is, formed by hand on a potter's wheel. With the introduction of molding techniques at midcentury, white earthenware dinner dishes were produced in large quantities, often with colorful transfer prints or hand-painted designs.

Three variants of white earthenware are yellow earthenware, produced in the same manner from a yellow clay; stoneware, so called because it was extremely tough and durable; and Rockinghamware, white or yellow earthenware covered with a brown glaze. Patterns and decorations were applied by transferring an ink design from tissue paper, or by applying paint either with a brush or sponge (spongeware).

The major manufacturers of earthenware in England were Adams and Sons, Samuel Alcock, Copeland, Doulton and Company, Martin Brothers, Mason, Minton, William de Morgan, Pratt and Company, and Wedgwood. In America, the

3-1 A Victorian dining table with china, silver, glass, and accessories. Note the front parlor in near distance. (Courtesy Bernhard House)

3-2 China serving dish with painted decorations. (Courtesy McHenry Mansion)

recognized names were American Pottery, Mayer, Norton, and Southern.

The best-quality and most expensive china found in better Victorian homes was porcelain imported from England (American manufacturers produced primarily decorative art porcelain). The widely recognized names of Coalport, Copeland, Derby, Minton, Ridgeway, and Worcester produced beautiful dinner sets with transferred and painted designs ranging from simple ribbon patterns to elaborate scenes with gilded borders.

Of primary importance to collectors of nineteenth-century ceramics is the recognition of marks found on the bottom of most pieces. These marks might include the manufacturer's name or hallmark, a diamond-shaped registration mark (used 1842 to 1883), or a registration number (since 1884). Several good books cataloging these marks are available.

Prices of Victorian dinner china are based on these factors: size and type of item; whether or not it is part of a set and if so, the number of pieces in the set; quality of artisanship; complexity of printed or painted design (if any); manufacturer; material used; condition; and market trends.

Price Ranges

Plates, American made, plain or with simple pattern
Earthenware: $2 to $25.
Ironstone: $2 to $25.
Rockinghamware: $25 to $50.
Spongeware: $50 to $175.
Yellow earthenware: $25 to $50.

Cup and saucer, American made, plain or with simple pattern
Ironstone: $10 to $75.
White earthenware: $4 to $25.
Yellow Earthenware: $10 to $75.

Copeland and Minton China
Copeland cup and saucer: $10 to $50.
Copeland plates: $5 to $30.

Minton cup and saucer: $25 to $150.
Minton plates: $75 to $175.

Covered Serving Dishes
Copeland $100 to $250+.
Minton $125 to $300+.
White earthenware with transfer print: $125 to $400.
Yellow Earthenware $45 to $85.

Porcelain, British made
Cup and saucer: $75 to $500+.
Dinner service: $750 to $3000+.
Plates: $50 to $500+. Elaborate designs by major manufacturers can bring up to $10,000.

Suggested Reading

Bagdade, Susan and Al. *English and Continental Pottery and Porcelain: An Illustrated Price Guide.* Radnor, Pa.: Wallace-Homestead Book Company, 1987.
Feild, Rachel. *McDonald Guide to Buying Antique Pottery and Porcelain: Authenticity, Technique, Dating, Reproduction.* Radnor, Pa.: Wallace-Homestead Book Company, 1989.

Cruets and Casters

There is probably no other table item more associated with the Victorian era than the caster, a small stand (usually silver or silver plated) containing colored or decorated condiment bottles called cruets. The term "caster" was used because items from the bottles—vinegar, salt, pepper, mustard, and other spices—were "cast" over the food.

During the second half of the nineteenth century, casters became quite popular and often quite elaborate. Silver-plated stands were decorated, in a process called "chasing," with ornately engraved patterns that frequently included figures or bells in the handle design. Glass bottles were cut or pressed with fancy patterns. Cut-glass or crystal stoppers were used on bottles meant to contain liquids, while spice bottles usually had silver caps. Small casters (called "breakfast casters" or "lunch casters") had three or four bottles, while large dinner casters had as many as seven.

3-3 Silver caster frame and glass condiment bottles with silver lids and crystal stoppers. (Courtesy McHenry Mansion)

Pickle cruets often had their own individual casters, and many cruet bottles were sold separately, without casters.

Prices of Victorian casters and cruets are based on size and complexity of stand, degree of chasing, number and style of condiment bottles, identification of manufacturer, and condition.

Price Ranges

Cruet bottles: $50 to $1000+.
Pickle casters: $75 to $500+.
Silver-plate casters: 3 bottles $75 to $250; 4 bottles $100 to $500; 5 bottles $100 to $750; 6 bottles $100 to $1000+; 7 bottles $150 to $1500+.

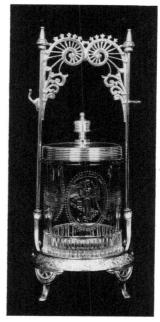

3-4 Pickle caster with pattern glass jar. (Courtesy McHenry Mansion)

In all categories, the highest prices are paid for bottles made of rare glass.

Suggested Reading

Heacock, William. *Encyclopedia of Victorian Pattern Glass, vol. 6, Oil Cruets.* Marietta, Ohio: Antique Publications, 1981.
Also see books on silver listed under Silver Service Items in this chapter.

Dining Tables

The dining tables found in Victorian homes were widely varied in style and size. Some Victorians preferred a round or square table with a one-piece top and a pedestal base with ornate carvings. Others preferred a lightweight rectangular extension table, which occupied a minimal amount of space and yet could expand to accommodate large dinner parties. In a house decorated entirely in Renaissance Revival or Eastlake furniture, one might find a massive dining table in the Empire or Gothic style.

If there is a definitive dining table of the late Victorian period, it probably is a rectangular extension table of Renaissance design with a pedestal base. This style was produced in large quantities by Grand Rapids manufacturers from the late 1870s. Some of these were designed to extend as much as twelve feet through the addition of numerous leaves. This type of table was also popular in the Eastlake style and with round or oval tops.

Prices of Victorian dining tables are based on style, complexity of design, number of leaves (if any), type of wood, size, and condition.

Price Ranges

American Eastlake dining tables: $750 to $1500.
Renaissance Revival dining tables: $1000 to $1500.

Suggested Reading

McNerney, Kathryn. *Victorian Furniture: Our American Heritage.* Paducah, Ky.: Collector Books, 1988.

Swedberg, Robert W. and Harriett Swedberg. *Victorian Furniture.* Vols. 1–3. Radnor, Pa.: Wallace-Homestead Book Company, 1984–85.

Glassware

Victorian period glassware is one of the most collected categories of antiques, primarily due to the extremely large array of styles and patterns

3-5 & 3-6 Two pattern glass goblets of the style produced in large variety during the Victorian period. (Courtesy McHenry Mansion)

that were produced. There are nearly three hundred major designs just in the popular pattern glass category. Sections on collectible glass often occupy more than one-third of the texts of major antiques price guides. (For additional information on the history and production of Victorian glass, see Decorative Glass in Chapter 2, The Front Parlor).

Glassware found in the dining room included goblets, tumblers, plates, platters, teacups, sugar bowls, creamers, serving dishes, pitchers, spoon holders, eggcups, butter dishes, saltcellars, compotes, marmalade jars, celery vases, honey dishes, cracker jars, cake stands, salt and pepper shakers, punch bowls, water carafes, and other specialty dishes too numerous to mention. While some of these items were manufactured in blown glass, most were made of molded pressed glass, which was produced in large quantities from the late 1860s.

Pressed glass items were made in a myriad of patterns to satisfy all tastes. Matching table settings were purchased along with serving dishes in the same pattern. Pattern names are identified with the particular manufacturer and the date produced, for example: Cupid and Venus, produced in the late 1870s by Hartley Glass; King's Crown, produced by Adams and Company during the 1890s; and Primrose, made by Canton Glass around 1880. Several excellent guides have been published for the identification of pattern glass (see Suggested Reading).

Pattern glass was produced in a variety of colors and finishes that may or may not affect the price of the piece, depending on the pattern and manufacturer. These colors and finishes include clear, frosted, canary or amber, ruby, emerald green, "maiden's blush" pink, apple green, vaseline, sapphire blue, milk, opal, and others. Some examples were trimmed in gold, silver, and even platinum.

In the 1870s the centuries-old art of glass cutting returned to popularity. Most of the dining room glass mentioned above was also produced in

3-7 Pattern glass sugar bowl and creamer. (Courtesy McHenry Mansion)

cut-crystal. (The term "crystal" refers to any fine-quality cut-glass of the period. Today crystal is a specific type of glass that contains at least one-quarter lead.) In this process, a glass "blank" was made of the particular item; then, using a type of grinding wheel, the artist cut the various patterns into the glass. Items produced by this method are considerably more valuable than pressed pattern glass, and the glass itself is usually of a much higher quality.

Prices of Victorian glassware are based on type and size of object, type and color of glass, complexity of design, condition, and identification of pattern and manufacturer.

Price Ranges

Pressed pattern glass (clear): goblet $20 to $200+; tumbler $10 to $200+; creamer $25 to $200+; pitcher $40 to $500+; compote $40 to $400+. Highest prices paid for certain colors and patterns. Cut crystal: goblet $50 to $1000+; tumbler $35 to $350+; sugar and creamer set $75 to $350; pitcher $85 to $2500+; compote $75 to $1000+. Highest prices paid for certain patterns and manufacturers.

Suggested Reading

Jenks, Bill and Jerry Luna. *Early American Pattern Glass, 1850–1910.* Radnor, Pa.: Wallace-Homestead Book Company, 1989.

Miles, Dori. *Wallace-Homestead Price Guide to Pattern Glass.* Radnor, Pa.: Wallace-Homestead Book Company, 1986.

Shuman, John III. *Collector's Encyclopedia of American Glass.* Paducah, Ky.: Collector Books, 1988.

Spillman, Jane. *American and European Pressed Glass.* Corning, N.Y.: Corning Museum of Glass, 1981.

Swann, Martha Louise. *American Cut and Engraved Glass.* Radnor, Pa.: Wallace-Homestead Book Company, 1986.

Highchairs

The basic design of the highchair has remained unchanged from Victorian times to the present day. The highchair is of a convenient height for feeding a child, and has a wide stance for stability and a tray to hold and catch food. Highchairs of the Victorian period were made entirely of wood and followed the styles of the day. They were manufactured with cane backs, slat backs, lyre backs, and spindles. Some even had wheels and were designed to collapse for use as a stroller (see Illustration 3-8). Some examples, primarily in the Renaissance Revival style, were upholstered. Victorian highchairs are available in nearly every style and substyle of the era.

Prices for Victorian highchairs are based on style, quality of artisanship, wood used, complexity of design, and condition.

Price Ranges

American Eastlake Highchair: $250 to $400+.
Renaissance Revival Highchair: $300 to $475+.

Highest prices are paid for examples that are adjustable and convertible to a crib or stroller.

3-8 Eastlake convertible highchair shown here in stroller configuration. (Courtesy Amador County Museum)

3-9 Elaborate French Revival side chair with carved crest. (Courtesy Leeper's Fantastic Antiques)

Side Chairs

When the dining table was purchased, it may or may not have come with matching chairs. In fact, the chairs surrounding the table were quite often of a different style and may not even have matched one another. Side chairs were often purchased individually as the family grew or when the need for additional seating was anticipated. The term "side chair" refers to a relatively narrow chair with a high back and no arms. Although it is commonly recognized as a dining chair, it was used in nearly every part of the Victorian home, usually sitting along the "side" of the room, against one wall.

The most popular style of side chair was a French Revival version with a balloon-shaped frame from the early Victorian era. Even after other furniture had been replaced by newer Revival styles, the balloon-back chair continued to find use, although it was extremely uncomfortable as it provided no back support other than that provided by the frame itself. Examples with carved or attached Rococo designs could actually be painful to sit in.

The appearance of mass-produced Renaissance

3-10 French Revival balloon-back side chair with finger roll.

3-11 French Revival balloon-back side chair with carved crest.

3-12 French Revival side chair with upholstered back and Gothic influence.

3-13 French Revival-influenced spool-turned side chair.

and Eastlake styles introduced padded and upholstered side chairs. While these were somewhat heavier and bulkier than the balloon backs, they were much more comfortable and saw even wider use as extra chairs in halls and parlors.

During the late 1850s, photography studios began to produce full-length portraits on a new form of paper photograph called the *carte de visite* (see Chapter 1, The Entry Hall). So that subjects would be more comfortable, various props upon which they could lean were provided. The easiest prop to come by was, of course, the common chair, which every photographer already had in his studio. Figures 3-10 through 3-17 take us on a trip back in time, providing us with not only a history of the Victorian chair but of Victorian clothing styles as well.

Prices of Victorian side chairs are based on style, complexity of design, wood used, type of upholstery, and condition.

3-14 French Revival upholstered side chair with crested balloon back.

3-15 French Revival fully upholstered lady's armchair.

Price Ranges

American Eastlake side chair: $150 to $350.
French Revival balloon-back side chair: $150 to $350, depending on complexity of carved or attached designs.
Renaissance Revival side chair: $200 to $450.

Suggested Reading

See Dining Tables, this chapter.

3-16 Eastlake upholstered side chair.

3-17 Eastlake folding side chair.

Sideboards

A Victorian dining room without a sideboard would be like a kitchen without a stove. The sideboard was a showplace for fine crystal and china, a storage cabinet for silver and linens, and a table from which the meal was served. Even the smallest dining room contained one of these often massive pieces of furniture.

The basic lines of the sideboard were similar to those of other tall pieces of furniture, such as hall trees and étagères. From a large table base with drawers and storage cabinets below, an ornate frame (often with a mirror in the center) rises up to a crowning pediment. Rows of shelves either flank the mirror or, if no mirror is present, cross the width of the frame from left to right. Sideboards range from six to eight feet in height and from four to six feet in length. Renaissance and Eastlake styles either can be very basic or highly

3-18 Renaissance Revival sideboard with carved deer head adornment. (Courtesy McHenry Mansion)

Silver Service Items

By the late nineteenth century, Victorians who could never have afforded even one item made of solid silver were now buying almost almost all of their service items in silver plate. A catalog from the 1880s shows a five-piece solid silver tea service for $375 and a similar six-piece service in "quadruple plated silver" for $48—"engraved free!"

Literally hundreds of items were available in plated silver for use in the dining room. Here is an abbreviated list from the aforementioned catalog:

baking dishes	napkin rings
berry bowls	nut bowls
butter dishes	nutcrackers
cake stands	nutpicks
call bells	pepper boxes
casters	pickle stands
coffee services	salad sets
cracker jars	spoon holders
cream pitchers	sugar bowls
crumb scrapers	sugar and cream dessert sets
crumb trays	syrup pitchers
cups	tea services
decanters	tea stands
fruit stands	tête-à-têtes
goblets	toothpicks
ice pitchers	tureens
ice swinging sets	water services
ice water sets	wine stands

ornate; however, larger examples tend to be of Renaissance style.

Prices of Victorian sideboards are based on style, size, complexity of design, wood used, presence of a marble top, and condition.

Price Ranges

American Eastlake sideboard: $1000 to $3000.
Renaissance Revival sideboard: $1500 to $5000.

Suggested Reading

See Dining Table, this chapter.

Many of these items were lined with gold plate (gilt) or porcelain; most were engraved with highly ornate patterns (called "chasing"). Single-plated items were very inexpensive, and extant pieces are usually worn through to the base metal. The most popular silver plated items of the Victorian period, and the most valuable on today's market, are quadruple-plated items.

Most of the pieces listed previously are still common in many twentieth-century homes; however, some are considered definitively Victorian.

Call bells—Large Victorian homes were seldom without at least one servant—a maid or a butler, or perhaps a manservant who performed all of the various household duties such as cooking and serving meals, cleaning, and even taking care of the children. Although most homes were equipped with a central bell or buzzer system for calling servants, silver call bells were convenient for bedside stands and dinner tables. These may have been standard bells, with a wooden or silver handle, or mechanical striker bells, sounded by hitting a button with the palm of the hand.

Crumb scrapers—One of the many jobs of Victorian servants was to make sure that the area around diners was kept neat during the meal. A silver crumb scraper is an elegant and discreet device with which a servant removed droppings from the table to a silver tray between courses. The crumb scraper looked like a small elongated shovel with a handle on the side. It was used to scrape small pieces of food onto a matching tray.

Napkin rings—While simple napkin rings are commonly used today, during the nineteenth century they often were quite elaborate and artistic pieces. Many examples are set on a platform base along with an ornate figure of a bird, flower, or cherub. Napkin rings usually are included in individual casters along with a saltcellar, a pepper or spice box, a call bell, and other items.

3-19 *Individual caster, shown in a Victorian catalog, includes napkin ring, condiment bottle, and saltcellar.*

3-20 *Crumb scraper and tray. (Courtesy Amador County Museum)*

3-21 Silver-plated napkin ring. (Courtesy Georgia Fox, Foxes Den)

3-22 Silver-plated swinging water set. (Courtesy Amador County Museum)

Spoon holders—A spoon used to stir a cup of tea cannot be placed back on the table without staining the tablecloth, and if it is placed on a plate, it sooner or later will be knocked off onto the table or floor. This dilemma of etiquette was solved in Victorian times by the use of a spoon holder, an elaborate two-handled miniature urn where the spoon could safely drain and wait for its next service.

Swinging sets—Among the most beautiful and elaborate of serving devices is the tilting ice water service—a large, ornate silver pitcher attached by a pivot to an equally ornate platform. Ice water can be easily poured into the matching goblets simply by tilting the pitcher forward. Excess water that dribbled from the spout might be caught in a slop bowl, which would rest on the stand behind the pitcher. Ice water sets were produced in a large variety of styles and configurations with or without matching trays, bowls, and goblets.

Pickle casters and stands—These are some of the most collected Victorian dinner accessories (see also Cruets and Casters, this chapter). Pickle casters were produced in cut and pressed glass (clear, frosted, or colored), had elaborate silver lids, and sat in silver stands with matching tongs. They were manufactured in both single- and double-caster configurations.

Victorian butter dishes—To one who is unfamiliar with Victorian dinner accessories, the butter dish is a puzzle. It quite often is a large and elaborate serving stand, seemingly too elaborate for a simple block of butter. For example, the catalog description for the example shown

3-23 Silver butter dish with typically elaborate etchings (chasing). (Courtesy McHenry Mansion)

3-24 Small silver container that may have been used for a variety of purposes. (Courtesy Georgia Fox, Foxes Den)

here reads: "Quadruple silver plated, plain satin, with engraved shield or elaborately chased butter dish; 14½ inches high with sliding top and patent glass drainer, at either $7 or $8."

Saltcellars—Before 1870 there were no salt and pepper shaker sets as we know them today. Salt was a valuable commodity in the early 1900s and was served in very small quantities in glass or silver dishes with perforated lids and tiny spoons. Even when salt became more plentiful the tradition of the saltcellar was maintained, either as part of a cruet set or as an individual service item. As the turn of the century approached, salt and pepper shakers became widely accepted, but the saltcellar saw continued use in upper-class dining rooms.

Collectors of nineteenth-century silver should become familiar with the various hallmarks indicating manufacturers of the period (see Suggested Reading). Prices of silver service items are based on complexity of design, quality of artisanship, quality of silver or plate, identification of manufacturer, condition, and fluctuations in the bulk silver market. The pricing of solid or sterling silver items is also greatly affected by place of origin (United States, England, the Continent, and so forth).

Price Ranges

Butter dishes: sterling $400 to $2200; plated $40 to $800.

Call bells: sterling $150 to $700.

Crumb scrapers: sterling $80 to $300.

Napkin rings: sterling $50 to $125; plated $15 to $150; figural $100 to $250.

Pickle casters: plated $80 to $250.

Saltcellars: individual sterling $55 to $425; plated $20 to $150; figural $30 to $750.

Swinging ice water set: plated $200 to $400.

Tray (approximately 10 to 20 inches): sterling $250 to $550+; plated $55 to $275+.

Suggested Reading

Bradbury, Fredrick. *Bradbury's Book of Hallmarks.* Cincinnati: Seven Hills, 1987.

Feild, Rachel. *McDonald Guide To Buying Antique Silver and Plate.* Philadelphia: Trans-Atlantic Publications, 1988.

Hagan, Tere. *Silverplated Flatware: An Identification and Value Guide,* third ed. Paducah, Ky.: Collector Books, 1986.

Heacock, William and Johnson. *Open Salts: A Collector's Guide.* Richardson Printing, 1982.

Rainwater, Dorothy T. and H. Ivan Rainwater. *American Silverplate.* rev. ed. West Chester, Pa.: Schiffer Publishing, 1988.

Schandig, Victor. *American Victorian Figural Napkin Rings.* Radnor, Pa.: Wallace-Homestead Book Company, 1971.

The Official Price Guide to American Silver and Silver Plate, fifth ed. Orlando: House of Collectibles, 1986.

Silver Flatware and Serving Utensils

As with many of the conveniences we today take for granted, the knife, spoon, and fork were born in the Victorian era. Prior to the mid–nineteenth century knives and forks were considered kitchenware. After the Civil War the Victorian

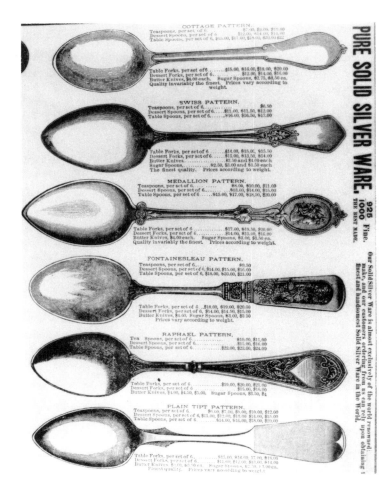

3-25 A sampling of silverware designs from a Victorian catalog.

place setting might have contained as many as six forks, eight spoons, and four knives.

The average setting generally contained a sugar spoon, teaspoon, dinner spoon, pickle fork, lettuce fork, meat fork, dinner fork, meat knife, dinner knife, and butter knife. Also included in the set, but not always used, was an oyster fork. Optional items included a sardine fork, cold-meat fork, cake fork, salt spoon, bouillon spoon, orange spoon, mustard spoon, preserves spoon, ice cream spoon, among many others. In addition to the small meat knife, there was a larger carving knife and individual knives for slicing cake, pie, bread, and fish.

The handles of Victorian silver flatware were decorated with a variety of both basic and elaborate designs, ranging from simple ribbon borders to ornate Rococo patterns. One of the most popular designs, called "Chantilly," was introduced by the Gorham Company of Providence, Rhode Island, in 1831 and is still being produced by popular demand. The various patterns used on flatware were seldom patented and were therefore often copied by other manufacturers in both sterling silver and silver plate.

A number of additional utensils were manufactured for various cutting and serving chores. There were ladles for serving sauces and gravies, pie servers, fish serving sets, berry spoons, grape shears for cutting small sprigs from the bunch, tea strainers, and nutpicks, just to name a few. There were also many novel and inventive devices, such as the bone holder, which attached to the bone of a ham or roast so that the meat could be held solidly during carving; the toast rack, which held four pieces of toast, an egg, and salt and pepper shakers; the egg coddler, which conveniently boiled eggs in a rack over a spirit flame; and even the coffee percolator. All of these items were produced in beautiful sterling silver or silver plate.

Silver Victorian flatware is seldom found in any sort of complete set. Collectors build their sets by first choosing a specific pattern and manufacturer, then locating the various items a few pieces at a time. As previously mentioned, certain patterns are still being produced today by the same manufacturers. Modern flatware is usually much lighter in weight than original pieces, but collectors should exercise caution.

Prices of Victorian silver flatware and utensils are based on quality of silver or silver plate, complexity of design, identification of manufacturer, condition, and supply and demand factors. All silver prices are affected by fluctuations in the bulk silver market.

Price Ranges

Fish knife set (serving knife and fork): sterling $250 to $500; plated $60 to $200.

Flatware: single pieces sterling $15 to $100+; single pieces plated $5 to $15+. Highest prices paid in both categories for rare patterns from well-known and respected manufacturers.

Ladle: sterling $60 to $500; plated $35 to $250.

Nut spoon: plated $75 to $300+. Highest prices paid for novel designs and gilt insets.

Tea strainers and balls: sterling $75 to $250; plated $20 to $100.

Suggested Reading

See Silver Service Items, this chapter.

CHAPTER 4

The Kitchen

In a formal home with servants, the Victorian kitchen was seldom seen by the family. It was the place where the hired help spent most of their day; the center of cooking, cleaning, and service-related activities. In less-formal homes, the kitchen was often the center of the household, where homemaking duties were performed and taught to daughters. Households that could not afford a cook or a maid were decidedly sexist in domestic structure. Almost all of the household chores were performed by the woman of the house and her daughters. The man of the house was the breadwinner and recognized master of his castle (although in many cases his wife wielded most of the decision-making power).

Many kitchens contained a small breakfast table where informal family meals were served, allowing the dining room to remain undisturbed. Family members would come and go throughout the morning and early afternoon, partaking of boiled-egg-and-toast breakfasts or finger-sandwich lunches. In wealthier homes all meals were served in the dining room by a servant. Everyone was expected to be on time and properly dressed.

While the kitchen was probably the room most widely varied from one home to another, certain items were common to all: sink, stove, *work table, icebox, cupboard, crockery* (for food and storage

preparation), *metalware* (for cooking), *mechanical devices* (for slicing, dicing, peeling, and pitting), and *utensils* (for cutting, stirring, and pressing). During the early part of the Victorian era, kitchens often were inconveniently tacked on to the back of the house or tucked away in the basement. The eighteenth-century custom of building the kitchen separate from the house to prevent the spread of fires became less common as the nineteenth century progressed. After the Civil War architects began to place more importance on designing light, airy, and more serviceable kitchens.

The kitchen was often the only access to the rear of the house, where deliveries were received and servants came and went. Two small rooms—the pantry, for storing foodstuffs and other items, and (after the introduction of indoor plumbing) the downstairs toilet—were often connected to the kitchen. From the kitchen one might cross the hall to the dining room, proceed to other rooms via the central hallway, or exit the house through the back door.

Boxes

A large variety of storage boxes found use in the kitchen. During the early part of the Victo-

63

rian era kitchen boxes were made primarily of wood. After the Civil War boxes made of tin or thin sheets of iron were coated with enamel or graniteware finishes. Metal boxes were better suited to keeping out moisture and household pests and did not absorb the odor of their contents as did wood boxes. Since many wooden kitchen boxes were tossed out with the advent of metal versions, examples found in good condition today often bring premium prices.

Probably the most common storage box was the bread box. Like most food storage devices its primary purpose was to keep its contents fresh while keeping out insects and mice. Locking versions, used for cakes and other sweets, kept out impromptu snackers. Styles ranged from simple, loaf-sized boxes with hinged covers to tall metal cabinets with several shelves or drawers and rolling tops. While bread boxes were used to store cakes, there were cake boxes designed specifically for the purpose. These enameled tin boxes are often easily identified by the word "cake" incorporated into the decorative design.

Candle boxes are especially popular with collectors. These generally were made of wood although metal versions were manufactured, and were usually made to hang on the wall. In the nineteenth century candles were like our flashlights of today, and it was important to keep a supply in an easily found storage place. Sizes of candle boxes vary, but they were commonly designed to hold six to eight candles.

The cheese box was actually more of a wooden barrel made of bentwood. These boxes were produced commercially for cheese manufacturers and for sale to individuals. After the cheese was removed or eaten, the boxes often found various uses throughout the home.

Dough boxes were used to hold bread dough during the kneading process and while it was

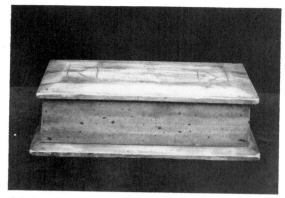

4-1 Candle box with incised decorations.

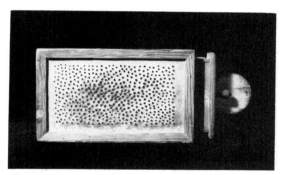

4-2 Dredge box for sprinkling flour. (Courtesy Amador County Museum)

being allowed to rise before baking. These usually are simple unfinished wooden boxes with slanted sides and covers. A pass under the nose often reveals the distinctive odor of yeast imbedded in the wood grain. Dredge boxes, or dredgers, were boxes with a perforated lid and were designed to hold and sprinkle flour.

Knife boxes were produced in a variety of styles and configurations. One style of knife box, beautifully produced in exotic woods with a cabinet-quality finish, was common in many upper-class Victorian homes and is often shown in related books. However, this distinctive knife box was actually produced prior to the period, in the late 1700s and early 1800s. Victorian period knife boxes often are similar to silverware boxes and have trays or slots inside and common hinged-top construction outside.

Pantry boxes are similar to cheese boxes—round or oval and made of bentwood. These commonly are called Shaker boxes by the antiques trade, and although the Shakers did produce this style of box, so did other manufacturers. Pantry boxes are often found in sets ranging in size from as small as three inches to as large as eighteen inches in diameter. Collectors are cautioned that this style of box has been continuously reproduced, even by the Shakers themselves.

Until the latter part of the nineteenth century, salt was difficult to obtain in quantity and was considered a precious commodity. Only small amounts were served at table (see Silver Service Items in Chapter 3, The Dining Room), and great care was taken in its storage. Salt boxes were produce in wood, glass, pewter, silver, and cast metal. Tin was seldom used because salt would eventually corrode it.

Spice boxes were designed to hold individual containers of spice. These containers may have been made of tin, wood, glass, or ceramic. Spice boxes took the form of a standard wooden box or cabinet or, more frequently, a large tin or bentwood box. They generally contained six or eight spice canisters, although some contained as many as sixteen. After all, what cook would want to be without a supply of cassia, marjoram, or celery powder?

Prices of kitchen boxes are based on a wide variety of factors, including size, shape, and purpose; condition of hinges, slides, and latches; condition of paint, enamel, or other finish; completeness of set (if part of a set); identification of date or name of manufacturer; existence of label or advertisement; and supply and demand.

Price Ranges

Bread boxes: wood $25 to 50; metal $15 to 75.
Butter boxes: bentwood $35 to 150.
Candle boxes: wood $35 to $500+; hanging metal $85 to $250.
Cheese boxes: $15 to $200+.
Pantry boxes: $20 to $500+, depending on size and identification of manufacturer.
Salt boxes: hanging wood $25 to $175+.
Spice boxes: $30 to $150+.

Suggested Reading

Franklin, Linda Campbell. *Three Hundred Years of Kitchen Collectibles.* Florence, Ala.: Books Americana, 1984.
Little, Nina. *Neat and Tidy: Boxes in Early American Households.* New York: E. P. Dutton, 1980.
Thompson, Frances. *Antiques from the Country Kitchen:* Radnor, Pa.: Wallace-Homestead Book Company, 1984.

Cane Chairs

Chairs with backs or seats of woven rattan are usually called "cane" chairs even though no cane was used in their manufacture. The idea for this type of chair came from Malaysia, where the natives made extensive use of the tough stems of the climbing palm in producing shades, baskets, and other useful items. The stems were sliced into long, thin strands of rattan, which were woven to create various objects.

The framework for Victorian cane chairs often was identical to other side chairs of the period. Instead of padding or upholstery, a woven rattan mat was attached to the frame, providing a flexible seat or back. Cane chairs were produced in all the major styles of the day, as well as simple ladder-back and spindle designs. Rattan insets were also used in rockers and folding lounge chairs.

Prices of Victorian cane chairs are based on

design, quality of artisanship, wood used in framework, and condition. While it is not impossible to find examples with original rattan mats, many pieces have had—or are in need of having—the weaving replaced. Whether original or restored, cane chairs with sturdy, functional insets bring the highest prices.

Price Ranges

American Eastlake cane chair: $100 to $250.
French Revival cane chair: $125 to $225.
Ladder-back cane chair: $75 to $150.
Renaissance Revival cane chair: $150 to $275.

Suggested Reading

McNerney, Kathryn. *Victorian Furniture*. Paducah, Ky.: Collector Books, 1988.
Plante, Ellen. *Kitchen Collectibles: An Illustrated Price Guide*. Radnor, Pa.: Wallace-Homestead Book Company, 1991.
Swedberg, Robert W. and Harriett Swedberg. *Victorian Furniture*. Vols. 1–3. Radnor, Pa.: Wallace-Homestead Book Company, 1983.

Canisters

Canisters traditionally are cans of various sizes used to store coffee, tea, sugar, flour, and other staples. During Victorian times they were manufactured in enameled tin, individually or in sets of four or six, with the name of the intended contents stenciled on the outside of each can. Although glass and ceramic storage jars were produced throughout the nineteenth century (see Crockery, next entry), canisters made of these materials are primarily a twentieth-century development.

Prices of Victorian canisters are based on size, completeness of set (if part of a set), and condition.

Price Range

Single canisters: single $15 to $35, six-piece set $50 to $150.

Suggested Reading

See Boxes, this chapter.

Crockery

The term "crockery" applies to jars, bowls, butter churns, and other kitchen items made of stoneware and earthenware. (Details of their manufacture and variety can be found under the heading Decorative Pottery in Chapter 2, The Front Parlor, and under China in Chapter 3, The Dining Room.) Most kitchen ceramics were sturdy and functional and produced in plain colors (white or yellow earthenware) or simple patterns (spongeware). The vast majority of kitchen crockery was produced in plain stoneware, with or without stenciled cobalt-blue decorations.

Whether or not the kitchen had a sink with a drain, slop jars were a necessity. This large, wide-mouthed vessel sat near the work area to hold wet waste materials until they could be disposed of outside. Slop jars were also used in bedrooms for the disposal of dirty water from washbowls.

Crocks were large storage jars used for a variety of purposes. They generally were straight sided, although some tapered in at the bottom. Straight-sided crocks measuring six inches or less in height were called "cake pots," and larger versions were called "butter pots." Crocks capable of holding thirty gallons or more, called "meat tubs," were produced in limited quantity. Wood or ceramic lids for crocks were purchased separately.

One of the more common storage vessels was called the "bean pot," although it was frequently used for other purposes. Bean pots resemble a large ceramic cup (five to eight inches high) with a handle and a lid. Examples without lids have considerably less value.

Preserve jars are a type of crock with sides slanting slightly outward then quickly curving in to a wide-lipped mouth. The jars (about six to

4-3 A typical "butter pot" crock.

4-4 Crockery jugs held more than just "moonshine." (Courtesy Williams Antiques)

twelve inches high) were filled with fruit or pre-serves, then sealed with a layer of hot wax. A similar jar with a somewhat narrower mouth was called a "corker" and was used for canning fruits and vegetables.

During the latter part of the nineteenth century most butter produced at home was made in glass jars with mechanical "butter beaters" (see Mechanical Kitchen Devices, this chapter). However, the device we most often connect with homemade butter is the "broom handle churn," a tall piece of crockery with a hole in its lid through which the handle of the "dasher" protrudes. As the dasher was raised and lowered, the milk or cream inside the crock was violently sloshed, causing butter to be formed on the dasher paddles. Crockery butter churns were produced in a variety of styles, and highly decorated versions are prized by collectors.

The most commonly available piece of Victorian crockery is the jug. Jugs for storing molasses, vinegar, cooking oil, and various mineral spirits were produced in large quantities. Plain stoneware jugs can be found nearly everywhere, but spongeware and other highly decorated examples are sought after by collectors.

Crockery pitchers and bowls were also pro-duced in large quantities and in a multitude of styles. Today these are collected to complete sets of yellowware, redware, Rockinghamware, spongeware, and other varieites of functional ceramics.

Prices of Victorian crockery are based on type of ceramic, complexity or novelty of decoration, identification of date or manufacturer (if any), condition, and supply and demand.

Price Ranges

Bean pots: $35 to $275+. Lowest prices are paid for plain redware.

Bowls: $10 to $200+.

Churns: $75 to $500+.

Crocks: $50 to $500+.

Jugs: $25 to $225+.

Pitchers: $35 to $385+.

Preserve jars and corkers: $40 to $325+.

Slop jars: $75 to $350+.

In all of these categories, the highest prices are paid for uniquely decorated pieces and for those identified as having been produced by important manufacturers.

Suggested Reading

Feild, Rachel. *MacDonald Guide To Buying Antique Pottery and Porcelain: Authenticity, Technique, Dating, Reproductions.* Radnor, Pa.: Wallace-Homestead Book Company, 1989.

Plante, Ellen. *Kitchen Collectibles: An Illustrated Price Guide.* Radnor, Pa.: Wallace-Homestead Book Company, 1991.

Raycraft, Don, and Carol Raycraft. *Country Stoneware and Pottery.* Paducah, Ky.: Collector Books; 1985.

Thompson, Frances. *Antiques from the Country Kitchen.* Radnor, Pa.: Wallace-Homestead Book Company, 1985.

Cupboards

Except for the pantry, storage areas or shelves were seldom built in a Victorian home. Wardrobes were used for storage in the bedroom, étagères and secretaries in the parlor and library, sideboards in the dining room, and cupboards in the kitchen. Kitchen cupboards may have been quality furniture in fine woods or functional pine pieces; they may have been painted, stained, or left unfinished. These generally resembled secretaries without the desk section, that is, tall shelving units covered by framed glass doors with drawers below and closed-front cabinets on the bottom. There were, however, a wide variety of kitchen cupboard styles, many of which were built to order to store flour bins and sifters, spice racks, and other such items. There were also smaller hanging cupboards and space-saving corner cupboards.

The primary purpose of a cupboard was, as its name implies, to provide shelving for dishes. However, since they often were the only storage unit in the kitchen, everything from pots and pans to foodstuffs were kept there. A shorter piece called a "jelly cupboard" had two drawers and double cabinets below a flat working surface. Its primary purpose was the storage of canned goods and other food items.

Kitchen cupboards with elaborate applied moldings and designs are rare. For the most part Victorian kitchen cupboards are found in designs called Country or Cottage furniture. Because many of these styles were produced from the eighteenth into the twentieth century, and because extensive restoration has often been performed, dating is sometimes difficult. Definitively Victorian Eastlake and Renaissance examples are prized by collectors.

Among the most sought-after kitchen cupboards is an elaborate two-piece design with a long door on one side containing a flour sifter, numerous cabinets and drawers, and a large enamelware or marble work surface. These cupboards, called "Hoosier cabinets," are not Victorian. They were produced mostly in Indiana, as the name implies, from the early 1900s and were used widely during the 1930s and 1940s.

Prices of Victorian kitchen cupboards are based on size and complexity of design, quality of artisanship, wood used, accuracy of dating, and condition. Prices in this category are greatly affected by local supply-and-demand factors; in certain areas examples may bring as much as twice the price listed here.

Price Ranges

American Eastlake cupboard: $750 to $1500+.
Corner cupboard: $450 to $1500+.
Jelly cupboard: $250 to $1000.
Kitchen cupboard: $350 to $1200+.
Renaissance Revival cupboard: $900 to $2000+.

In all of these categories, the highest prices are paid for examples of quality construction in prime condition.

Suggested Reading

Plante, Ellen. *Kitchen Collectibles: An Illustrated Price Guide.* Radnor, Pa.: Wallace-Homestead Book Company, 1991.

Swedberg, Robert and Harriet. *Country Pine Furniture: Styles and Prices.* Radnor, Pa.: Wallace-Homestead Book Company, 1976.

————. *Country Furniture and Accessories with Prices.* Vol. 2, *Furniture.* Radnor, Pa.: Wallace-Homestead Book Company, 1982.

Iceboxes

The primary method of keeping food and drink cool during the nineteenth century was to store it in the cellar. If one wanted ice, one had to go where the ice was. In the summer this meant a long journey to the shady side of the highest mountain peak. Ice was cut from ponds and streams during the winter and stored for as many months as possible, but it seldom survived until the summer, when it was most needed.

As the turn of the century approached, technology to produce ice in blocks developed. These blocks could be stored in a metal-lined box along with perishable items requiring cool temperatures. While this method was not especially efficient, it was considerably more convenient than the cellar, and iceboxes thus became the rage of the 1890s.

Victorian iceboxes were made primarily of oak with tin linings and ornate brass or iron hinges and handles. Most had at least two sections: one for ice and one for storage. Some elaborate units had several ice compartments and storage shelves.

Price ranges of Victorian iceboxes are based primarily on size and condition. Other influencing factors include the wood used, complexity of hardware design, and accuracy of dating. Antique iceboxes are in demand and often command high prices; with patience bargains can be found.

Price Range

Iceboxes: $500 to $1500+.

Suggested Reading

Jones, Joseph C. *American Ice Boxes:* Shawnee Mission, Kans.: Jobeco Books, 1981. Information also can be found in books on Country furniture; see Cupboards, this chapter.

Irons and Trivets

Many centuries ago people decided that clothing looked better without wrinkles. (Today we buy some clothing prewrinkled, proving that things often come full-circle.) It was obvious that the way to remove these wrinkles was to press them out with something heavy: iron was a good choice for the job. Someone then discovered that heated iron worked even better, and the iron as we know it came to be.

The easiest way to heat an iron was to place it in contact with fire. Of course this meant that one had to constantly stop and reheat the iron throughout the ironing process. Being the century of invention, the 1800s provided several possible remedies to the situation. Irons were invented that held burning embers, and that were made of metals that stayed hot longer. In the latter part of the century irons that burned gas or spirits were manufactured.

These early irons are often called "sadirons" ("sad" as a synonym for "heavy") and were produced in an endless variety. Collectors look for highly ornate examples or those of unusual de-

4-5 Sadiron with silver-plated top and removable handle. (Courtesy Williams Antiques)

sign. While most are made of iron, some were produced in brass, copper, pewter, and silver plate.

To protect working surfaces from irons at rest, ornate holders called "trivets" were used. These were also produced in various materials but were primarily cast iron. Trivet designs are seemingly endless, ranging from elaborate Rococo scrollwork to various animals and characters. Many were produced as promotional pieces and contain designs or wording relating to a product or service.

NOTE: Collectors are cautioned that trivets have been continually reproduced throughout the twentieth century.

Prices of Victorian sadirons and trivets are based on complexity of design, material used, condition, and accuracy of dating.

Price Ranges

Sadirons: $20 to $200+.
Trivets: $15 to $175+.
Prices in excess of $400 have been paid for certain rare examples in both categories.

Suggested Reading

Berney, Esther. *Collector's Guide to Pressing Irons and Trivets.* New York: Crown Publishers, 1977.
Glissman, A. H. *The Evolution of the Sad Iron.* Self-published, 1970.
Jewell, Brian. *Smoothing Irons: A Collector's Guide.* Radnor, Pa.: Wallace-Homestead Book Company, 1977.

Mechanical Kitchen Devices

Of the hundreds of thousands of patents issued for new inventions during the Victorian era, a large percentage were for mechanical kitchen aids. For centuries cooking chores were performed with a sharp knife and a wooden

4-6 Mechanical apple peeler. (Courtesy Amador County Museum)

spoon, but in the latter part of the nineteenth century the average kitchen contained numerous devices for peeling, coring, grinding, whipping, and sifting.

For the most part these machines were a conglomeration of gears, blades, and handles, and they often attached to a table top or work counter with a screw-type clamp. These included apple parers, apple corers, cherry pitters, bean slicers, coconut graters, fruit presses, food grinders, meat grinders, grape and raisin seeders, butter churns, egg beaters, coffee grinders, and various mixers and mills. The apple peeler/corer is the most collected of these, perhaps because it was produced in such a wide variety of configurations. The cherry pitter is second in popularity. Until the invention of the electric food processor during the last decade, antique meat grinders were still regularly used in country homes.

Prices of Victorian mechanical kitchen devices are based on purpose of object, novelty of design, condition, and supply and demand.

4-7 Mechanical butter beater or churn. (Courtesy Williams Antiques)

Price Ranges

Apple peeler/parer/corers: $25 to $125+. Prices in excess of $250 have been paid for elaborate or unusual configurations.

Cherry pitters: $15 to $75+. Prices in excess of $175 have been paid.

Food/meat grinders: $15 to $100+. Highest prices are paid for certain examples with interchangeable graters and slicing drums.

Grape/raisin seeder: $15 to $75+. In excess of $300 has been paid for certain examples.

Mechanical butter churn: $30 to $85+.

Mills (coffee, spice, flour): $35 to $300+.

Suggested Reading

Franklin, Linda Campbell. *Three Hundred Years of Kitchen Collectibles.* Florence, Ala.: Books Americana, 1984.

Plante, Ellen. *Kitchen Collectibles: An Illustrated Price Guide.* Radnor, Pa.: Wallace-Homestead Book Company, 1991.

Thompson, Frances. *Antiques from the Country Kitchen.* Radnor, Pa.: Wallace-Homestead Book Company, 1984.

Metalware

Included in this category are those nonmechanical items made of metal used to measure, mix, strain, and cook. Most of these items were made of tin or sheet iron, often with an enamelware or graniteware finish. The process of applying hard enamel finishes to iron originated in Germany in the early 1800s but was not widely used in the United States until after the Civil War. The name "graniteware" refers to those enameled pieces with a speckled finish resembling granite. Enameled pieces with a marbleized finish of two or more colors commonly are called "splashware."

Collecting enamelware and graniteware is based primarily on colors. The most common colors are white and grey followed by blue, green, red, brown, purple, and beige.

4-8 Enamelware kitchen tools, including spoon, turner, funnel, and cream pitcher. (Courtesy Williams Antiques)

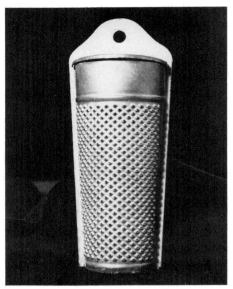

4-9 Spice grater. (Courtesy Amador County Museum)

NOTE: Collectors are cautioned that ena-melware has been reproduced throughout the twentieth century. Nineteenth-century examples are much heavier in weight and sometimes have cast-iron handles.

Prices of Victorian metalware are based on purpose of object, type of finish, color and pattern of finish (if any), condition, and supply and demand.

Price Ranges

Graniteware coffeepot: $20 to $75.
Graniteware colander: $15 to $50.
Graniteware pie pan: $15 to $35.
Graniteware spoon (large): $15 to $35.
Splashware coffeepot: $45 to $100+.
Splashware colander: $40 to $175+.
Splashware gooseneck teapot: $45 to $100+.
Splashware pie pan: $35 to $75+.
Splashware spoon (large): $25 to $50+.
Tin colander: $10 to $30.

Tin pie pan: $5 to $25.
Tin spoon (large): $5 to $25.

Suggested Reading

Franklin, Linda Campbell. *Three Hundred Years of Kitchen Collectibles.* Florence, Ala.: Books Americana, 1984.
Vogelzang and Welch: *Graniteware Collector's Guide.* Radnor, Pa.: Wallace-Homestead Book Company, 1981.

Pie Safes

In an era when professional exterminators were unheard of, mice and insects were a problem even in the best-kept homes. Foodstuffs left unattended quickly became a feast for unwanted pests. Every item therefore had its secure place in the cupboard, the preserves cabinet, boxes and canisters, or, in the case of fresh baked goods, in the pie safe.

As even any modern cook or homemaker knows, making fresh baked goods from scratch is no simple matter. In Victorian times an entire day was set aside for baking, and a quantity of items, enough to last until the next baking day, was produced. These items were then placed in a cabinet with double doors and numerous shelves called a "pie safe." Pierced tin insets in the doors and along the sides allowed air to circulate, cooling the goods and allowing moist air, which would quickly spoil the goods, to escape.

Pie safes were typically of "Country pine" construction and, like many kitchen furnishings, often were left unfinished. In the South they may have received a red clay stain, and occasionally they were painted, although most painting of Victorian kitchen furniture has been done by later generations. Collectors look for unfinished original pieces in good condition and are especially drawn to examples with novel patterns (other than the expected stars, hearts, and so forth) pierced in the tin panels.

NOTE: Pie safes were used well into the twentieth century, and dating is often difficult.

Price Range

Victorian pie safes: $200 to $500+.

Suggested Reading

See Cupboards, this chapter.

Tables

Several types of tables could be found in the kitchen, but the most common was the drop-leaf design, which allowed the table to be increased or decreased in size as needed. A kitchen table had to be sturdy and functional. It might be used as a breakfast table in the morning, a baking table in the afternoon, and a meat-processing table in the evening. While drop-leaf tables were produced in the styles of the day, those used in the kitchen usually were very plain. Fancy attached moldings and incised decorations would have been difficult to keep clean in the working atmosphere of a kitchen.

A number of styles of working tables were also produced for kitchen use. These were solidly built Country pine tables and sometimes included drawers and cabinets below.

Prices of Victorian kitchen tables are based on size, design, wood used, and condition. Prices of all Country furniture are greatly affected by regional supply and demand.

Price Ranges

Drop-leaf table (simple turned legs): $250 to $600+.
Country pine work table: $175 to $850+. Highest prices are paid for sturdy examples with drawers or cabinetry underneath.

Suggested Reading

See Cupboards, this chapter.

Utensils

Literally hundreds of instruments and implements saw use in the Victorian kitchen. Victorian inventors worked hard to come up with new tools to make life easier for cooks, servants, and homemakers. Many of these devices had been around for centuries and are still used, and taken for granted, today.

Among the most collected kitchen tools are rolling pins. These devices for rolling out pie crusts and cookie dough were produced in wood, glass, metal, and ceramic. They were glazed, carved, incised, variegated, and corrugated. Some had double rollers or automatic flour dispensers; one contained a set of additional tools inside.

Also extremely popular with collectors are butter molds and stamps (also called "butter prints"). Making home-churned butter was a laborious and time-consuming job, and after all this effort the maker wanted his or her finished product to look its best on the butter dish. The butter was molded into a particular shape in butter molds (usually made of wood, although glass and ceramic examples were produced) and then imprinted with an artistic design from a relief-carved wooden butter stamp.

Collectors like items produced in a variety of styles, and probably no kitchen collectible has more variety than the cookie cutter. Early examples were made of sheet iron or tin shaped into the forms of people, animals, geometric designs, and holiday-oriented items. These usually did not have handles, as do most modern examples, and often had a hole or holes in the top to facilitate removing the dough after it was cut. Early examples that appear to be homemade (or at least handmade) are prized by collectors. These homemade shapes often are unique pieces. While most cookie cutters are two to five inches in diameter, some were as large as twelve inches or more. Cookie cutters were also produced in wood, copper, glass, and ceramic.

Several interesting devices were manufactured for producing a fancy crimped edge on pies. Called pie crimpers or pastry jaggers, these zigzag wheels were found in nearly every Victorian kitchen. They are now quite popular with country kitchen collectors, as are pie birds—metal, glass, or ceramic vents shaped like birds placed in pies to facilitate the cooling process. Pie birds apparently were conceived by someone who had read the children's nursery rhyme that contains the line "Four and twenty blackbirds baked in a pie."

While not actually a kitchen tool, the rug beater was used by the servant or housekeeper and is often shown in the kitchen section of antiques shops. Rug beaters are paddles, usually made of wire woven into fancy shapes, with wood, metal, or ceramic handles. Carpets were placed over a sturdy line outside and then vigorously whacked with the beater until dust ceased to spew forth. This rug cleaning method was used well into the twentieth century, until vacuum cleaners became widely affordable. Rug beaters were also produced with wicker paddles.

An enormous variety of additional tools and utensils, too numerous to mention here, were used in the Victorian kitchen. Those interested in collecting a complete Victorian kitchen should purchase one of the many extensive volumes available on the subject (some suggestions follow). Prices of Victorian kitchen tools and utensils are based on size, design, and purpose of object, materials used, condition, and supply and demand.

Price Ranges

Butter molds: $20 to $150+. Highest prices are paid for mechanical press molds and those with carved designs.

Butter stamps (prints): $50 to $350+. Prices are greatly affected by supply and demand. Butter stamps frequently sell at auction for prices well in excess of the range listed here.

Cookie cutters: $20 to $225+. Highest prices are paid for those handmade examples positively identified as nineteenth century in origin.

Pie birds: $15 to $100+. Highest prices are paid for detailed pieces and those in rare glass and or ceramic.

Rolling pins: $15 to $250+. Highest prices are paid for examples in rare glass and ornately carved wood.

Rug beaters: $15 to $65.

Suggested Reading

Franklin, Linda Campbell. *300 Years of Kitchen Collectibles.* Florence, Ala.: Books Americana, 1984.

Gould, Mary Earle. *Early American Wooden Ware.* Rutland, Vt.: Charles E. Tuttle Company, Inc., 1962.

Kindig, Paul. *Butter Prints and Molds.* West Chester, Pa.: Schiffer Publishing, 1986.

Plante, Ellen. *Kitchen Collectibles: An Illustrated Price Guide.* Radnor, Pa.: Wallace-Homestead Book Company, 1991.

Thompson, Frances. *Antiques from the Country Kitchen:* Radnor, Pa.: Wallace-Homestead Book Company, 1984.

CHAPTER 5

The Back Parlor

Depending on the design of the house and the whims of its owner, the back parlor may have been called the music room, the den, or the library. In most Victorian homes the term "family room" would have been most appropriate, because this room was the center of family life. In homes with large families the back parlor was extremely crowded, because each family member brought the objects essential to his or her favorite pastime to this room to display and to use. Musical instruments, games, books, stereo viewers, stationery, photograph and autograph albums, and scrapbooks all were found in the back parlor.

The furniture found in the back parlor consisted of the same pieces found in the front parlor (settees, parlor tables, étagères, and stands), except that here durability and function were more important than style and appearance. Decorative items were more personal and less intended to impress than those in the front parlor. Cheap souvenirs of summer vacations and weekend excursions often were found in every nook and cranny of the room. However, in certain wealthy homes, especially those with few or no children, the back parlor was barely distinguishable from the front parlor except for signs of wear resulting from more frequent use. In these homes, the man of the house found personal refuge in the library, the woman of the house in her sewing room, and the children, if any, in their bedrooms.

Armchairs

Chairs that were larger than a side chair and usually fully upholstered were called armchairs, although many did not have arms. In fact, in matching sets the lady's armchair is distinguished from the gentleman's by the lack of arms to accommodate women's clothing. These large chairs were often the most comfortable seating in a Victorian home and were found not only in both parlors but also in libraries and bedrooms as well.

Armchairs were produced in all the popular styles of the period. Prices are based on style, size, wood used in the frame, upholstery, and overall condition.

Price Ranges

French Revival armchair: $375 to $600.
Renaissance Revival and Eastlake: $225 to $500.

Suggested Reading

See Davenports, this chapter.

5-1 French Revival lady's (left) and gentleman's (right) arm-chairs. (Courtesy McHenry Mansion)

Autograph Albums

The men and women of nineteenth-century literature, politics, and theater were the celebrities of the era, admired by most and emulated by many. Then as today teenagers were their biggest fans, and an autograph obtained at a reading or performance was a prized possession. Albums were manufactured for keeping autographs, and their design has remained relatively unchanged to this day. Celebrities unfortunately were not easily accessible, and most albums of the period are filled with the writings of friends and family.

As the autograph album fad became widespread in the early 1870s, coming up with new and unused poetry or prose to accompany one's signature presented quite a challenge. What indignant looks must have been received by those who returned the album signed simply "best wishes" or opening with the line "Roses are red,

Violets are blue." Those who were up to the challenge would ask that the album be left with them while they produced an original piece especially for the owner. Others would plagiarize something from another album or modify an old standard. Whatever the origin, the composition usually was poetic or contained sage advice.

Today, these albums are an excellent way to discover the thoughts and feelings of the Victorian people, who, through sickness and war, had discovered that life is rewarding but fleeting, and that friends are the greatest possessions. They also displayed the superb Spencerian-influenced penmanship of the period, which often incorporated drawings of birds, flowers, or other subjects. Many albums contain colorful chromolithographic scraps as well.

The standard format for autograph albums is 4½ inches by 7 inches, although other sizes were produced. Some albums are beautifully illustrated with lithographic prints and may have

5-2 Autograph albums came in an endless variety of styles.

elaborately pressed, inlaid, or painted covers. Prices are affected by size, quality of artisanship, complexity of design, number of autographs, and condition.

Price Range

Autograph albums: $8 to $35+. Highest prices are paid for very ornate albums and those containing autographs of known celebrities.

Suggested Reading

Hart, Grossman, and Dunhill. *Victorian Scrapbook.* New York: Workman Publishing, 1989.
Sanders, George and Helen, and Ralph Roberts. *Collector's Guide to Autographs.* Radnor, Pa.: Wallace-Homestead Book Company, 1990.

Bird Cages

Very few pets were allowed in a proper Victorian home. The occasional gift kitten or bunny was quickly sent outside or to the country. Birds, however, required relatively little maintenance and were an attractive addition to a room, especially if the bird was kept in a fancy cage.

Today, antique bird cages are still collected both to keep pet birds and as decorative items. Unless a cage is dated or can be attributed to a particular manufacturer, the time period is often difficult to determine. Iron and wood bird cages have been produced for many centuries, while brass and wicker cages were popular during the 1930s.

Many Victorian bird cages are Oriental in origin and design. A few cages were produced showing the characteristics of period styles such as French Revival and Eastlake, and these are quite valuable.

Prices of Victorian bird cages are based on size, style, materials, identification of manufacturer, reliability of dating, and condition.

Price Range

Bird cages: $35 to $500+. Highest prices are paid for large, elaborately designed cages positively identified as Victorian.

Cased Photographs

Photography was introduced just one year after the young Queen Victoria took her throne by Louis-Jacques-Mandé Daguerre of France. His invention, called the daguerreotype, provided Victorians with a method to produce their exact likenesses on silver plates. Portrait studios quickly spread throughout the United States during the 1840s, and by 1850 millions of daguerreotype portraits had been taken. Because the image could be erased from the plate with just a touch, daguerreotypes were housed in beautiful brass frames and leather or plastic cases. These cases were convenient for carrying and for displaying on tables and shelves.

Two new methods of photography were introduced in the 1850s: the ambrotype (on a glass

5-3 A daguerreotype, the world's first practical form of photography.

plate), and the tintype (on a varnished iron plate). Portraits by these processes were also placed in cases for protection and ornamentation. During the Civil War paper photographs began to replace cased photographs (see *Carte de Visite* in Chapter 1, The Entry Hall), and by 1867 they seldom were made.

Today cased photographs are widely collected throughout the world, both as representations of the earliest photographic processes and for their importance as historical records of the Victorian era. Because large quantities were produced collectors look for features that make a particular image stand out from others of its type. Portraits of blacks, native Americans, persons dressed in uniform or occupational clothing, corpses, and well-known personages are highly collectible, as are photographs by well-known photographers.

Outdoor portraits and scenic views are prized by collectors, as are large-size images (4½ by 5½ inches or larger).

Cases also play an important role in the value of a cased photograph. Leather cases with flowers and birds are generally common. Cases with mother-of-pearl inlays and painted designs are uncommon, as are most plastic cases.

Price Ranges

Cased ambrotypes: $20 to $500+.
Cased daguerreotypes: $30 to $2500+. Highest prices are paid for large images by or of well-known persons and outdoor scenes.
Cased tintypes: $10 to $250+.

Suggested Reading

Mace, O. Henry. *Collector's Guide to Early Photographs.* Radnor, Pa.: Wallace-Homestead Book Company, 1989.

Newhall, Beaumont. *Daguerreotype in America:* New York: Dover Publications, 1976.

Taft, Robert. *Photography and the American Scene.* New York: Dover Publications, 1964.

Wood, John. *Daguerreotype: A Sesquicentennial Celebration.* Iowa City, Iowa: University of Iowa Press, 1989.

Davenports

The name "davenport" has caused some confusion over the years because of its connection with three separate items: Davenport china, manufactured in England from 1794 to 1887; the davenport sofa, a large couch that converts to a bed (invented in the late nineteenth century but particularly popular in the United States during the 1950s); and the davenport desk, a popular choice for libraries, children's rooms, and back parlors during the Victorian era.

The accepted history of the davenport desk is that it was designed by Captain Davenport of the British Royal Navy and produced by Gillow and Company of London in the eighteenth century. The design is distinguished from other desks in

Entry hall, McHenry House.

Front parlor, McHenry House.

Dining room, Banning Mansion.

Back parlor, McHenry House.

Back parlor, Bernhard House.

Library, McHenry House.

Lady's bedroom, Armstead Brown House, Amador County Museum.

Lady's bedroom,
Armstead Brown House,
Amador County Museum.

Lady's bedroom, Bernhard House.

that the drawers are located on the side. The top of the desk is a hinged writing slope (also called a "book slide" in period advertising) with a storage area beneath. Various versions were produced and Victorian examples (often called a "lady's desk" in period advertising) may have swiveling tops and secret drawers. While the basic design was based on the original British example, American davenports of the late nineteenth century frequently incorporated Renaissance Revival and Eastlake adornments.

Davenport desks often were used by school-age children for studying because of their abundant storage area and because they resembled the desks they used at school. Victorian children were required to study in the library or back parlor; where their progress could be monitored by their parents. Only in later years, when their diligence could be trusted, were they permitted to study in their own rooms.

Prices of davenport desks are based on size, design, and complexity of style, as well as wood used and condition.

Price Range

American davenport desks: $650 to $2000.

Suggested Reading

McNerney, Kathryn. *Victorian Furniture: Our American Heritage.* Paducah, Ky.: Collector Books, 1988.
Swedberg, Robert W. and Harriett Swedberg. *Victorian Furniture.* Vols. 1–3. Radnor, Pa.: Wallace-Homestead Book Company, 1984–1985.

Footrests

The back parlor, like our family rooms today, was a place to relax. Father often was found there in the evening, wearing his slippers and puffing on his pipe, reading the newspaper or a good book. Chances are his feet would be resting comfortably on a footstool or footrest. These functional pieces of furniture usually were simple four-legged low

stools with or without padded and upholstered tops. The design is so basic that footstools often were the first building project of young boys.

There were, however, fine-quality footrests produced by furniture manufacturers in the styles of the period. These were made in fine woods and may have been ebonized or gilded. Padded tops were upholstered in quality needlework, often with fancy fringes. The top frequently was hinged to provide a storage compartment beneath (such stools were also called "slipper stools"). These elaborate footrests apparently were the exception rather than the rule—for extant examples, especially those in good original condition, are quite rare.

Prices of Victorian footrests are based on size and complexity of design, woods and other materials used, finish, and condition.

Price Ranges

Basic footstools: $25 to $100.
Renaissance Revival and American Eastlake footrests: $150 to $450+. Prices in excess of $1500 have been paid for ornate examples in near-original condition.

Suggested Reading

McNerney, Kathryn. *Victorian Furniture: Our American Heritage.* Paducah, Ky.: Collector Books, 1988.

Game Tables

Tables in dozens of styles were produced for playing games. Many of these incorporated holes or slots for various game pieces and may have had game board patterns painted on the surface. However, the definitive Victorian game table was an extremely popular multipurpose folding table, which found use in nearly every room of the house. It retains that popularity even today and can frequently be found in rooms with Victorian-based decor. While they were produced in all the styles of the period their basic design remained the same: a plain flat surface (round, rectangular, or nonpariel in shape) hinged so that one half can be dropped out of the way or lifted to lean against a wall. The surface may be supported by narrow legs or a pedestal base.

While game tables, especially pedestal versions, occasionally show influences of the styles of the period, most are very basic pieces with spool-turned legs. Some versions may include a storage drawer underneath.

Prices of Victorian game tables are based on style, size, complexity of design, wood and finish used, and condition. Round versions are especially desirable.

Price Range

Game tables: $275 to $750.

Suggested Reading

See Davenports, this chapter.

Games

In a world without television, video games, or stereos, children entertained themselves with activities that kids today probably would consider boring. They collected scrap, butterflies, and other bugs; painted; played musical instruments, and read books and children's magazines. In addition to toys (see Chapter 10, The Children's Room), card and board games and puzzles were the primary indoor entertainment for children. While these diversions actually were invented centuries earlier, the new mass-production technology and chromolithographic (color) printing process of the nineteenth century popularized them.

In the 1850s the firms of W. and S. B. Ives and McLoughlin Brothers began publishing many of the popular games of the period. These early board games usually were designed to teach and often had religious, moral, or educational themes. Later in the century the familiar names of Parker Brothers and Milton Bradley began their long-lived and prolific game-publishing empires.

While there were a few foreign competitors, the board game business was primarily an American enterprise.

Today there are many factors involved in collecting Victorian board games and puzzles. Early games, such as McLoughlin Brother's Mansion of Happiness (the first such game of the nineteenth century) and The Man in the Moon have brought premium prices—from $1000 to $5000. In addition to age and manufacturer, condition is a primary factor. A game or puzzle must retain all of its original pieces, be contained in its original box, and exhibit a minimum of fading, warping, and general wear to bring the highest price.

The games most common to the back parlor were, of course, checkers, chess, and cards. The game manufacturers previously mentioned were also the major makers of these items as well. Because games have been produced in such quantity for so many years, Victorian examples often can only be identified by the manufacturer's imprint or by comparing them to examples in publications on antique toys and games.

Price Ranges

Board games: $50 to $1000+. Lowest prices are paid for simple games with few pieces. Condition is of primary importance.

Card decks: $20 to $500+. Highest prices are paid for decks in top condition with original boxes.

Picture puzzles: $35 to $500+. Again, condition is the primary factor. Naturally, elaborate examples with many or all pieces bring the highest prices.

Suggested Reading

Bell, Robbie. *The Board Game Book.* Los Angeles: Knapp Press, 1979.

Dennis, Lee. *Warman's Antique American Games.* Warman Publishing, Co., Inc., 1986.

Williams, Anne D. *Jigsaw Puzzles: An Illustrated History and Price Guide.* Radnor, Pa.: Wallace-Homestead Book Company, 1989.

Music Boxes

Before the invention of the phonograph by Thomas Edison in 1877, the only way to have music in the home was to play either an instrument or a music box. The basic concept for the music box came from Switzerland around the beginning of the Victorian era, and novelty music boxes are still being produced today. At the heart of the design is a metal comb, the teeth of which produce various musical tones when struck by pins on a rotating cylinder. By careful placement of these pins, a repetitive melody can be produced. Elaborate versions that played long and complicated tunes were manufactured. Some have interchangeable cylinders. Some examples have a multitude of bells, chimes, drums, and other tone-producing mechanics that give the effect of a full orchestra.

In 1886 Paul Lochmann of Germany invented a music box that used interchangeable disks with bent prongs that struck the teeth of the comb and produced musical tones. The listener could choose a favorite tune from a collection of discs in the style of the modern long-playing record. Even with the increasing interest in Edison's invention, this style of music box achieved the height of popularity just prior to the turn of the century. Even an automatic self-changing version—a forerunner of the jukebox—was introduced for commercial use.

The cabinetry in which a music box is encased, with its fine woods, ebonized finishes, and linings of colorful chromolithographic prints, often is as beautiful as the music it produces. Some have mechanical dancers twirling about, characters playing tiny instruments, or chirping birds. The best early units were produced in Germany with names like Symphonium (average cost is $3000 today), Polyphon (average $1500), and Kaliope (average price not available). But the American Regina (average $2500 to $3500) and Olympia gave the German makes a run for their money.

Prices of Victorian music boxes are based on size and complexity of design in both mechanics and cabinetry. Also important are identification of the manufacturer and condition of the piece.

Price Ranges

Cylinder-type music boxes: $225 to $3000+. Prices in excess of $20,000 have been paid for elaborate examples from well-known manufacturers.

Disc-type music boxes: $250 to $5000+. Prices in excess of $10,000 have been paid for certain pieces.

Suggested Reading

Tallis, David. *Music Boxes: A Guide for Collectors.* Stein & Day, 1971.

Web, Graham. *Musical Box Handbook.* Vestal, N.Y.: Vestal Press, 1986.

Musical Instruments

Pianos, guitars, violins, accordions, organs, and flutes were the musical instruments commonly found in Victorian homes. Other instruments associated with the period—banjos, harps, horns, and drums—were used mostly by professional musicians. Music of the period was classical—operas, waltzes, and marches. Every young lady was required to learn to play at least one musical instrument, usually the piano, and to be able to perform a flawless impromptu recital for visiting friends. Ladies with great musical talents were particularly admired by the social circle. As for young gentlemen, musical ability was encouraged but not necessarily a requirement.

Collecting musical instruments is a very specialized field that requires a thorough knowledge of nineteenth-century manufacturers and their work. Quality pieces often cost in excess of $10,000. Those interested in this field should obtain a thorough reference library and subscribe to the appropriate auction catalogs from major houses, such as Sotheby's and Christie's.

5-4 An early violin or fiddle.

Basic examples of unmarked Victorian pieces such as violins and wooden flutes can be obtained for reasonable prices and displayed as decorative items. Prices of these pieces are affected primarily by condition.

Price Ranges

Violins: $50 to $300.
Wooden flutes: $10 to $125.
Guitars: $75 to $300.
Tambourines: $35 to $100.
Prices listed are for basic unmarked or mass-produced instruments whose primary value is decorative.

Suggested Reading

Evans, Tom and Mary Anne Evans. *Official Price Guide to Music Collectibles.* New York: Ballantine, 1986.

Parlor Desks

If one were to walk into ten antique furniture stores and ask to see their parlor desks, one would probably be shown ten different types of desks. Today the name "parlor desk" has come to encompass all Victorian desks that cannot be placed in a specific category. These desks range from a simple writing slope on a trestle base to heavy drop-front cabinets. In the 1880s, however, the term "parlor desk" was applied to a desk with a three-drawer base and a storage compartment covered by a hinged writing slope. The desk portion often is detachable, and these pieces have been sold separately over the years.

Parlor desks were used in both parlors, but, like all parlor furniture, they received heavier use in the back parlor, especially in homes without a library or study. Here household bills were paid, children's homework done, and letters written. Drawers were used to store important papers and business or personal correspondence.

Prices of parlor desks are based on style, size, wood used, and condition. The price range listed below applies to all styles of desks categorized as parlor desks.

Price Range

Parlor desk: $500 to $1500+. Examples showing decorative influences of popular period styles (French Revival, Renaissance Revival, Eastlake) are highly sought after by collectors and often bring premium prices.

Suggested Reading

See Davenports, this chapter.

Phonographs

As the turn of the century approached, Thomas Edison significantly transformed Victorian daily life. His electric light bulb revolutionized the lighting industry, and his "talking machine"—the phonograph—brought the music of real orchestras into hundreds of parlors. Within months of the first demonstration in 1877, dozens of manufacturers were producing their own versions of the phonograph. These were manufactured under a variety of names, including Gramophone (Berliner), Graphophone (Columbia,

McDonald), Grafanola (Columbia), Junophone, Victrola (Victor Company), Zonophone, and Amberola (Edison). Most of these were produced well into the twentieth century.

Early examples of Edison's machine were very basic in design. Sounds were recorded onto a plastic-coated cylinder (produced in quantity after 1889) and played back through a pick-up needle attached to a wooden or metal horn that amplified the sound. This concept remained unchanged until near the turn of the century, when the configuration was altered and flat discs replaced the cylinders. (The term "flat" as used here is somewhat of a misnomer, since these early records were thin and heavily warped and required a center weight to hold them down.)

As with music boxes, the cabinetry built around a phonograph was often of the best quality, with beautifully applied wood veneers, painted horns, and inlays of silver, brass, and mother-of-pearl. Prices of nineteenth-century phonographs are greatly affected by supply and demand and are often inflated. Other important factors include size, style, woods used, identification of manufacturer, and condition.

Price Ranges

Cylinder phonographs: $250 to $2000+.
Early disc phonographs: $150 to $1500+.

Suggested Reading

Gelatt, Roland. *The Fabulous Phonograph.* New York: Macmillan Publishing Company, 1977.

5-5 An Edison roll-type phonograph. (Courtesy Bernhard House)

Photo Albums

Photo albums were invented shortly after the introduction of calling card-sized portraits called *"cartes de viste"* (see Chapter 1, The Entry Hall). These albums were covered in leather or velvet and contained pages with die-cut openings to hold images of family and friends or celebrity

5-6 A small photograph album, circa 1870, designed to hold cartes de visite.

portraits and travel views purchased from photographic galleries. (A "gallery" in the nineteenth century was a photographic studio where portraits were taken and mass-produced photographs sold.)

After the Civil War a larger card portrait called the "cabinet card" was introduced. From that time on most albums contained pages cut to fit both this new format and the still-popular *carte de visite.* During the latter part of the century albums became increasingly ornate, with gold or brass adornments and other fancy trimwork, and they had ornate stands to hold them. Some even played music in the style of a music box.

Today these early albums are used primarily as decorative pieces or to hold collections of card photographs from the period. The page format is incorrect for most modern photographs, although some people try to make them work and often ruin the album in the process. Because most of these albums have been in heavy use for over one hundred years, those in near-mint condition,

especially highly ornate examples, usually command the highest prices.

Some Victorian albums contain photographs of historical importance—images of politicians, actors, royalty, and significant places and events. Complete albums of this type often command premium prices at auction. Those interested in collecting such albums should subscribe to the catalogs of dealers and auction houses that regularly present them for sale (Sotheby's, Swann Galleries, Christie's, and others).

Price Range

Photo albums: $30 to $250+.

Suggested Reading

Darrah, William C. *Cartes de Visite in Nineteenth-Century Photography.* Self-published, 1981.
Mace, O. Henry. *Collector's Guide to Early Photographs.* Radnor, Pa.: Wallace-Homestead Book Company, 1989.

Pianos and Organs

The piano was the instrument of choice for Victorians. Any household that could afford a piano had at least one. The best examples were placed in the front parlor while less-expensive pieces were installed in the back parlor (which often changed its name to "music room," even though little else in the room pertained to music). Every young lady who expected recognition in social circles, or who expected to attract a young man, knew how to play the piano and had practiced at least one piece well enough to appear accomplished. Impromptu recitals were an important part of social gatherings, and competition among young ladies often was quite fierce.

Organs were also popular although not nearly as much as the piano, possibly because of their association with churches, funerals, and sideshows. Some examples were quite large and elaborate, with numerous pedals and pulls to change tones. Pump organs required continuous motion

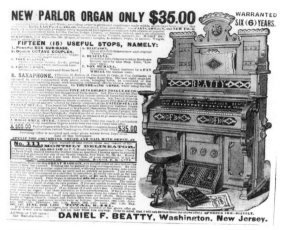

5-8 Nineteenth-century magazine ad for a parlor organ.

of the foot pedals to produce the pressure needed for operation.

Prices of nineteenth-century pianos and organs are based primarily on complexity of design, identification of the manufacturer, and condition of the piece.

5-7 Victorian piano with French influence. Stool is in Renaissance Revival style. (Courtesy McHenry Mansion)

Price Ranges

Organs: $250 to $3500+. Many pump organs can be found for under $1000. Certain examples have brought more than $10,000.

Pianos: $1000 to $6500+. A few examples can be found for as low as $400. Some pieces have brought more than $10,000.

Suggested Reading

Michel, N. E. *The Organ Atlas.* Self-published, 1969.
————. *The Piano Atlas.* Self-published, 1961.

Scrap Albums

One of the leading technological advances of the nineteenth century was the invention of the chromolithographic printing process. Prior to its invention pictures were printed in black and white from highly detailed engravings by skilled artists. Colors occasionally were added to individual pictures in the form of transparent watercolors, but because of the time and expense involved this practice was reserved for special "limited edition" pieces.

As with many innovations of the day, chromolithography in the United States coincided closely with the Victorian period itself. The process, while simple in theory, is somewhat difficult to describe. Artistic designs were drawn in reverse using a special ink on smooth limestone slabs; one stone was needed for each design and color. These printing stones were then coated first with water and then with ink; which clung to the previously inked design but not to the water. The various stones were then pressed to paper, creating the layers of colored patterns that made up the finished picture.

The process was used to create advertisements (often attached to boxes or other packaging); to illustrate books and magazines; and to create colorful cards, calendars, and decorative hangings. Embossed chromolithographic overlays were used on greeting cards and calling cards and as seals for correspondence. Whether or not the Victorians were aware of the painstaking process that created these little works of art, they apparently did appreciate their beauty, for they collected much of it in scrap albums.

Today both albums and individual examples of chromolithographic art are cherished by collectors of paper ephemera. Some specialize in a particular type, such as cigar boxes or orange crate labels; others collect only embossed overlays or valentines. Still others collect subjects, such as cats, babies, or flowers.

Because they were equally cherished in the nineteenth century, much chromolithographic ephemera has survived in near-mint condition. Worn, torn, or folded pieces should be ignored unless they are rare or extremely unusual. While scrap albums often are themselves in disrepair, it is the condition of the art that is important.

Price Ranges

Chromolithographic art: 25¢ to $100+. Highest prices are paid for large or elaborate cutout cards and valentines and certain advertising art.

Scrap albums: $25 to $250+. Prices are greatly affected by emotional appeal to individuals, and certain persons will pay more than $1000 for a particular album.

Suggested Reading

Hart, C., J. Grossman, and P. Dunhill: *Victorian Scrapbook.* New York: Workman Publishing, 1989.
Lee, Ruth Webb. *A History of Valentines.* Santa Ana, Calif.: National Valentine Collector's Association, n.d.

Sheet Music

Musicians of the nineteenth century obtained their music just as those of today do—from a music shop, in the form of thin booklets called "sheet music." Victorian sheet music is somewhat larger than modern versions and often has very artistic lithographic (and later photo-

5-9 Sheet music cover for "Fireman's Song," circa 1850s.

graphic) covers. Among today's collectors the covers can be of more value than the music contained within.

High prices are also paid for contemporary publications of famous show tunes and standards. While very few examples of sheet music can be considered rare, few early pieces have survived in good condition. Therefore, the older the sheet music is, the better.

Price Range

Sheet music: $15 to $50+. Prices in excess of $1000 have been paid for certain rare compositions by well-known composers of the period.

Suggested Reading

Dillon, Debbie. *Collector's Guide to Sheet Music.* L-W Promotions, 1988.

Priest, Daniel. *American Sheet Music: A Guide to Collecting.* Radnor, Pa.: Wallace-Homestead Book Company, 1978.

Stereo Viewers and Stereographs

Even prior to the invention of photography in 1839, artists and scientists were experimenting with ways to produce three-dimensional representations on a flat surface. A binocular (two-lens) camera was invented around 1849, and at London's Crystal Palace Exhibition in 1851, stereoscopic daguerreotypes were shown in a viewer that produced the illusion of dimension.

With the advent of paper photographs in the mid-1850s stereography became commonplace, and by the 1860s mass producing stereographs (also called "stereo cards" or "stereo views") was a major industry in the United States and Great Britain. E. and H. T. Anthony and Company of New York purchased thousands of negatives from both professional and amateur photographers, which were printed and mounted in their huge production facilities. These included many series containing as few as six or as many as fifty or more stereographs pertaining to a particular subject.

5-10 Hand-held stereo viewer and card depicting Montreal, Canada.

The stereograph has been called the television of the nineteenth century. While this is a considerable exaggeration, there are many similarities. Most Victorian parlors had one or more stereo viewers (also called "stereoscopes") and a large selection of stereo cards. Through the stereoscope the viewer could be transported to a far-off land or enjoy a funny story, such as "The New French Cook" or "The Wedding."

Because stereographs were produced throughout the second half of the nineteenth century, and because of the variety of photographic processes and subjects they represent, they offer a wider variety of collectibles than any other photographic format. Those using early, one-of-a-kind processes (daguerreotypes, ambrotypes, tintypes) are the most valuable. Early stereo cards (1850s) using paper processes are also sought after by collectors. Mass-produced examples (post-Civil War) are collected by subject or series. The highest prices are paid for examples in mint or near-mint condition.

Price Range

Stereographs: $1 to $100+. The average good-quality stereograph of an unusual subject sells for around $15. Prices in excess of $1000 have been paid for certain rare examples.

Suggested Reading

Darrah, William C. *World of Stereographs*. Self-published, 1977.

Mace, O. Henry. *Collector's Guide to Early Photographs*. Radnor, Pa.: Wallace-Homestead Book Company, 1990.

Waldsmith, John. *Stereo Views: An Illustrated History and Price Guide*. Radnor, Pa.: Wallace-Homestead Book Company, 1991.

CHAPTER 6

The Sewing Room

In a home where most of the rooms were considered masculine, the sewing room belonged solely to the madam of the house. Men seldom entered there and seldom wanted to. Everything it contained was the property of a lady, and woe be it to those who removed or disturbed anything from its assigned place. Although it properly was called the sewing room, it was in truth the lady's sanctuary—a place to rest, read, write, gossip, enjoy hobbies, and, yes, even occasionally to sew.

The wallpaper in this room usually was the most floral, the drapes the laciest, and the carpet the most colorful of any room in the house. Hanging on the walls one would probably find decorative needlecraft and other homemade art and favorite photographs or paintings of family members—especially the children. There would be a comfortable armchair or rocking chair where those children were rocked, fed, and lullabied during their infancies. There might be a small desk or secretary containing beautifully printed stationery for writing to sisters or cousins in distant towns. Of course, there would be a *sewing stand,* which would be either simple or elaborate, depending on the ability or inclination of its owner. Within its drawers was a treasury of sewing accessories.

On the opposite side of the chair from the sewing stand one might find a *magazine rack* containing the latest copy of *Godey's Lady's Book, Home Journal, Art Amateur,* or the latest catalog from Tiffany and Company, Mermod and Jaccard Jewelry, or Sears Roebuck.

Elsewhere around the room there might be a free-standing sewing machine or a smaller version sitting atop a *work table.* On this table one might also find a *sewing bird,* a table clamp for holding material in place while it is being worked on; a *pincushion doll,* used to hold the easily lost pins and needles; and a work box, sometimes used instead of or in addition to the sewing stand to hold *scissors, thimbles,* and other *sewing implements.* Early in the Victorian era, and even in later years in small towns where cloth was difficult to obtain, the sewing room would include a *spinning wheel* for turning cotton into yarn, a skein holder for winding the yarn, and a loom for weaving the yarn into cloth.

The personality of a Victorian lady could be easily determined by the contents and arrangement of her sewing room. Some were neat and tidy, every item in its place. In many sewing rooms there was hardly room to walk; bolts of cloth would be strewn across furniture and paper patterns and yarn stuck in every nook and cranny. As the turn of the century approached women were fighting for the freedom to choose their places in a society that had always lived by the doctrine "A woman's place is in the home." In that home, the only place that was really her's was the sewing room.

Buttons

Probably no other collectible comes in such varied quantities as buttons. There is also probably no other collectible that allows the accumulation of such a large and varied collection for so little money. Buttons can be found in nearly every shape and size imaginable, made of nearly every material imaginable, and decorated with a wide array of painted, embossed, engraved, and applied adornments. A collector will likely never come across a box of buttons that does not contain at least one he or she had never seen before.

In ancient times most clothing was held in place by string or rope ties. By the sixteenth century buttons were in use but served more as decorative embellishments than functional fasteners. From that period on buttons attained wider use and, by the mid-nineteenth century, were the common way to fasten shirts, coats, and pants. Most early buttons were hand carved from wood, shell, ivory, or bone. In May 1851, Nelson Goodyear patented a button made from India rubber. This was not a true rubber as we know it and is now believed to have been the first plastic product ever produced. One year later a similar process was being used in the production of daguerreotype cases, and this "thermoplastic" was also used to make buttons. This is the substance incorrectly called "gutta-percha," a name properly applied to a kind of tree sap from which buttons and other items—but not daguerreotype cases—were made.

During the second half of the century buttons were also produced in brass, iron, silver, tin, enamel, china, porcelain, glass, horn, leather, pewter, and gold. These materials were also combined to produce certain decorative examples. A variety of paints and platings were applied as well. Decorative relief patterns were pressed, applied, or engraved on the various surfaces. Buttons with holes through the surface are called "sew-throughs." Other buttons may attach by means of a shank, which may be part of the button (self-shank) or attached to the button (metal or loop-shank). Jewels and other stonelike settings were set into a rimmed metal base called a "collet."

Today buttons are collected by material, shape, or a particular decorative design. Those made of precious materials or set with rare or unusual settings are, of course, the most valuable. Even though prices in excess of $1000 have been paid for a single button, prices for desirable pieces seldom top $40, and the average collectible button sells for about $3.50. Prices are affected by size, shape, construction material, decorative design, condition, and supply and demand.

6-1 Hand-painted ceramic buttons. (Courtesy Georgia Fox, Foxes Den)

Price Range

Buttons: 25¢ to $35+.

Suggested Reading

Luscomb, Sally. *Collector's Encyclopedia of Buttons.*
New York: Crown Publishers, 1967.
Also see Suggested Reading under Ladies' Work
Boxes, next entry.

Ladies' Work Boxes

As we shall see later in this chapter, the Victorian lady usually owned a large variety of sewing tools and implements. Most of these were kept in a sewing stand (noted later in this chapter), but the smaller, most often used tools might be kept in a work box (also called a sewing box, needlework box, or sewing tool case). Work boxes were often homemade and inlaid with shells or bits of colored wood (called tunbridgeware). Other examples made of wood, glass, ceramic, silver, or other metals were purchased with the various tools included in special trays designed to hold each implement in its place. The tools themselves may have been made of silver or plated with silver or gold (see Sewing Implements, this chapter).

Work boxes were made in such variety that, unless they contain tool trays or tools, they are often not recognized as work boxes. One style, produced from just after the Civil War until well into the twentieth century, had a wooden frame top into which a fashion print from one of the contemporary women's magazines was placed. Other work boxes were produced as representations of small pianos, cottages, or even coffins.

Today the most sought-after work boxes are those with lift-out trays containing tools. Examples with most or all of the original implements are rare and prized by collectors. Otherwise, prices of Victorian ladies' work boxes are based on complexity of design and embellishments, accuracy of dating, identification of manufacturer (if any), and condition. High-quality homemade examples are unique and can bring premium prices.

Price Range

Ladies' work boxes: $35 to $500+. Basic frame-style boxes can be found for as little as $15, while prices in excess of $1000 have been paid for novel examples including tools.

Suggested Reading

Clabburn, Pamela. *The Needlework Dictionary.* New York: William Morrow and Company, Inc., 1976.

6-2 Victorian sewing room setting includes work box (on floor), work table and early treadle sewing machine. (Courtesy Bernhard House)

Clement, Joyce. *Official Price Guide to Sewing Collectibles.* New York: Ballantine, 1987.

Zalkin, Estelle. *Zalkin's Handbook of Thimbles and Sewing Implements.* Radnor, Pa.: Wallace-Homestead Book Company, 1988.

Magazine Racks

One of the more recognizable pieces of Victorian furniture, the wooden magazine rack has remained relatively unchanged in design to this day. The sides of the rack rise out at sharp angles from a narrow base. Some early examples were connected on the end by chains so that the unit could be folded up; however, most had solid end

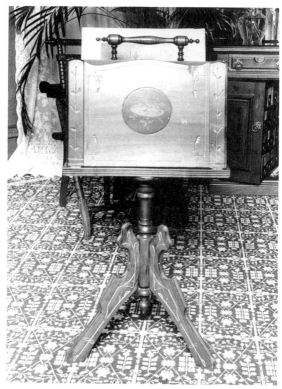

6-3 Eastlake folding magazine rack. (Courtesy McHenry Mansion)

pieces. Most racks have a handle across the top and legs of various heights, although some sit flat on the floor.

Victorian magazine racks were produced in the styles of the period; however, only Eastlake examples are common. Many racks were homemade or produced by amateur cabinetmakers. Today prices of Victorian magazine racks are based on size, style, and condition.

Price Range

Magazine racks: $75 to $250+. Highest prices are paid for manufactured pieces in the styles of the period.

Suggested Reading

Swedberg, Robert W. and Harriet Swedberg. *Victorian Furniture.* vol. 1, rev. ed. Radnor, Pa.: Wallace-Homestead Book Company, 1984.

Magazines and Catalogs

There were few forms of home entertainment in the nineteenth century. If one were not entertaining guests, one might read a book, peruse a stack of stereographs, listen to music, play a game, or engage in a hobby. One of the most popular pastimes of the period, especially for ladies, was reading one or more of the large variety of magazines available in Victorian times. While the gentlemen were more interested in news magazines, such as *Harper's Weekly* or *Peterson's,* the ladies had a number of publications produced especially for them.

Probably the most popular and most influential ladies' magazine of the period was *Godey's Lady's Book,* published from 1830 to 1895. Although it was produced in the United States, its abundant fashion plates were European in origin and chosen specifically for the American reader. The *Monitor of Fashion* and *Harper's Bazaar* were also rich in fashion prints.

Also popular with ladies was the *Delineator: A Journal of Fashion, Culture, and Fine Arts.* This

6-4 Harper's Bazaar *ladies' magazine; December 1876.*

relatively thick monthly magazine included information on the latest fashions for ladies, gentlemen, and children; artistic needlework; home decoration; travel; entertaining, and sports. Also included were book reviews, recipes, short fiction, and a large advertising section. The *Art Amateur* and the *Art Exchange* were popular magazines of a similar content but with extensive coverage of home decor, drawing, painting, and other art themes.

Harper's, the best known Victorian publisher, produced several different magazines: *Harper's Weekly,* which was heavily weighted toward news, travel, and fiction; *Harper's Monthly Magazine,* which contained less news and more fashion and fiction; and *Harper's Bazaar,* which was

geared more toward the lady of the house. *Harper's, Godey's, Century Magazine,* and others also produced compendiums, usually containing edited versions of the magazine's previous six month's issues. These were often beautiful leather-bound volumes with marbleized end papers and colorful, hand-tinted or chromolithographic illustrations. Many of these have survived in excellent condition and are prized by book collectors and historians.

Catalogs from the nineteenth century usually have not faired as well. Most of those still in existence are badly torn and stained; therefore, examples in good condition often bring relatively high prices. However, great caution must be exercised since many have been reproduced in their original forms throughout the twentieth century. This is especially true of the Sears Roebuck catalog, whose early reproductions are now considered antiques.

Both magazines and catalogs from the nineteenth century are valuable not only as collectibles but as historical artifacts. They enable us to visualize and comprehend the life-style and economy of the Victorian era from a firsthand source. Prices for Victorian magazines and catalogs are greatly affected by condition. Other factors are date, title, size, number of pages, and supply and demand. Art Nouveau covers and large engravings by famous artists such as Will Bradley, Winslow Homer, or Thomas Nast also greatly increase a magazine's value.

Price Ranges

Catalogs: $25 to $250+.

Magazine compendiums (bound): $25 to $100+. Highest prices are paid for Civil War-period issues.

Magazines (individual): $10 to $75+. Highest prices are paid for Civil War period issues and those with extensive use of color.

Suggested Reading

Le Fontaine, Joseph R. *Turning Paper To Gold: How To Make Money with Old Books, Magazines, Comics,*

Sheet Music, and Other Printed Paper Collectibles. Crozet, Va.: Betterway Publications, 1988.

Romaine, Lawrence B. *A Guide to American Trade Catalogs 1744–1900.* New York: R. R. Bowker, 1960.

Pincushion Dolls

Antique dolls are one of the largest and most varied collectible categories. One of the most popular and unique dolls is the pincushion doll (also called the half-doll, tea cosy, egg cosy, bust, tea bust, dresser doll, and whiskbroom doll), produced in glazed porcelain by manufacturers in the United States, Europe, and Japan from the mid-1890s until the middle of the twentieth century. Early Victorian examples were produced in England, France, and Germany and were attached to thick skirts that were placed over teapots to help keep the tea warm. When the dolls were imported to the United States, clever Americans found a multitude of additional uses for them. The smallest versions (about one inch high) were attached to tiny skirts and used as egg cosies to keep a boiled egg warm until it was eaten. The larger sizes (up to nine inches) were used as tops for whisk brooms, bottle corks, and—most often in Victorian times—pincushions.

Because production began so late in the period, and because the same molds were used for many years, it is nearly impossible to date specific half-dolls to the Victorian era. However, high-quality German examples molded in the form of eighteenth-century French ladies of fashion are representative of the period. Of course, these are also the half-dolls that maintain the highest value. The most collectible pincushion dolls are in mint or near-mint condition. Those with cracks or chips are worth considerably less. The existence of original pincushions and clothing in good condition add to the value of the piece.

Price Range

Pincushion dolls (high-quality examples with German porcelain marks): $200 to $1000+.

Suggested Reading

Marion, Frieda and Norma Werner. *Collector's Encyclopedia of Half-Dolls.* New York: Crown Publishers, 1979.

6-5 Half-doll whisk broom (left), and pincushion doll (right).

Rocking Chairs

Sometime in the mid–eighteenth century, someone took a ladder-back chair and attached two curved runners to the legs to make it rock. The arrangement caught on, and the rocking chair became a standard offering in furniture catalogs, especially in the nineteenth-century United States.

Victorian rocking chairs were made in a wide variety of styles and configurations. The most popular style of the period, and the most recognized today, probably is the Boston rocker with its S-shaped arms, curved seat dipping from the

6-6 Renaissance Revival rocker with Eastlake influence. (Courtesy Jensen's Antiques)

aissance and Eastlake influences are common in late nineteenth-century platform rockers.

Many Victorian-style rockers have been reproduced continuously throughout the twentieth century. Therefore, dated or signed examples that can be specifically attributed to the period are especially desirable. Prices of Victorian rocking chairs are affected by style, size, wood used, and condition. Upholstered examples either should have their original cloth in good condition or should be properly reupholstered in cloth of the period style.

Price Ranges

Boston (Country) rockers: $135 to $325.
Caned-back rockers: $175 to $375.
Folding (carpet) rockers: $150 to $275.
Lincoln rockers: $350 to $550.
Platform rockers: $250 to $450.
Standard Renaissance or Eastlake rockers: $200 to $350.

Prices in excess of $2000 have been paid for rockers that are highly ornate or made of high-quality woods, as well as for unique rockers by highly reputable furniture makers of the period.

Suggested Reading

McNerney, Kathryn. *Victorian Furniture: Our American Heritage:* Paducah, Ky.: Collector Books, 1981.
Swedberg, Robert W. and Harriett Swedberg. *Victorian Furniture,* vols. 1–3. Radnor, Pa.: Wallace-Homestead Book Company, 1984–1985.

Sewing Birds

The Victorian age, being the "age of invention," produced many mechanical conveniences for use in various rooms in the house. The one item from the sewing room most recognized as Victorian today is the sewing bird, a device that clamped to the work table and held material in place while it was being sewn. The upper portion of the clamp is in the form of a metal bird with a spring-hinged mouth to hold the cloth. A silk-

back and scrolling over in front, and high spindle back with carved ornamental panel depicting leaves, flowers, or fruit. These are now commonly categorized as "Country" rockers. There were also bentwood rockers with cane seats and backs; thickly upholstered folding "carpet rockers"; padded, leather-upholstered "Lincoln rockers" (the president's favorite); and a variety of mechanical rockers attached by springs to a solid platform base.

Rocking chairs were also produced in the well-known styles of the period: balloon-back and finger-roll versions of French Revival influence, examples with extensive applied ornaments and crests in the Renaissance style, and straight-lined Eastlakes with incised decorative patterns. Ren-

6-7 Brass sewing bird. (Courtesy Georgia Fox, Foxes Den)

or velvet-covered pincushion usually also was incorporated into the design.

Sewing birds were made in a variety of styles, some highly ornate and decorative, others basic and functional. Like many other sewing tools, some were silver plated or gilded. Most were brass or nickel-plated metal. In addition to birds, flowers, and other animals might be included in the design of more elaborate versions.

Prices of Victorian sewing birds are affected by complexity of design, size, condition of metal or finish, and identifying marks. Pricing is also greatly affected by regional supply and demand.

NOTE: High-quality modern sewing bird reproductions exist.

96

Price Range

Sewing birds: $55 to $200+. Average: $125 to $150.
Prices in excess of $500 have been paid for elaborate or dated examples.

Suggested Reading

See Ladies' Work Boxes, this chapter.

Sewing Implements

Only the most avid couturier would recognize all of the unusual tools to be found in the Victorian sewing box. An abbreviated glossary of nineteenth-century sewing implements, many of which are still produced for use today in their original or modernized forms, follows.

Buttonhole scissors—Their function is their name. Several types were made, but the most common type resembles a pair of scissors with short, hatchet-shaped blades. Other versions have a single blade that feeds through a slotted base.
Crochet hooks—Crocheting is a form of knitting in which loops of thread are interwoven with a hook-ended needle. Called crochet hooks,

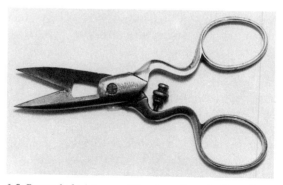

6-8 Buttonhole scissors. (Courtesy Georgia Fox, Foxes Den)

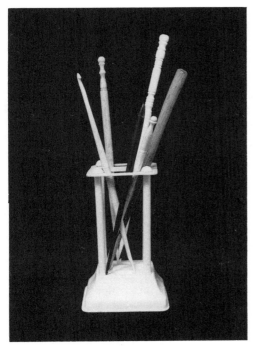

6-9 *A variety of knitting needles in a celluloid holder.* (Courtesy Georgia Fox, Foxes Den)

6-10 *Wooden darner with storage compartment inside.*

these needles were produced in a variety of sizes, from three or four inches to twelve or more inches in length, and made either of metal or wood.

Darner—In households where money for new clothes was scarce, holes in socks and other clothing were repaired by darning the hole closed. The darner (also called darning ball or darning egg) was a ball or egg-shaped object made of glass, ceramic, wood, or metal placed inside the garment during the darning process to keep the needle from catching other areas of the material.

Embroidery hoop—Ornamentation was added to pillows, towels, and other cloth items by sewing colorful thread to form pictures, initials, or symbols in a process called embroidery. Two interlocking loops held the cloth taut during the embroidery process. In earlier years

these were made primarily of wood; later both wood and metal versions were used.

Hem gauge—The most common work done in the sewing room probably was the rehemming of pants and dresses, either because they had been accidently torn loose or because the hemline needed to be lengthened or shortened. A device called a hem gauge acted as a guide to keep the distance from hem to stitch, or hem to floor, equal all the way around. Hem gauges were produced in wood, cast iron, and silver.

Scissors—Although scissors were produced in an endless variety (some were for trimming paper, cooking, gardening, hair cutting, or manicures), there only are a few basic types used by the Victorian seamstress. Probably the most recognized and collected scissors of the period were the "stork" scissors. These were shaped like the familiar bird, with cutting blades repre-

97

6-11 Silver-plated stork scissors used for embroidery work. (Courtesy Georgia Fox, Foxes Den)

senting the beak and handles forming the wings and legs. Scissors with long thin blades were used for embroidery, and those with one sharp-pointed and one blunt-pointed blade were trimming scissors. Large shears were used for cutting material.

Seam cutter—The only way to remove an old hem or seam is to cut through each stitch. A very sharp knife or razor can be used, but it often accidentally snags the material. The Victorian seam cutter has a V-shaped cutting point that slipped between the pieces of cloth to cut only the threads.

Shuttle—Any device around which thread is wound for storage and use can be called a shuttle. Over the years, however, the term most frequently has been used to describe large commercial spools and tatting shuttles, which are flat, elongated winders that look somewhat like

spearheads. These were produced in a variety of materials, including bone, ivory, celluloid, tortoise shell, whale bone, and silver. They often had carved, embossed, or painted decorations.

NOTE: Do not confuse shuttles with thread winders, which are listed later in this section.

Spools—Thread was purchased wound on wooden spools of various sizes (as small as one inch or as large as twelve inches), and additional spools made of wood, bone, or ivory could be purchased for thread storage. High-quality or unique spools often also are called "shuttles."

Stiletto—Holes for small eyelets were made with a thin, sharp tool—a sort of tiny sword called a stiletto. They were primarily made of steel, but other materials such as ivory, bone, and silver were occasionally used.

Tape measure—Tape measures were produced of leather, cloth, or paper and enclosed in often highly ornate cases of metal, wood, ivory, or celluloid. Collectors are interested in the overall quality of the piece, and in imprints of companies who often gave them away as promotional items.

Thread winder—Loose or measured amounts of thread can be wound onto any piece of stiff, flat material for storage. These "thread winders"

6-12 Celluloid tatting shuttle with tatting. (Courtesy Georgia Fox, Foxes Den)

6-13 Commercial-type wooden spools, also called "shuttles."

6-14 Wooden knitting needles.

were made of wood, ivory, bone, cardboard, shell, celluloid, and other materials cut into a variety of commonplace or unusual shapes to keep the thread in place.

Thread waxer—Waxing thread strengthens it and makes working with it easier. Several types of containers were manufactured in Victorian times to hold the beeswax while the thread was pulled across it. These generally were cylinder shaped, had caps or bases of wood, ivory, shell, or silver, and sometimes had a pincushion incorporated in the design. Today thread waxers are among the rarest of nineteenth-century sewing collectibles.

All of these items from the Victorian sewing room are now highly collectible. Wooden items such as knitting needles, darning balls, and spools can be found in abundance. Tools that often came in sets (lucets, netting tools, stilettos, hem gauges, and so forth) are sometimes difficult to locate and often are incorrectly identified.

Prices of Victorian sewing implements generally are based on purpose of tool, materials used, complexity of design, completeness of set (if any), and condition. Prices are greatly affected by supply and demand.

Price Ranges

Buttonhole cutter: $25 to $75.

Crochet hooks (wood): $15 to $50 a pair. Prices in excess of $200 have been paid for certain ivory or whalebone examples.

Darners and darning balls: $10 to $100+. Prices of $200 or more have been paid for examples in rare woods or glass and for dated examples.

Embroidery hoops (wood): $10 to $75. Prices in excess of $150 have been paid for Shaker and other rare examples.

Hem gauge: $15 to $50.

Scissors (ordinary): $10 to $50.

Scissors (decorative handles, silver or gold plated): $35 to $150+.

Shuttles and thread winders: $5 to $75+. Highest prices are paid for ivory or scrimshaw examples.

Spools: wood $1 to $15, ivory $25 to $75.

Stork scissors: $20 to $75+. Lower prices for brass, higher for sterling silver.

Tape measures: $10 to $100+. Average: $35.

Wooden needles: $5 to $25.

Suggested Reading

See Ladies Work Boxes, this chapter.

Sewing Machines

Various mechanical devices to aid the seamstress in her needlework were introduced in the eighteenth century, but the sewing machine as we know it was patented on September 10, 1846, by Elias Howe, Jr., of Cambridge, Massachusetts. He used a needle and shuttle of novel design and combined them with a holding surface, feeding mechanism, and other components brought together for the first time in one machine. Surprisingly many of these features had been invented previously by others unknown to Howe, and yet they were brought together into one machine for the first time by him. Numerous improvements to Howe's design were made throughout the remainder of the century. By the beginning of the Civil War there were a number of major manufacturers, primarily (in order of sales): Wheeler and Wilson; Grover and Baker; the familiar L. M. Singer and Company; Wilcox and Gibbs; Ladd and Webster; the inventor A. B. Howe; Bartholf, Leavitt and Company; and Finkle and Lyon.

The earliest sewing machines had a hand crank, and although machines were produced with this antiquated feature into the twentieth century, most Victorian period examples used the pumping power of a foot pedal called a "treadle." Many reliable treadle machines are still in use today and are sought after by collectors both for their historical value and for their beautiful, solidly built, and often elaborate cabinetry.

Turn-of-the-century models such as the Burdick, White, New Queen, Howard, Minnesota, and, of course, the early Singer are easily found at antiques and estate sales. Prices are based on brand, complexity of design (both of machine and cabinetry), construction materials, age, and condition.

Price Range

Sewing machines: $35 to $1500+. Average: $175 to $225. Highest prices are paid for unusual machines designed to produce a specialized type of stitch (for example, lace, netting, and so forth) and those with cabinetry of special note.

Suggested Reading

See Ladies' Work Boxes, this chapter.

Sewing Stands

Sewing tables and stands were manufactured in a wide variety of styles, from a simple pedestal table with a single drawer to massive, multidrawered cabinets. Some stands contained compartments specifically designed to hold tools, spools, and other sewing necessities. These usually are more valuable than other styles that often are simply called "work tables," because they do not have features specifically associated with sewing.

Early Federal sewing stands were quite popular with Victorians and remain so with today's collectors. These heavy pieces with rolling, veneered designs are still easy to locate but often are accompanied by a hefty price tag. French Revival designs with curved legs and, usually, a lifting lid were also quite popular and are reasonably priced on today's market. Renaissance and Eastlake sewing stands were produced but were not as popular then or now. A large variety of Victorian sewing stands do not fit into any specific group or style or may combine features from a variety of styles. Some unique and beautiful sewing stands also were produced in wicker and in wrought iron.

Prices of Victorian work tables and sewing stands are based on style, complexity of design, woods used, manufacturer (if known), and condition.

Price Ranges

Federal sewing stands: $2500 to $10,000+.
French Revival sewing stands: $450 to $1500+.
Generic Victorian sewing stands: $175 to $1000+. Average: $275 to $325.
Renaissance and Eastlake sewing stands: $275 to $1000+.

Suggested Reading

Clement, Joyce. *Sewing Collectibles*. New York: Ballantine, 1987.

McNerney, Kathryn. *Victorian Furniture: Our American Heritage.* Paducah, Ky.: Collector Books, 1988.

Swedberg, Robert W. and Harriet Swedberg. *Victorian Furniture,* vols. 1–3. Radnor, Pa.: Wallace-Homestead Book Company, 1984–1985.

Spinning Wheels

The old method of spinning cotton into thread was to attach a bunch of the processed fiber to the end of a forked stick called a "distaff," which was held under the left arm. The cotton was drawn out and twisted with the right forefinger and thumb, the size and quality of the yarn produced regulated only by delicacy of touch. The thread was wound on a stick called a "spindle." This was the work of the spinsters of old England until the spinning wheel was introduced from India during the reign of Henry VIII. On the spinning wheel the spindle itself turns at high speed, twisting the yarn as it winds.

The spinning wheel has a distinctive profile that is universally recognized and immediately associated with history. It was made in a variety of sizes and from a variety of woods, many with ornate carvings or applied ornamentation. Some have parts made of bone or ivory, and some, mostly from northern countries, are attractively painted. Large versions are called "wool wheels" and smaller ones "flax wheels," designating the type of raw material spun.

On today's market spinning wheels are in high demand as decorator items. Prices are based on woods used, complexity of decoration, and condition. Size is a secondary price factor. Missing or replacement parts detract heavily from the value. Collectors are cautioned that spinning wheels have been continuously produced throughout the twentieth century, and superb reproductions of early designs have been made.

Price Range

Spinning wheels: $150 to $2500+. Average: $450.

Suggested Reading

See Sewing Stands, this chapter.

Thimbles

Quite likely, the person who invented the needle invented the thimble a few seconds later, after the first needle prick. We do know that thimbles have been around as long as history has recorded such things, and they have been made from nearly every imaginable material. Because of their small size and enormous variety, they have been collected for almost as long as they have been used.

Thimbles of the Victorian period were made of

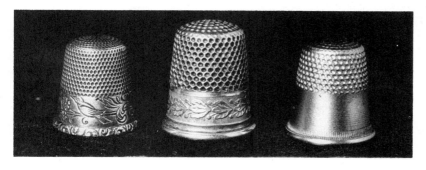

6-15 Three thimbles (left to right): silver, silver plate, and brass.

metal, glass, porcelain, and other carved or molded materials. The following list is provided to give the collector an idea of the variety of Victorian thimbles currently in collections.

abalone, inlaid	ivory, painted
bone, plain	ivory, scrimshaw
bone, scrimshaw	ivory, silver inlay
brass, advertising	mother-of-pearl, inlaid
brass, embossed	papier-maché, jappaned
brass, engraved	pewter, engraved
bronze, etched	pewter, molded
celluloid, embossed	porcelain
celluloid, painted	porcelain, painted
celluloid, plain	silver, commemorative
celluloid, swirl	silver, embossed
china, advertising	silver, enameled
china, molded	silver, engraved
china, painted	silver, inlaid
glass, amber	silver, jeweled
glass, crystal	silver plate, embossed
glass, cut	silver plate, engraved
glass, pressed	silver plate, inlaid
glass, ruby	silver plate, jeweled
glass, Tiffany	silver, Tiffany
gold, embossed	tin, advertising
gold, enamel design	tin, jappaned
gold, engraved	tin, painted
gold, jeweled	tin, pressed
gold, plate	tortoise shell, inlaid
gold, solid	wood, carved
hard rubber	wood, encised
iron, nickel-plated	wood, inlaid
iron, painted	wood, painted
ivory	

Prices of Victorian period thimbles are based on construction materials, size, complexity of design and applied decorations, manufacturer (if known), and condition. Values are greatly affected by supply and demand. Thimbles with advertising and commemorative themes are prized by specialty collectors. It is highly recommended that those interested in this area of collecting obtain one or more of the many definitive books on the subject in order to recognize and evaluate specific pieces.

Price Range

Thimbles: $5 to $2500+. Prices range widely in all categories. A price guide should be kept at hand for reference to particular pieces. The average collectible thimble sells for around $20 to $35.

Suggested Reading

Greif, Helmut. *Talks About Thimbles.* Wilmington, Del.: Dine-American, 1983.

Lundquist, Myrtle. *Book of a Thousand Thimbles.* Radnor, Pa.: Wallace-Homestead Book Company, 1970.

———. *Thimble Americana.* Radnor, Pa.: Wallace-Homestead Book Company, 1981.

———. *Thimble Treasury.* Radnor, Pa.: Wallace-Homestead Book Company, 1975.

Von Hoelle, John. *Thimble Collector's Encyclopedia:* Radnor, Pa.: Wallace-Homestead Book Company, 1986.

Zalkin, Estelle. *Zalkin's Handbook of Thimbles and Sewing Implements.* Radnor, Pa.: Wallace-Homestead Book Company, 1988.

CHAPTER 7

The Library

Nearly every Victorian home had a library. It may have been called a study or an office, or it may have been only a small corner of the back parlor. However, in many homes it was the largest room and, being primarily the domain of the master of the house, it was decidedly masculine. Rich woods were frequently used for fireplace mantels, built-in bookshelves, and trim. Carpets were often dark, with large, bold designs. Wall coverings in libraries also frequently had dark patterns, although plain lighter coverings were used as well. The basic concept of Victorian library decor was understated (for the period), quiet, and masculine. There were, of course, exceptions, in homes where male dominance was not so severe, there was a greater degree of feminine influence.

If the library was a separate room, the children usually were not allowed to be there unattended. Cherished books and important papers were stored there and had to be kept from destructive if playful fingers. Even if *bookcases* were built-in, there also often were free-standing examples with locking doors for additional protection. *Secretaries,* with shelves for books, drawers for papers, and a *desk* for writing, were common here, although there may have been several scattered throughout the house. A variety of desks, from large plantation types to small roll-tops, also could be found in the library.

Other furniture found in the library was identical to those items, previously described, in parlors: side chairs, armchairs, settees, center tables, parlor stands, and so forth. While mantel clocks frequently were found in libraries, large *wall clocks* were seen as well.

Male visitors often were invited to the library after dinner to talk, relax, have a glass of sherry, and smoke. Items related to these activities—*liquor cabinets, decanters, pipes, humidors, snuff boxes, spitoons,* and so forth—would be stored or on display. If the master of the house were a hunter or shooter, a variety of new or antique *guns* might be hanging on the wall. Nearly every Victorian adult male owned a set of dueling pistols, although this dangerous yet romantic custom quickly wained after the Civil War.

Family business was conducted in the library. Bills were paid and collected, mail orders placed, and various correspondence prepared. Desk drawers were filled with a variety of *writing implements,* as well as *ink bottles, wax seals, magnifying glasses,* and *spectacles* (reading glasses). Important papers might be kept in a locked drawer of the desk or secretary or in a more portable *document box.* Individual family members often had their own private *lap desks,* which could be closed and locked, and which had storage compartments for writing materials and correspondence.

The primary use of any library is, of course, to store *books.* The nineteenth century produced many of the most famous names in literature, and reading was the most common pastime of the period. Printing methods were constantly improving, and publishing houses took great pride not only in the quality of the published material, but in the quality of the bindings as well. A row of books bound in natural leathers with bright red insets and gold-embossed titles symbolizes Victorian ideals.

If the famous Sherlock Holmes wanted to learn as much as possible about the residents of a house, he first would head for the library. From the books they read to the papers they wrote, the library held the past, present, and future of a Victorian family.

Bookcases

Books could be stored in built-in bookcases, in secretaries, or in free-standing bookcases. Free-standing types generally were about eight or nine feet high, with two long framed glass doors exposing a half-dozen or more shelves inside. Most of these also had two drawers side by side in the base. While bookcases were produced in the styles of the period (French Revival, Renaissance, and Eastlake), many were very plain, with little or no adornments such as pilasters, pediments, medallions, and so forth.

Prices of Victorian bookcases are based on factors of size, style, wood used, and condition, with size being a primary factor.

Price Range

Bookcases: $500 to $1500.

Suggested Reading

McNerney, Kathryn. *Victorian Furniture: Our American Heritage:* Paducah, Ky.: Collector Books, 1981.
Swedberg, Robert W. and Harriett Swedberg. *Victorian Furniture,* vols. 1–3. Radnor, Pa.: Wallace-Homestead Book Company, 1984–1985.

Books

Victorian period books are collected for their beauty: many were bound in fine leather bindings that now exhibit a natural rustic appearance. They are collected for their content: some of the most famous and widely read authors of literature were Victorian. Finally, they are collected for their monetary value: certain rare first editions can bring six figures. Famous Victorian authors of period poetry and prose included

Hans Christian Anderson
Charlotte Brontë
Emily Brontë
Elizabeth Barrett Browning
Robert Browning
Lewis Carroll
James Fenimore Cooper
Charles Dickens
Mary Mapes Dodge
Arthur Conan Doyle
Thomas Hardy
George Washington Harris
Bret Harte
Nathaniel Hawthorne
Oliver Wendell Holmes
Victor Hugo
Washington Irving
Henry James
Charles Kingsley
Rudyard Kipling
Henry Wadsworth Longfellow
Herman Melville
Edgar Allan Poe
William Sydney Porter (O. Henry)
George Bernard Shaw
Robert Louis Stevenson
Harriet Beecher Stowe

Alfred Lord Tennyson
William Makepeace Thackeray
Henry David Thoreau
Leo Tolstoy
Mark Twain
Jules Verne
Walt Whitman
Oscar Wilde
William Wordsworth
Willam Butler Yeats

Many magazines of the period published compendiums or condensed versions of their literary publishings in bound form. *Harper's Monthly Magazine* volumes contained six months of news, fashion, and literature by many of the major writers of the time. These volumes (published from 1851) are prized as a source of firsthand information about Victorian life and literature and nineteenth-century history. *Godey's Lady's Book, Les-*

lie's, and others also were produced in bound volumes.

A variety of technical books, schoolbooks, Bibles, and other works by unknown Victorian period authors have survived in reasonably good condition and have limited appeal to collectors. All pre-1900 books have historical value and should be protected while stored, transported, and displayed.

Prices of Victorian period books are based on age, type of book, content, author, quality of bindings and papers, edition, publisher, and condition. Book prices are greatly affected by supply

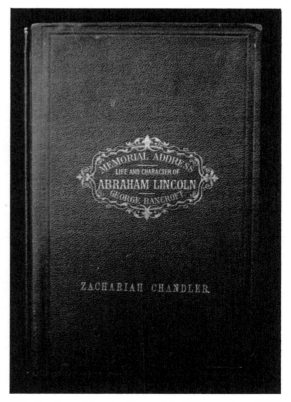

7-2 Abraham Lincoln Memorial Address, circa 1866. Formerly the property of Zachariah Chandler, who later became an aide to President Grant.

7-1 A sampling of nineteenth-century books, including a Harper's Magazine *compendium circa 1859, an 1855 dictionary, a* Godey's Ladies Book *sampler, a first edition of Mark Twain's* Roughing It, *and two small Testaments circa 1860.*

and demand. Certain books lie unnoticed for decades, suddenly becoming a valued collector's item simply because of a change in demand for that type of book or author.

Price Ranges

First editions: $25 to $1000+. Average: $150 to $300. Prices in excess of $100,000 have been paid for certain nineteenth-century first editions.

Harper's Monthly Magazine six-month compendiums: $20 to $65. Average: $35.

Schoolbooks: $5 to $50. Average: $15.

Examples

The following examples show the wide variety of pricing in the collectible book field. Accordingly, serious collectors should familiarize themselves with current trends by purchasing one of the many excellent guides to book collecting and subscribing to a periodical in the field.

David Copperfield by Charles Dickens, 1850: $250 to $300.

Kidnapped by Robert Louis Stevenson, 1886: $75 to $125.

Luck of Roaring Camp by Bret Harte, 1872: $50 to $100.

Representative Men by Ralph Waldo Emerson, 1850: $50 to $75.

Roughing It by Mark Twain, 1872: $75 to $100.

Treasure Island by Robert Louis Stevenson, 1883: $300 to $350.

Suggested Reading

Ahearn, Allen. *Book Collecting: A Comprehensive Guide.* Putnam Publishing Group, 1989.

LeFontaine, Joseph R. *Turning Paper To Gold: How To Make Money with Old Books; Magazines, Comics, Sheet Music, and Other Printed Paper Collectibles.* Crozet, Va.: Betterway Publications, 1988.

Old Book Value Guide, second ed. Paducah, Ky.: Collector Books, 1990.

Decanters

Liquor and spirits were seldom dispensed from their original containers. They were transferred to fine-quality glass or crystal decanters, which were then displayed on a table or kept in a cabinet or box. Each decanter usually had its own identifying tag in silver or gold plate held in place by a small chain that encircled the neck of the bottle (these decanter tags are a popular collectible in themselves).

High-quality decanters were made by most of the major glass manufacturers of the period, such as New England Glass and Boston and Sandwich. (For more information on glass manufacturers, styles, and collecting, see Decorative Glass in Chapter 2, The Front Parlor, and Glassware in Chapter 3, The Dining Room).

Prices of Victorian glass decanters are based on size, pattern, manufacturer (if known), type and color of glass, and condition. The glass stoppers used in most decanters were easily lost or broken; therefore, those with original stoppers command higher prices than those with replacements.

Price Ranges

Cut-crystal decanters: $125 to $350+.

Pressed pattern glass decanters: $45 to $275+.

Suggested Reading

See Glassware in Chapter 3, The Dining Room.

Desks

There are probably more styles of Victorian desks than of any other type of furniture. Many nineteenth-century homes contained a desk of some sort in nearly every room, and many of the desks used by businesses were identical to those used at home. The widespread popularity of the desk led designers and manufacturers to come up with new designs that incorporated convenience, security, and abundant storage capabilities.

The most recognizable Victorian period desk probably is the roll-top. Roll-tops have a flexible cover made of small strips of wood held together by a cloth backing. The cover can be pulled out

7-3 A Wooton desk with "turning" storage compartments. (Courtesy McHenry Mansion)

over the top of the desk to protect its contents. This cover conforms to the shape of the end supports and is either half-round or S-shaped. Roll-tops evolved from earlier covered desks with slanted drop-fronts and solid half-round cylinders. Many desks without covers were produced in the same layout: a flat desk surface with a thin drawer beneath and a back piece containing small drawers and pigeonholes (open-front storage slots), all supported by two stacks of drawers on either side of the central leg space. Drop-front (slant front) desks do not have a leg space since the desk top extends out from the edge when it is dropped. Therefore, they usually have large drawers extending the full width of the front.

One of the most famous Victorian desks was the Wooton "Wells Fargo," an extremely large desk with massive doors containing a multitude of storage boxes. These doors open to reveal a large number of drawers and pigeonholes and a drop-front desk surface. All Wooton desks are notable for their abundant storage compartments and high quality of construction. Wooton desks are now quite rare and are considered investment-quality antiques.

Many styles of desks were produced in table models, with legs instead of drawer stacks. These usually are smaller than "leg space" versions and are substantially lower in price.

Prices of Victorian desks are based on style, size, complexity of design, wood used, manufacturer (if known), and condition.

Price Ranges

Cylinder desks: $1000 to $2500+.
Drop-front desks: $500 to $1500+.
Roll-top desks: $2500 to $4000+.
Table desks: $200 to $750+
Wooton Wells Fargo: $10,000 to $16,000+.

Suggested Reading

See Bookcases, this chapter.

Document Boxes

Locking storage boxes were produced in a variety of configurations in both wood and metal. The only protection these boxes afforded was to keep the contents safe from prying eyes, for if someone wanted to steal the papers inside they could sim-

7-4 Typical locking document box in pine with brass corners.

ply take the entire box to a place where they could break it open. Wooden boxes and their contents burned up in fires. Metal boxes sometimes survived, but their contents did not (perhaps inspiring the term "internal combustion").

Just about any small box (about twelve inches in length) dating from the nineteenth century that does not have an identifiable purpose can be called a document box. Similar boxes, such as tea caddies, humidors, ladies' work boxes, and jewelry boxes had linings of some sort; document boxes usually did not. Because they saw frequent use and were handled often, they usually exhibit extensive wear, giving them a character not seen on other boxes. Many document boxes were quite ornate—inlaid with mother-of-pearl, painted with colorful figures or scenes, or covered in fine leather. Sometimes the words "deed," "papers," or "doc" are painted or incised in the top.

Document boxes should not be confused with tin money boxes or spice boxes produced from about the turn of the century. These were painted black and usually had a gold, silver, or red line running around the top about one inch from the edges. These are frequently found today without their original money trays or spice tins, and their value is about $15 apiece.

Prices of Victorian document boxes are based

on size, materials used, complexity of decoration (if any), and condition. Locking boxes with working keys are especially desirable.

Price Range

Document boxes: $100 to $250+. Prices in excess of $500 have been paid for certain highly ornate examples.

Suggested Reading

Klamikin, Marian. *Collector's Book of Boxes.* New York: Dodd, Mead & Company, 1970.

Documents, Papers, and Autographs

Until recently, estate handlers would peruse old papers quickly and then discard those deemed unrelated to current or future family affairs. Today each item is carefully studied for possible historical or collectible value. These papers are sought after not only by collectors but by museums, archives, libraries, and universities around the world.

Documents with the greatest market value are those concerning specific historical events or signed by historical figures. However, many old papers are collected for their emotional appeal (love letters, for example) or aesthetic value (as a framed and hanging decoration). A number of firms archivally mount and frame historical papers and make them available to the general public at remarkably high prices.

The chances of discovering a famous autograph among a stack of old papers is not as unlikely as you might think. Until after the Civil War secretaries and personal aids were not commonly used, and many important government officials produced and signed all of their own correspondence. Although the president did have a personal secretary who often signed his name to documents of lesser importance, it was not uncommon for the president to personally answer letters from the common populace.

7-5 Land grant dated 1859.

The various factors that affect the value of an old document or letter include length, date, addressor and addressee (if any), subject or purpose, and condition. As previously mentioned, historical relevance is a primary factor, as is supply and demand. The popularity of certain figures has made their autographs rare although they were prolific writers; other autographs are scarce simply because the subject produced very few signed documents, often due to early death.

Price Ranges

Divorce decrees, deeds, wills, and so forth (not deemed of historical import): $1 to $35. Highest prices are paid for large, older documents in good condition and suitable for framing.

Historical documents: $15 to $10,000+. Lowest prices are for documents involving a historical event but not containing reference to a significant person, place, or event, or a signature of a recognized figure.

Suggested Reading

Rawlins; Ray. *The Stein and Day Book of World Autographs.* Chelsea, Mich.: Scarborough House, 1978.
Sanders, et al. *Collector's Guide to Autographs.* Radnor, Pa.: Wallace-Homestead Book Company, 1989.

Guns and Weapons

The first weapons used to fire a projectile through a tube by means of explosive powder were cannons produced in the thirteenth century. By the 1800s two reasonably efficient (and much smaller) handheld versions had evolved: a shoulder arm, called the musket, and a pistol. During the first half of the century muskets were heavy and slow to load and fire. After pouring a measured amount of highly explosive "black powder" into the barrel, the projectile, a lead ball approximately one-half inch or larger in diameter, was rammed down the barrel with a rod. A small amount of powder was also placed in a hole near the base of the barrel to act as a kind of fuse. When the trigger was pulled, a hammer containing a piece of flint fell forward and, striking near the hole, produced a spark that ignited the powder in the hole, which in turn ignited the powder in the barrel and fired the lead ball. Pistols operated in the same manner but, as they had much shorter barrels, were extremely inaccurate at distances of more than a few yards. These weapons are called "flint lock muzzle-loaders."

7-6 Ball-and-cap type pistol with solid silver trimwork, circa 1850s.

The Victorian period brought three important improvements to gun design: widespread use of "rifling," the percussion firing mechanism, and the "minie ball" bullet. Rifling was a series of grooves cut into the barrel interior that caused the bullet to spin, and made the gun's aim much more accurate at longer distances. The percussion system, which replaced the flint-and-powder firing mechanism, featured a small nipple onto which an explosive cap was placed. When the hammer struck the cap, a spark from the explosion traveled down the nipple and ignited the powder in the barrel—a faster, more reliable, and much cleaner method. The minie ball was the first true bullet. It was cone shaped and hollow at the base to facilitate expansion into the rifling grooves of the barrel. Guns with these improvements date from the 1850s through the Civil War period and are called "percussion muzzle-loaders." (Other terms used include "rifle muskets" and "ball-and-cap" rifles or pistols.)

During the early 1850s a pistol was invented with six revolving chambers, providing the convenience of six shots before reloading. The inventor was Samuel Colt, and the gun, called the 1851 Colt Navy, is one of the most highly prized—and widely reproduced—collectible American weapons. The name "Colt" is now synonymous with early American Western gunlore, primarily attributed to his "Peacemaker" .45 caliber cartridge revolver of the 1870s.

Cartridge-type ammunition (with powder, bullet, and ignition cap contained in a single unit) was experimented with as early as 1812 but was not perfected until the Civil War period. Due to the high cost of refitting troops with the new arms and ammunition, cartridge weapons did not see extensive military use until after the war. Rifles and revolvers using the new metal cartridges gradually began to replace percussion weapons in the late 1860s, and by the turn of the century muzzle-loaders were generally obsolete.

During the Civil War literally millions of rifles were produced in a wide variety of configurations and calibers. The infantry generally carried some version of the M1861 Springfield rifle (model numbers indicate the year certain improvements were made), and the cavalry carried one of several carbine rifles (Sharps, Spencer, Burnside, Starr, Remington, and others). Calibers varied, especially during the early years of the war when weapons of any type were in great demand, causing severe difficulty in supplying ammunition to the troops.

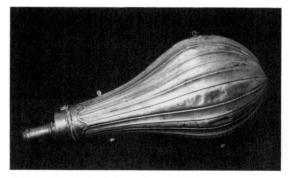

7-7 Powder flask of the style needed for most guns produced before 1865. (Courtesy Amador County Museum)

Pistols, while not carried by all the troops, were produced in an equal array of configurations. Colt and Remington were in direct competition as the major suppliers of military handguns. Both produced a .36 caliber "Navy" and .44 caliber "Army" percussion pistol, with improvements in each successive model year. Also popular with collectors today are the limited-production LeMat revolver, which has a nine-shot cylinder as well as a central buckshot barrel, and early pistols from a name well known in the modern gun market—Smith and Wesson.

It was not unusual for certain Victorian ladies to carry small derringer pistols in their handbags for personal protection. These one- or two-shot pistols were usually highly engraved and often were plated in silver with ivory or mother-of-pearl handles. Fancy Victorian derringers are prized by collectors.

Victorian gentlemen were frequently armed—during the early years with single-shot percussion pistols and after the Civil War with small revolvers. A gentleman might also carry a fancy dagger, possibly with a jeweled handle and fine-leather or velvet scabbard. Gentlemen usually owned a set of fine-quality dueling pistols (single-shot flintlock or percussion), even though he might have no intention of ever using them. He also probably would own several hunting rifles and shotguns. If he were a frequent hunter or woodsman, he would own a large bowie knife.

Prices of Victorian-period weapons are based on a variety of factors, the most important of which are condition and rarity. Those who wish to specialize in this complicated field should obtain as many current books on the subject as possible and familiarize themselves with the variety of arms manufacturers and configurations. The collector is cautioned that a small variation in two similar weapons can make a difference of several thousand dollars in value. It is also important to know that excellent reproductions of these early weapons have been and are being made for display and use by reenactment groups and filmmakers. (See also Civil War Artifacts in Chapter 11, Miscellaneous Victorian Collectibles.)

Price Ranges

Cartridge revolvers: $100 to $10,000+.
Cartridge rifles: $250 to $5000+.
Cartridge shotguns: $300 to $5000+.
Flintlock muskets: $500 to $5000+.
Flintlock pistols: $450 to $5000+.
Percussion pistols: $250 to $5000+.
Percussion revolvers: $350 to $5000+.
Percussion rifles: $300 to $5000+.
Percussion shotguns: $300 to $5000+.

Prices well in excess of the high end of this range have been paid for certain rare or desirable guns.

Suggested Reading

Flayderman, Norm. *Flayderman's Guide to Antique American Firearms.* Northbrook, Ill.: DBI Books, 1987.

Hogg, Ian V. *Weapons of the American Civil War.* New York: Crown Publishers, 1987.

Madaus, Michael H. *Warner Collector's Guide to American Longarms.* New York: Warner Books; 1981.

Lap Desks

Letter writing was an important activity among Victorian ladies. They used the finest-quality stationery they could afford and honed their penmanship skills in the finest Spencerian style. These letters, both incoming and outgoing, were considered personal and private and were kept safe from prying eyes in the lady's private lap desk (also called a portable writing slope), which is a locking box, usually of the finest wood and often inlaid with brass, silver, or mother-of-pearl. The box opened to reveal a writing slope padded with leather, velvet, or felt. Compartments beneath each flap of the slope provided storage for stationery and treasured correspon-

7-8 Typical Victorian lap desk with storage compartments.

dence that would be tied with silk ribbons. A sectioned area at the front of the slope contained compartments for the inkwell, blotter, pens and pencils, wax seals, and so forth.

Lap desks were also used by other family members as well as businessmen and students. These desks were produced in a variety of styles, from very inexpensive basic pine boxes to elaborate inlaid examples, and with a variety of interior configurations. They came as small as six by nine inches and as large as sixteen by twenty-four inches (closed). The common lap desk found in antiques stores is about 7½ inches wide by 11 inches long by 4½ inches high and sells for around $85 to $125.

Prices of lap desks in today's antiques market are affected by size, type of wood, and type and quality of inlaid decorations. Condition is of primary importance. Exteriors with noticeable marks or missing inlaid pieces and interiors with missing compartment dividers or torn or missing slope pads greatly detract from the value. Lap desks with the original fitted inkwells and blotters are highly prized.

Price Ranges

Lap desks: $50 to $1500+. Lower prices are paid for pine school desks; higher prices are paid for large or elaborately decorated examples in fine woods.

Suggested Reading

Coe, Brian. *Boxes.* San Mateo, Calif: Pitman Publishing, 1976.

Little, Nina. *Neat and Tidy: Boxes.* New York: E. P. Dutton, 1980.

Liquor Cabinets and Boxes

In the Victorian home, just as in homes today, spirits may or may not have been made available depending on the whims or the moral or religious ideas of the master and madam. Evidence suggests, however, that it would have been unusual if guests of a Victorian dinner party were not offered a predinner sherry, a fine imported red wine with dinner, and an after-dinner cognac or perhaps a shot of good Kentucky bourbon.

Large collections of wine were kept in a wine cellar beneath the house. Smaller collections might be kept in a "cellarette"—a cabinet built especially for wine—or in cabinets beneath an étagère, secretary, or sideboard with other spirits or liquors. Liquor cabinets were seldom advertised by manufacturers of the period; however, many pieces intended for other purposes, such as music cabinets, bedside cabinets, and small cupboards in fine woods, were easily converted. A lock was of prime importance to keep out children and impromptu nippers.

Fine spirits were usually transferred from their original bottles to crystal or cut-glass decanters. These often were part of a set that included silver tags indicating the type of liquor and a handsome storage box with birds-eye maple veneers or inlaid silver or mother-of-pearl designs. Other liquor chests looked much like tall lap desks with brass straps and corners and perhaps even a handle on top. Still others, usually imported from the

South Seas, were made of woven rope or rattan or were designed to look like small trunks.

Today prices of antique Victorian liquor cabinets and chests are based on size, wood used, complexity of design, and condition. Chests with the original fitted decanters are highly prized.

Price Ranges

Liquor cabinets: $350 to $850+. Highest prices are paid for quality examples with burlwood and birds-eye veneers or those in the styles of the period, such as French Revival, Renaissance Revival, and Eastlake.

Liquor chests: $100 to $850+. Highest prices are paid for large pieces, those with quality wood veneers or inlaid designs, and for those with original decanters.

Suggested Reading

Knopf Collector's Guides to American Antiques, vol. 2, *Furniture.* New York: Alfred A. Knopf, 1982.

Feild, Rachel. *Victoriana.* New York: Ballantine, 1988.

Pipes, Humidors, and Smoking Items

Smoking tobacco was introduced in Europe during the sixteenth century by various adventurers (notably Sir Walter Raleigh) who had seen the natives of the American continents smoking it in pipes. The earliest commercially manufactured smoking pipes were made of clay, and even into the Victorian period clay pipes were available for those who wanted a cheap but efficient smoking device. By the nineteenth century, however, attractive wood and meerschaum pipes were the order of the day, as pipe smoking was widely accepted in most circles.

Elaborately carved meerschaum pipes imported from Turkey and Persia were collected by Victorian gentlemen, and both antique and recently manufactured examples are still popular with collectors today. Meerschaum, a lightweight porous stone, is highly suited for pipe bowls, providing a cool, continuous burn and lending itself well to elaborate, deep-relief carvings. Famous faces, animals, erotica, and even landmarks have been reproduced on beautiful white meerschaum pipes. The famous if fictitious nineteenth-century sleuth Sherlock Holmes surely would never have solved a crime without his "Calabash," with its polished gourd stem and wide-brimmed meerschaum bowl. Pipes were also produced in bone, ivory, glass, porcelain, and briar. The bowls of some wood pipes were lined in silver or porcelain, and many early pipes also had valuable silver, gold, or amber mouthpieces.

Often equally elaborate were the pipe tamps used to press the tobacco into the bowl. These were both manufactured and handmade in a wide variety of materials, including bone, brass, silver, glass, wood, ivory, and scrimshaw. Victorian period tamps can frequently be found in the "smalls" cases of antiques shops at quite reasonable prices.

Also popular among Victorian gentlemen—but not nearly as well accepted by Victorian ladies—was the cigar. Fine-quality cigars were produced in Virginia and the Mid-Atlantic states, but in the nineteenth century, as now, the finest cigars came from Cuba. Several items produced in connection with the smoking of cigars are now quite collectible.

While the rogue might bite off the end of his cigar and spit it into the fireplace, the gentleman was never without his cigar cutter or "tipper." Near the end of the century these were often included in a box of cigars as an advertising gimmick; however, quality examples were manufactured as jewelry in sterling silver and other metals. Both versions are highly collectible today, with prices in excess of $500 being paid for certain brand-name advertising cutters.

Both cigars and pipe tobacco were kept fresh in airtight "humidors." Humidor boxes were often lined with glass, porcelain, or enamel. Humidor jars were made of these same materials

113

No. 3452.   CIGAR BOX. $8.00

NICKEL PLATED, CENTRE PLACE FOR SPONGES, HOLDS FIFTY CIGARS.

No. 3453, same as above. but much larger, $13.50, more ornamental and with Candlestick on top, place for Sponge, and holds 100 Cigars.

7-9 Nineteenth-century advertisement for fancy cigar humidor.

with elaborately painted, cut, or molded surface decorations. Tins of copper, lead, and other materials also served the purpose.

Cigarette lighters were manufactured during the end of the nineteenth century, but these are extremely rare. Many examples marked as Victorian actually date from the period after 1910, when cigarette smoking achieved widespread popularity.

Prices of Victorian pipes and smoking items are based on complexity of design, materials used, accuracy of dating, condition, and supply and demand.

Price Ranges

Cigar cutters: (advertising) $50 to $500+; (pocket or jewelry) $25 to $250.

Humidor boxes: $25 to $250+. Highest prices are paid for certain examples in quality woods or veneers or with elaborately inlaid decorations.

Pipe tamps: $15 to $250. Highest prices are paid for tamps made of quality materials (ivory, silver, and so forth) and unique designs.

Smoking pipes: $25 to $500+. Highest prices are paid for unique carved meerschaum examples that can specifically be dated to the period.

Suggested Reading

Rappaport, Benjamin. *Complete Guide to Collecting Pipes.* West Chester, Pa.: Schiffer Publishing, 1979.

Hyman, Tony. *Handbook of American Cigar Boxes.* Claremont, Calif.: Treasure Hunt Publications, 1979.

Secretaries

The Victorian secretary was a large piece of furniture with a desk area and numerous locking cabinets and drawers. The design was so convenient that some homes had one in nearly every room. Libraries sometimes had both a large working desk for business affairs and a secretary for personal or home-related work.

Secretaries were produced in a wide variety of configurations, but they generally have a centrally located desk area with a fold-out slant-top or cylinder-type cover. Above the desk is a group of bookshelves behind framed glass doors, and below the desk is a set of drawers or cabinets. While secretaries were produced in the popular styles of the period (French Revival, Renaissance Revival, and Eastlake), many less-ornate designs (what we today would call generic) were pro-

7-10 Renaissance Revival secretary with pull-out writing surface. (Courtesy McHenry Mansion)

duced in quantity. These generally have straight, applied moldings and a basic slanted cornice. Better-quality pieces have burl or birds-eye veneered panels.

Prices of Victorian secretaries are based on size, woods used, complexity of design, and condition. Secretaries with cylinder-front desks are slightly higher than slant-front or pull-out versions.

Price Ranges

Secretaries: $1500 to $3000.

Suggested Reading

McNerney, Kathryn. *Victorian Furniture: Our American Heritage.* Paducah, Ky.: Collector Books, 1988.
Swedberg, Robert W. and Harriett Swedberg. *Victorian Furniture,* vols. 1–3. Radnor, Pa.: Wallace-Homestead Book Company, 1984–1985.

Snuff Boxes

In the sixteenth century European explorers made note of the several methods being used by native Americans to consume tobacco. Leaves were shredded and smoked in pipes (see Pipes, Humidors, and Smoking Items, this chapter), chewed (see Spitoons, this chapter), or ground into a fine powder and sniffed into the nose. Tobacco in this latter form was known as "snuff," which became quite popular with the British—especially the aristocracy of the seventeenth and eighteenth centuries—thereby making its way back to the American colonies.

While the taking of snuff declined in popularity during the nineteenth century, its use was still widespread. The proper gentleman carried his supply in a small hinged box with a black japan varnish finish. A pinch was placed in the crease at the base of the thumb and discreetly sniffed into the nostrils. The rogue or the dandy may have carried a far more ornate box and used a tiny jeweled silver or gold spoon much like those used in recent years by consumers of cocaine.

Snuff boxes are now a popular collectible, primarily due to their abundance and variety. Examples can be found inlaid with silver, gold, or brass wire; mother-of-pearl; and tortoise shell. Boxes

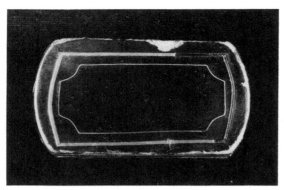

7-11 Lid of small snuff box with silver wire inlays.

with painted or lithographed scenes are especially desirable. Elaborate examples in solid silver or gold or inlaid with jewels may date from the eighteenth century.

Snuff bottles were used by the Chinese, who found them convenient for dipping snuff with their long fingernails. These often elaborately carved bottles were produced from a variety of materials, including jade, coral, ivory, and semiprecious stone. Because they were individually carved, most are unique and are prized by collectors.

Prices of Victorian snuff boxes are based on complexity of design, materials used, and condition. Some examples were homemade or produced specifically for an individual by a manufacturer, making them unique. The average collectible piece, as found in antiques shops in abundance, usually sells for around $65 to $100.

Price Ranges

Chinese snuff bottles: $75 to $1500+.
Victorian snuff boxes: $35 to $500+.

Suggested Reading

LeCorbeiller, Clare. *European and American Snuff Boxes.* New York: Viking Press, 1966.

Bedford, John. *All Kinds of Small Boxes.* New York: Walker and Company, 1965.

Spectacles and Magnifying Glasses

The use of glass magnifying lenses to aid those with poor vision probably came into being in the thirteenth or fourteenth centuries. (Many people believe Benjamin Franklin invented spectacles; this misconception comes from the fact that Franklin published a paper called the *Spectacle,* and that he invented the bifocal lens.) Numerous improvements were made over the centuries, and by Victorian times the wearing of spectacles, as eyeglasses were then called was common among adults and children. These generally were wire-rimmed glasses with round, oval, or octagonal lenses. Also popular were lorgnettes, spectacles with a handle and fancy frames of gold, silver, mother-of-pearl, onyx, or other materials.

Victorian magnifying glasses were also produced in a variety of styles, from small versions with tin frames to large examples with handles of precious materials like those mentioned previously. Small magnifying lenses were also produced in the form of jewelry, worn on a long cord about the neck by ladies or at the end of a watch chain by men.

7-12 Typical brass wire-rimmed spectacles.

Prices of Victorian spectacles and magnifiers are based primarily on the complexity of the frames, the materials used in their construction, and their overall condition. "Granny glasses" with wire-rimmed octagonal frames are common-but-popular collectibles and usually sell for $10 to $20.

Price Ranges

Magnifying glasses: $20 to $250+.
Spectacles: $10 to $500+. Highest prices are paid for certain elaborate examples with frames of precious metals or other novel materials.

Suggested Reading

Kelly, Alberta. *Lenses and Spectacles: The Story of Vision Aids.* Nashville: Thomas Nelson Publishing, 1978.

Spitoons

The white man emulated the native American's use of tobacco, but preferred to smoke it or sniff it (see Pipes, Humidors, and Smoking Items,

7-13 Spongeware ceramic spitoon, circa 1870s.

as well as Snuff Boxes, this chapter). Chewing tobacco, always the least-common form of the product, traditionally has been used almost exclusively by working-class people and farmers. While native Americans were seen using this method of consumption, the leaves they chewed likely had a more medicinal or narcotic effect.

Tobacco juice, if swallowed in quantity, has a noticeably negative effect on the human digestive system; therefore, a spitoon was provided for its disposal. Spitoons are distinctive round, wide-mouthed bowls in glass, metal, and ceramics. Tin and brass versions were common and have since seen frequent use as flower pots. Those made of pottery, porcelain, or enamelware are highly collectible.

Prices of Victorian spitoons are based on size, material used, decorative design, and condition.

Price Ranges

Brass Spitoons: $15–50.
Ceramic Spitoons: $50–300.
Enamelware Spitoons: $35–200.

Suggested Reading

See Crockery and Metalware in Chapter 4, The Kitchen.

Wall and Shelf Clocks

Clocks of the nineteenth century came in a variety of styles and sizes, but there were primarily four popular types: the tall case clock (see Chapter 1, The Entry Hall), the mantel clock (see Chapter 2, The Front Parlor), the shelf clock, and the wall clock. These last two clocks were in many cases, interchangeable—designed to either hang or sit on a shelf.

One of the most popular clocks of this style is called the "O.G." or ogee, a term for the S-shaped curve used in its case design. Being a

7-14 O.G.-type wall clock with hand-painted decorations on glass door. (Courtesy Bernhard House)

making was a major American industry. Large firms such as the New Haven Clock Company turned out over one hundred thousand clocks a year. Gothic styles were among the most popular: the "round Gothic" is somewhat bullet shaped; and the "sharp" or "steeple Gothic" has a pointed top and two sharp, pointed columns on either side. These were produced in combinations of fine woods and wood veneers, with colorful designs hand painted on the glass doors.

Probably the most recognized—and most reproduced—Victorian clock is the domestic "Regulator" of the style popularized by Seth Thomas during the 1870s. Regulator clocks, first manufactured during the early 1700s, were the most accurate of clocks—the ones by which all other clocks might be set. While the domestic Regulator did not provide the high degree of accuracy associated with the name, they were good-quality clocks and highly popular for both commercial and home applications.

The classic domestic Regulator had a large round or octagonal face with a narrow, glass-fronted pendulum case below. This is the type of wall clock commonly seen in Western and Victorian period movies and television shows. Many other nineteenth-century wall clocks are easily identified by their descriptive names, such as the lyre clock, the banjo clock, and the keyhole case clock.

Prices of Victorian wall and shelf clocks are based on size, style, materials used, maker, designer, and condition of both case and works. The fine wood veneers used on many of these clocks are highly susceptible to cracking, chipping, and warping. Therefore, working clocks with quality cases in mint or near-mint condition are most desirable. (For more information about the manufacture and design of Victorian clocks, see Mantel Clocks in Chapter 2, The Front Parlor.)

basic rectangle with a flat bottom, the O.G. was appropriate for a shelf, mantel, or wall. The numerals and other decorations often were painted directly onto the framed glass door, some versions having beautiful hand-painted scenes in the lower section. O.G.s were manufactured primarily in the United States by most of the major clock companies of the day, such as Seth Thomas, Ingram, and Ansonia Clock.

Despite the Victorian decorator's propensity for Rococo mantel clocks (see Chapter 2, The Front Parlor), U.S. clockmakers concentrated primarily on the basic wood case shelf clock. During the second half of the century, clock-

Price Ranges

Gothic shelf clocks: $150 to $1500+.
O.G. clocks: $200 to $750+.
Wall clocks (including domestic Regulators): $250 to $2000+.

Suggested Reading

Swedberg, Robert W. and Harriett Swedberg. *American Clocks and Clockmakers.* Radnor, Pa.: Wallace-Homestead Book Company, 1989.

Smith, Alan. *Clocks and Watches: Antique Collector's Guide.* New York: Outlet Book Company, 1975.

Clock price guides have been published by the Antique Collector's Club, L-W Promotions, Heart of America Press, and House of Collectibles (Ballantine).

Writing Implements

The Declaration of Independence and the Bill of Rights quite likely were signed with quill pens.

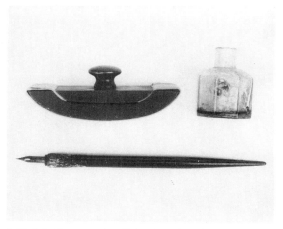

7-15 Ink blotter and well (top), and early pen of enameled wood and cork (bottom).

Made from the feather of a goose or other large bird, it had been the standard writing instrument for many centuries, and even with the invention of steel-tipped pens in England around 1780, it would continue to be the writing instrument of choice well into the Victorian period. It is interesting that although extensive commercial production of metal-tipped pens began in England as early as 1822, they were not widely used in the United States until after midcentury. By the 1870s barrel pens were in common use, followed by fountain pens in the 1880s—more than thirty years after their invention. Even then goose quill pen production had not waned and their price had not come down.

Graphite pencils were quite popular during the Victorian era, especially among shop owners and those who required a reliable and easily accessible writing instrument. Mechanical pencils were invented for military use during the Civil War and quickly became popular with the general public afterwards. Ladies frequently kept small mechanical pencils on chains or cords tucked into their waist pockets.

Victorian pens and pencils were produced in a large quantity of styles and configurations. Collecting these items today requires a thorough knowledge of both design and current supply and demand factors. Therefore, those interested in this field should obtain one or more of the detailed works listed in the Suggested Reading section.

Prices of Victorian pens and pencils are based on style, construction materials, decorations or adornments, accuracy of dating, condition, and rarity.

All early pens needed to be dipped frequently in ink. This could be done directly from the bottle or from an attractive ink well designed specifically for the purpose. These ink wells and the stands on which many of them sat are also widely collected. Early examples are simple, containing

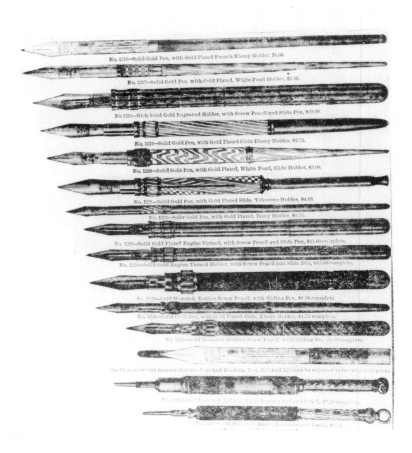

No. 1216—Solid Gold Pen, with Gold Plated French Ebony Holder, $3.00

No. 2217—Solid Gold Pen, with Gold Plated, White Pearl Holder, $3.50

No. 1218—Rich Solid Gold Engraved Holder, with Screw Pencil and Slide Pen, $28.00

No. 1219—Solid Gold Pen, with Gold Plated Slide Ebony Holder, $2.75

No. 1220—Solid Gold Pen, with Gold Plated, White Pearl, Slide Holder, $3.00

No. 1221—Solid Gold Pen, with Gold Plated Slide, Telescope Holder, $4.00

No. 1222—Solid Gold Pen, with Gold Plated, Ivory Holder, $1.75

No. 1223—Solid Gold Plated, Engine Turned, with Screw Pencil and Slide Pen, $13.00 complete

No. 1224—Solid Gold Engine Turned Holder, with Screw Pencil and Slide Pen, $13.00 complete

No. 1225—Gold Mounted, Rubber Screw Pencil, with Sliding Pen, $6.50 complete

No. 1226—Solid Gold Pen, with Gold Plated Slide, Ebony Holder, $1.75 complete

No. 1227—Gold Mounted, Rubber Screw Pencil, with Sliding Pen, $5.00 complete

28—This shows the manner that the Pens and Holders, Nos. 1215 and 1216 can be adjusted to be carried in pocket

No. 1229—Gold Mounted, Rubber, Magic Reverse Pen and Pencil, $7.50 complete

No. 1230—Gold Mounted, Magic, Rubber Screw Pencil, $2.50

7-16 A selection of pens and mechanical pencils from a Victorian catalog.

only a section to hold the well and a slot or hole in which to store the pen when not in use. From the 1870s until after the turn of the century these stands were produced in a variety of elaborate decorative configurations and often included a storage drawer and inkwells made of art glass or ceramic.

Prices of Victorian inkwells and stands are based on design, materials used, age, and condition.

One of the more romantic items of the Victorian era is the letter seal, a metal stamp with a letter or symbol on the bottom. Hot wax was allowed to drip onto the back of the envelope at the point of the flap; the seal was then quickly pressed into the soft wax, sealing the letter shut and leaving the impression of the sender's initial or symbol. Victorian seals are usually made of silver or silver plate, pressed or engraved with an elaborate design, and topped with a small figure

7-17 Advertisement for fancy brass inkstand, circa 1880s.

or semiprecious stone. Prices of antique Victorian letter seals are today based on complexity of design, materials used, and condition.

Price Ranges

Ink pens: $15 to $500+. Lowest prices ($15–$25) are paid for basic metal-tipped pens with plain painted wood or cork shafts. The average Victorian pen as found in antiques stores usually sells for around $50 to $75.

Ink well stands: $50 to $500.

Letter seals: $25 to $250.

Mechanical pencils: $10 to $500+. Highest prices are paid for quality examples in silver or gold.

7-18 Silver-plated wax sealer with jeweled crown.

Suggested Reading

Lawrence, Cliff. *Fountain Pens: History and Values.* Paducah, Ky.: Collector Books, 1977.

Revira, Betty and Ted Revira. *Inkstands and Inkwells: A Collector's Guide.* New York: Crown Publishers, 1973.

Walley, Joyce. *Writing Materials and Accessories.* Detroit, Mich.: Gale Research, 1975.

CHAPTER 8
Her Bedroom

In most cases the Victorian master and madam of the house had separate bedrooms. This was arranged out of a desire for privacy and personal space and certainly did not mean that couples always slept in separate beds. If a couple were to adhere to the strict religious rule of the day, he would sleep in his bed and she in hers, and they would come together only for the purpose of procreation. Fortunately, this was the exception rather than the rule.

Until the latter part of the century the bedroom in most Victorian homes was also the dressing room, powder room, bathroom, and toilet. A large bowl and pitcher for personal bathing were kept atop a *wash stand* or *commode* with a *slop jar* inside for disposal. A *chamber pot* was kept discreetly beneath the bed or commode. A servant would make sure water was readily available throughout the day and would empty and clean the slop jar and chamber pot regularly.

The central piece of furniture in the bedroom was, of course, the *bed*. These followed the styles of the time but were often massive wooden structures with ornately carved figures (see color section). The bed may have had a matching *armoire* (wardrobe), often quite massive as well, which served as the closet in Victorian bedrooms. Other clothing storage was made available in a variety of forms, such as bureaus, *chiffoniers, dressing cases,* and *dressers.* The dresser was also where the lady kept such necessities as a *brush and comb,* various *hair ornaments;* a *hatpin holder* to keep those decorative pins in order; a *hair receiver* to hold hair taken from brushes and combs for later use making jewelry and wreaths; various *boxes* for *jewelry* and *gloves;* and a variety of *perfume bottles* and *powder* and *cream jars.*

Bedside stands (or *somnoes*) held lamps and contained additional drawers for storage. If the room were large enough, there might also be a *fainting couch,* where the lady might take a short rest in privacy. If there were a child, a *crib* or *cradle* would stay in the mother's bedroom during the child's infancy.

Unless a separate dressing room was provided, the lady would change her clothing behind a *dressing screen* then view herself in a large standing mirror or adjustable *cheval* mirror. The average Victorian lady would change clothing at least three times a day, more if it were an especially active day. There were specific types of clothing for different periods of the day and for different activities. There were also numerous accessories, including *pelerines* (large lace collars), shawls, caps or bonnets, gloves, *parasols,* and the always-present handkerchief. At her waist she might wear a *scent bottle* for use in case the wind brought some unpleasant odor her way, or a *chatelaine* from which she might hang a watch, letter seal, magnifier, key, locket, or any number of small items of personal importance.

Purses of various types were used, although their absence in most photographs and illustrations of the period indicate that they were not especially important as fashion accessories. Within a Victorian lady's reticule (a woven cloth, beadwork, or metal mesh purse) one might find a *calling card case,* a *vinaigrette* (containing a sort of smelling salts), a note pad and pencil, and perhaps a cased photograph of a loved one. Face powder or other cosmetics would not be found, for these were properly applied only in the privacy of the lady's boudoir. Items of this type needed on a lengthy trip or overnight stay were carried, along with *button hooks, manicure sets,* decorative *hair accessories,* and selected jewelry, in a portable *dressing case.*

Events of the day were recorded in the lady's *diary* or journal, usually kept in the bedside stand or secreted away under quilts in a blanket chest or storage trunk.

For the Victorian lady the bedroom was of primary importance. It was her sanctuary, a place of intimacy for her and her spouse. Because personal appearance was among her greatest concerns, the bedroom was the scene of some of her heaviest activity of the day—primping. In most cases her children were conceived there, born there, and nursed there. When the time came, she closed her eyes for the last time in this room.

Armoires

Victorian homes seldom had built-in storage areas other than the pantry, cellar, and attic. Closets were an architectural luxury of the future, but a wonderful piece of furniture called an armoire (wardrobe) served the same purpose. (The name came from a storage cabinet in which the French stored their armor—not a totally inappropriate comparison if one has ever seen a Victorian lady's corset.) Designed to hold a lady's (or gentleman's) wardrobe, the armoire, then as now, is any free-standing closet. The Victorians, however, had a penchant for the romance of the French language and made the word "armoire" the one commonly used to describe the piece.

Armoires were manufactured in a wide variety of shapes, sizes, and configurations, from a simple boxlike cabinet to enormous, highly decorated examples the size of a small room. Common examples found today are in the Renaissance Revival, Eastlake, and Country (or Cottage) styles. Again, sizes vary widely, but an average piece might be seventy-five to eighty inches high, forty-five to fifty inches wide, and twenty to thirty inches deep. (Deep units without a central dividing piece in front are in demand for use as entertainment centers to hide televisions, VCRs, stereo equipment, and other appliances in otherwise Victorian-decorated rooms.) Many examples include one or more drawers in their design, both above and below the closet area.

During the latter part of the nineteenth century armoires were included as part of a bedroom set along with a bed, two night stands, and a dresser or dressing case of the same style. Some examples (primarily of French or Renaissance Revival influence) have highly artistic hand-carved figures and other elaborate decorations, often carved by the same artisans who produced ships' figureheads. When changing styles brought a change of furniture, many preferred to chop these heavy pieces into firewood rather than haul them away in one piece.

NOTE: Antique bedrooms sets should be kept together. They are much more valuable as a set than as individual pieces.

Prices of Victorian armoires are based on size, style, configuration, manufacturer (if known), and condition. Basic examples are usually in the Eastlake or Country styles and occasionally in Renaissance style. Elaborate pieces are usually influenced by Rococo French or Renaissance Revival styles.

Price Ranges

Basic armoires: $400 to $1000.
Elaborate armoires: $1200 to $3000+.

Suggested Reading

McNerney, Kathryn. *Victorian Furniture: Our American Heritage.* Paducah, Ky.: Collector Books, 1988.
Swedberg, Robert W. and Harriett Swedberg. *Victorian Furniture,* vols. 1–3. Radnor, Pa.: Wallace-Homestead Book Company, 1984–1985.

Bed Warmers

A long time before electric blankets, clever Victorians devised a way to warm cold feet by placing a covered brass or copper pan filled with hot coals beneath the covers before going to bed. Pans manufactured specifically for the purpose were called "bed warmers." (They were originally called "bed pans," a name now associated with an item having a much less romantic purpose.)

8-1 Ceramic bed warmer. (Courtesy Georgia Fox, Foxes Den)

Another style of bed warmer was made in the form of a ceramic bottle that could be filled with hot water. Both types of bed warmers are now quite rare and this is reflected in their price, which is also based on materials used, construction, complexity of engraving or embellishments, manufacturer (if known), and condition.

NOTE: Reproductions are common.

Price Ranges

Victorian bed warmers: $100 to $350+.

Beds

Like all bedroom furniture, Victorian beds varied widely in size and style. Some examples (sold separately or as a set with other matching pieces—see Armoires, this chapter) were massive pieces with elaborate hand-carved adornments and figures. The most basic examples were in Eastlake designs (although ornate beds with Eastlake influence do exist) or Spool designs (often called "Jenny Lind" beds). While a few Renaissance Revival beds are somewhat basic in design, most have highly ornate pediments and applied moldings. While not as elaborate as many Renaissance versions, the Rococo carvings on French Revival headboards are quite impressive. The classic curling shell motif is often seen in ornate French Revival carvings on beds, armoires, and bedroom sets.

Canopy and four-poster beds, while often associated with the Victorian period, are actually of colonial origin. They remained popular as antiques well into the nineteenth century, especially in the South. (A bed with a short overhang, called a half-tester, was produced in the late nineteenth century for use in areas where mosquito drapes were required.) Another style of bed from the first

8-2 Eastlake bed. (Courtesy Bernhard House)

half of the century, the sleigh bed, was also quite popular with the Victorians and with collectors today. Many of these early beds were so high off the floor that getting into them required a special stool.

Brass and iron beds, although introduced late in the Victorian era, did not become widely accepted in the United States until the Edwardian period, after the turn of the century. Their use in the late nineteenth century was primarily limited to children's rooms, lower-income homes, and hotels. Few existing pieces can be positively identified as originating before 1901.

Prices of Victorian beds are based on size, style, woods used, complexity of embellishments, identification of manufacturer (if any), and condition.

Price Ranges

Basic Beds (Spool and simple Eastlake and French or Renaissance Revival styles): $300 to $1500.

Elaborate Beds (large, ornate French or Renaissance Revival styles): $1500 to $5000+. Prices in excess of $50,000 have been paid for certain examples with novel adornments.

Suggested Reading

Knopf Collectors' Guides to American Antiques, Furniture. vol. 1, New York: Alfred A. Knopf, 1982. See also Armoires, this chapter.

Bedside Stands

Small cabinets designed for use next to the bed were often included as part of a "chamber suit," as bedroom sets were called in the nineteenth century. These bedside stands, called "somnoes" by manufacturers (from Somnus, the Roman god of sleep), usually have a single drawer beneath the top and a locking cabinet below. On some versions, the top lifts to reveal a small storage area.

8-3 Eastlake bedside stand with Egyptian Renaissance influence. (Courtesy Leepers Fantastic Antiques)

Bedside cabinets were also incorporated into the design of many beds, being attached to, or conforming to the shape of, the oversized headboard.

Then as now, somnoes found use throughout the house, wherever a small stand or cabinet was needed. They were produced in all of the styles of the period, with the better pieces having veneer panels and elaborate moldings.

Prices of antique bedside stands are based on style and complexity of design, woods used, and condition.

Price Range

Bedside stands: $150 to $750 each. Highest prices are paid for well-made examples with elaborate moldings and burlwood or birds-eye veneers.

Suggested Reading

See Beds and Armoires, this chapter.

Blanket Chests

The use of a large wooden chest to hold blankets and bedclothes was popularized during the seventeenth and eighteenth centuries, primarily by the pioneers and early settlers. It would not have been unusual for a lady of the late Victorian period to have her grandmother's "six-board" blanket chest, or perhaps a more contemporary manufactured version, sitting at the foot of her bed. Six-board chests were originally made of six wide, rough-hewn boards (one each for top and bottom, two sides, and two ends) that were hand cut with a saw or ax. In later years the style was produced by furniture manufacturers in finely finished woods.

Many of the blanket chests of Victorian vintage are much taller and have one or two drawers underneath. Blanket chests of all configurations are found most commonly in basic Country or Shaker styles.

Prices of antique blanket chests are based on whether they are handmade or manufactured, the woods used, quality of construction and finish, size, style, and condition.

Price Ranges

Blanket chest with drawers: $350 to $1500+. Prices in excess of $3000 have been paid for verified original Shaker blanket chests.
Manufactured three-board chests: $250 to $850.

Suggested Reading

Raycraft, Don and Carol Raycraft. *American Country Antiques.* Radnor, Pa.: Wallace-Homestead Book Company, 1986.
————. *Shaker: A Collector's Sourcebook.* Radnor, Pa.: Wallace-Homestead Book Company, 1980.

Brushes, Combs, and Hand Mirrors

To Europeans, the term "toilet" still means what it did to our Victorian ancestors—that is, all items and activities related to grooming and dressing. (As usual, the modern American relegation of the term is far less romantic.) The lady's dressing table and the numerous items upon it were her toilet, and sets containing brushes, combs, mirrors, and other hair-grooming necessities were called "toilet sets." Combs were made of shell, bone, or ivory; later examples may also have been hard rubber or plastic (both of these compounds were invented mid-century), and the best combs were always trimmed in silver or silver plate. Brushes were made of bristle, the best coming from wild boar, and set into silver-trimmed ivory, hard rubber, or plastic bases. Hair brushes were made with and without handles. Mirrors were manufactured primarily using mercury as the reflective coating, although silver was occasionally used. The best mirror frames and handles were decorative silver or silver plate.

Silver toilet sets came in a variety of configurations and decorative designs, ranging from simple embossed or engraved floral patterns to such high-relief molded figures as Cupids or Venuses. (These latter versions usually date from the Art Nouveau period at the turn of the century.) Silver-plated versions often have lost much of the plating, allowing the grey base metal to show through. Collectors should avoid these, unless they are of novel design or extremely cheap, as better-quality pieces can be easily found.

Near the end of the century toilet sets were frequently produced in celluloid, a plastic manufactured to resemble ivory, tortoise shell, or other more-expensive materials. The collector is cautioned that these celluloid items were produced

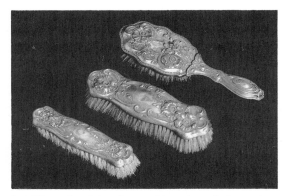

8-4 Silver-plated brush set with embossed decorations. (Courtesy Georgia Fox, Foxes Den)

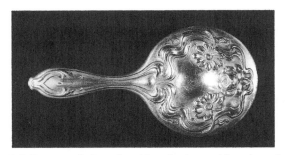

8-5 Reverse of silver-plated hand mirror with embossed design.

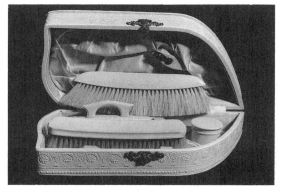

8-6 Celluloid dresser set, brushes, and presentation box. (Courtesy Georgia Fox, Foxes Den)

with little change in design well into the twentieth century. (See also Glove Boxes, Manicure Sets, and Decorative Hair Pins and Ornaments, this chapter.)

Prices of ladies' toilet sets and individual pieces are based on materials used, complexity of design, and condition. Complete sets in their original presentation cases are most desirable.

Price Ranges

Individual combs, brushes, mirrors (solid silver mounts): $75 to $1000+ each. Prices in excess of $10,000 have been paid for certain unique examples in solid silver.

Individual pieces (celluloid): $5 to $50.

Individual pieces (Silver plate): $20 to $150.

Toilet sets (celluloid): $25 to $250+.

Toilet sets (silver plate): $45 to $250+.

Toilet sets (solid silver mounts): $250 to $5000+. Prices in excess of $10,000 have been paid.

Suggested Reading

Feild, Rachel. *McDonald Guide to Buying Antique Silver and Plate.* Philadelphia: Trans-Atlantic Publications, 1988.

Rainwater, Dorothy T. and H. Ivan Rainwater. *American Silverplate.* West Chester, Pa.: Schiffer Publishing, 1988.

Button Hooks

Button hooks frequently were part of a dresser or toilet set but are given separate notice here because of their definitively Victorian link and their popularity as a separate collectible.

Victorian clothing and shoes used the button-and-loop fastening system. Getting the sometimes several dozen buttons through the loops was a long and tedious process, especially on shoes and the backs of dresses. By pushing a button hook through the loop and pulling the in-

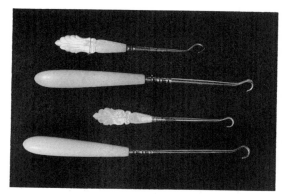

8-7 Buttonhooks with mother of pearl, ivory, and celluloid handles. (Courtesy Georgia Fox, Foxes Den)

tended button into place, the process was made quicker and easier.

A simple and easily recognizable tool, button hooks were made with a variety of attractive decorative handles made from silver, shell, ivory, plastic, and other materials. The numerous unique designs from U.S. and European manufacturers make the button hook a popular collectible on both continents.

Prices of Victorian button hooks are based on material used, uniqueness of design, identification of manufacturer (if known), and supply and demand.

Price Range

Button hooks: $10 to $100+.

Calling Card Cases

Calling cards (also called visiting cards) were a must for the Victorian socialite (see Chapter 1, The Entry Hall). Cards were left on silver receivers in homes and places of business and were passed out to new friends and acquaintances.

8-8 Purse-type silver calling-card holder with engraved design. (Courtesy Georgia Fox, Foxes Den)

Both ladies and gentlemen carried their cards in attractive cases (usually of silver or silver plate) made especially for the purpose. Such a case may have been of a plain, classic style engraved with the owner's initials, or an elaborately embossed or molded piece with floral designs and figures (the latter dating primarily from the Art Nouveau period at the turn of the century).

The collector is cautioned that several other items from this and later periods, including ladies' compacts, cigarette cases, and especially match safes, often resemble calling card cases. In addition to silver, cases were produced in ivory, scrimshaw, mother-of-pearl, tortoise shell, celluloid, and plastic.

Prices of Victorian calling card cases are based on material used, complexity of design or decoration, and condition.

Price Ranges

Calling card cases: $35 to $250. Highest prices are paid for ivory and silver pieces.

Suggested Reading

Riley, Noel. *Visiting Card Cases.* Cincinnati: Seven Hills, 1983.

Also see Suggested Reading for Brushes, Combs, and Hand Mirrors, this chapter.

Commodes and Wash Stands

Indoor plumbing came late to most of the United States and Europe in the Victorian era. Even after bathrooms with sinks, tubs, and running water were introduced just prior to the turn of the century, many ladies still preferred to freshen up in the privacy of their boudoir using the traditional washbowl and pitcher. Two pieces of furniture were designed to hold these items: the commode and the washstand.

Commodes have a flat surface, usually with a standing splash board at the back. The surface and backboard often are made of waterproof marble. There is usually a combination of one or more drawers and cabinets underneath. Some contain a hidden sink or "stepped" interior, which provided space for the bowl and pitcher. Commodes were produced in the styles of the period, including many in Country (Cottage) styles.

Wash stands are much smaller than commodes. They also have a flat top and splash board but are open below, and they have a single shelf for storing the pitcher and bowl. Some versions have a small drawer below the shelf. Wash stands can also be found in the various styles of the period, in addition to basic Country style units.

Both commodes and wash stands were also

129

8-9 Renaissance Revival commode with mirror. (Courtesy Williams Antiques)

produced by Shaker artisans. These are highly sought after by collectors and often bring premium prices.

Prices of Victorian commodes and wash stands are based on size, style, wood used, presence of

marble surface, and condition. Because of frequent wetting due to spillage, condition should be carefully checked. Watch for repairs and replacement boards, which lower the value of the piece.

Price Ranges

Commodes: $250 to $1000+. The highest prices in this range are paid for marble-top units with large splash boards. The average commode sells for around $400 to $500. Prices in excess of $7000 have been paid for Shaker versions.

Wash stands: $100 to $1000+. The average basic wash stand sells for around $150 to $200. Highest prices are paid for ornate pieces in the styles of the period.

Suggested Reading

See Armoires, this chapter.

Cradles

Cradles and infant beds were produced in quantity in all the major styles of the period, yet today they are among the rarest and most sought-after Victorian furniture pieces.

Country styles are the most common. A Country cradle is basically a long box, slightly wider at the top than at the base, and may have rockers on the bottom. These can be found in a variety of woods, although pine is common for all Country-style furniture. Some versions have a hood over the head of the cradle. Shaker examples of this style bring premium prices.

Both fancy cradles and infant beds (often a miniature of adult versions) were produced in Eastlake and French or Renaissance Revival styles. Collectors lucky enough to come across one of these should not be shocked by the price. Quality examples are prized.

Prices of Victorian cradles and infant beds are based primarily on regional supply and demand. Wood used, style, and condition also affect price.

Price Ranges

Country cradles: $200 to $500. Prices in excess of
$5000 have been paid for Shaker versions.
Cradles (styles of the period): $250 to $1000.
Infant beds: $50 to $500+.

Suggested Reading

See Armoires, this chapter.

Decorative Hairpins and Ornaments

Ladies' hairstyles changed just as frequently in
Victorian times as they do today, but, as a general
rule, the style for adults was always "up." Rarely
was hair allowed to fall about the shoulders—
possibly only during a country outing or at bed-
time. To keep the hair up, a variety of plain or
fancy hairpins and combs were used.

Among the earliest and most frequently used
decorative combs was the *peineta,* a kind of
woven tiara worn by Spanish ladies, which stood
up at the back of the head, in front of the obliga-
tory bun. Later versions produced by U.S. manufacturers were called simply "back combs."

As the century progressed ringlets and falls
were proper at the back of the neck, but, as always, the hair was pulled back from the face and
pinned at the back of the head. The classic Victorian hairpin, a somewhat dangerous-looking two-
pronged fork, was made in silver, silver plate,
hard rubber, ivory, bone, plastic, and, at the turn
of the century, celluloid. The crown of the pin

might have been small and plain to hide in the
hair, or it might have been decorated with applied
figures or precious or semiprecious jewels.

Prices of Victorian hairpins and ornaments are
based on style, materials used, age, and condition.
The highest prices are paid for silver and ivory
hairpins, and those set with precious jewels.

Price Range

Hairpins and ornaments: $10 to $250+. Lowest prices
are paid for costume pieces from the turn of the
century. An average fine-quality hairpin exemplify-
ing the style and period usually sells for $50 to $125.

Suggested Reading

Haertig; Evelyn. *Antique Combs and Purses.* Carmel,
Calif.: Gallery Graphics Press, 1983.

Diaries and Journals

Victorians, both gentlemen and ladies, frequently kept a journal of daily events. It is unfor-
tunate that this practice declined in popularity
during the present century, for these diaries are
invaluable to historians. They relate common elements of everyday life that cannot be found in any
other source: descriptions of jobs and working
conditions, reactions to historic or political
events, courtship practices, and details of social
events. The personal thoughts and emotions of a
variety of personalities from a bygone era are to
be found in the Victorian journal.

Although there were numerous volumes designed specifically for the purpose, almost any

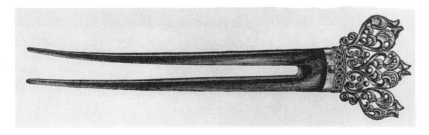

*8-10 Ladies hairpin with fancy
silver crown, from a Victorian
catalog.*

collection of clean, bound paper might have been used as a journal. Various ledgers, account books, and notebooks were used; some diaries were simply a collection of loose sheets of paper kept in a box or tied with string or ribbon. However, the diaries of most Victorian ladies were small, nicely bound books, often covered with silk, velvet, or fine leather. Some came with hooks, straps, or buckles to keep them securely closed; some even had locks.

Today diaries and journals from the Victorian era are prized by collectors, museums, and historians. Many journals, especially those of notable persons or those containing detailed information about a particular place or event, find their way into state and local archives. Because of this widespread interest, fine examples are hard to find on the open market. Estate sales and flea markets present the best chance for discovering an interesting or important journal.

Prices of Victorian diaries and journals are based on age, notability of the writer, the historical or entertainment value of content, and condition.

NOTE: It cannot be stressed enough that these items are of historical and often of genealogical importance. When selling a journal or diary, it is proper to offer the first chance to purchase it to the family of the writer (if known), or to an appropriate museum or archive.

Price Range

Journals and diaries: $20 to $1000+. Basic personal diaries dating from the end of the Civil War to the end of the century, without notable author or content, usually sell for around $35 to $150.

Suggested Reading

Mallon, Thomas. *A Book of One's Own.* New York: Ticknor and Fields, 1984.

Dressers, Dressing Cases, Bureaus, and Chiffoniers

The average Victorian lady's daytime costume might consist of as many as fifteen pieces of clothing (including bonnet and shoes): bloomers, stockings, petticoats or underskirt, overskirt, cor-

8-11 Renaissance Revival dressing case. (Courtesy Amador County Museum)

set, chemisette (false shirt front), bodice, crinoline or bustle, pelerine or collar, undersleeves, and jacket or shawl. This was the standard costume for midday wear—for visiting or receiving guests, shopping, and so forth. A different set of clothing was worn for the morning hours at home, and yet another set for the evening. There were clothes for riding, clothes for picnicking, clothes for mourning, clothes for entertaining—and ball gowns for every type of ball. There were winter clothes, summer clothes, and special outfits for Easter, Christmas, and the Fourth of July. As you can see, this adds up to literally hundreds of items of clothing.

Where was all of this stored? Most hanging items were kept in an armoire (see Armoire, this chapter). Everything else was stored in drawers, and Victorian furniture manufacturers made a variety of pieces with drawers, starting with the familiar dresser. The dresser was designed for storage and as a table for the lady's toilet (grooming aids). Most dressers had a large central mirror that pivoted to adjust the angle. The dresser might have any number of drawers, depending on its height and configuration. They generally had three or four long drawers below and sometimes two short drawers atop the table on either side.

The dressing case was similar to the dresser except that the table portion sat in a deep well formed by a stack of short drawers on either side. The central surface might be anywhere from near floor level to chest-high, depending on the configuration of the unit. Behind this central well was a large, pivoting dressing mirror.

Bureaus and chiffoniers were simply large chests of drawers. Bureau wash stands were equipped with a mirror or a splash board. Chiffoniers were quite tall, with five or more long drawers, and were usually narrower than a bureau or dresser. (The collector should be aware that confusion abounds over these various names, and, by appearance, some examples could fit into several categories. Dealers and advertisers frequently use the blanket term "chest of drawers."

To add to the confusion, in Europe a bureau is a desk and a dressing case is also a lady's overnight case.)

All of these pieces of furniture were manufactured in the various styles of the period, with varying degrees of decorative embellishment. All were included at various times as part of the "bedroom suits" advertised by many furniture stores.

Today, prices of Victorian chests of drawers and dressers are based on style, woods used, size, configuration, and condition. The highest prices are paid for pieces with fine wood veneers and elaborately framed mirrors.

Price Ranges

Dressers: $250 to $1000+. Examples with original mirrors are more valuable than those without.
Dressing cases: $450 to $1000+.
Bureaus: $250 to $500.
Bureau wash stands: $350 to $750.
Chiffoniers: $450 to $1000+.

Suggested Reading

See Armoires, this chapter.

Dressing Screens

The proper Victorian lady always changed clothes behind a screen, even in the privacy of her boudoir. The dressing screen also provided extra privacy while bathing or using the chamber pot. Despite what Hollywood would have us believe, the proper lady never undressed when a gentleman was present, with or without a screen. If the master of the house was to visit the madam's boudoir, it would be after madam was dressed in nightclothes and in bed. Behavior to the contrary might indicate a "loose" upbringing.

Comprised of three or more framed panels, the dressing screen was manufactured in a variety of sizes and configurations. Most were designed to be decorative as well as functional, with quality wood frames in the styles of the period. The inset panels were made of a variety of materials (for example, wood, leather, metal) but were usually of cloth. The fabrics ranged from imported silks and tapestries to homemade needlepointed fabrics.

On today's market prices of Victorian dressing screens are based on size, style, wood used in the frame, type and design of material used in inset, and condition. Torn or heavily soiled insets should be replaced only with like materials in a pattern of the period. Examples with original insets in good condition are most desirable.

Price Range

Dressing screens: $75 to $1000+. The average dressing screen with original tapestry in good condition sells for $250 to $500. Highest prices are paid for quality examples with elaborate embellishments in the styles of the period.

Fainting Couches

Another piece of furniture readily associated with the Victorian era is the fainting couch, also called the chaise lounge by devotees of the Romance languages. Photographers made extensive use of the chaise lounge (French for "long chair") in photographing the more liberated ladies of the 1880s and 1890s, who posed in what would appear to be a very uncomfortable lounging position, with one arm behind the head and the other tucked behind the back. Actually, the fainting couch—in essence a large, heavily padded version of our modern outdoor lounge chair—was quite comfortable. The name came from the tendency of certain Victorian ladies to pass out with almost predictable frequency. While it is a sad fact that many women of the era were in poor health, it is also true that these fainting spells seldom occurred when no one was around to see them.

Fainting couches were manufactured in a variety of styles but almost always have plush upholstery (primarily velvet). Some versions look exactly like a typical easy chair, but with an elongated seat of five to six feet in length. Other versions look like a narrow bed or cot with a slightly raised head cushion at one end. The latter style may also have a wood-frame back with applied moldings and incised designs in the style of the period.

Today Victorian fainting couches are not difficult to locate, although it may take some time to find a particular style. Although many have been reupholstered, quite a few have survived the century with the original material in reasonably good condition. As always, the more original a piece is, the more valuable. Other factors affecting price include size, style, and wood used.

Price Range

Fainting couches: $350 to $1500+.

8-12 Fully upholstered fainting couch. (Courtesy Bernhard House)

Suggested Reading

Swedberg, Robert W. and Harriet Swedberg. *Victorian Furniture,* vol. 1, rev. ed. Radnor, Pa.: Wallace-Homestead Book Company, 1984.

Fans

The properly dressed Victorian lady was never without her fan. She had a fan to fit every occasion—perhaps a bright ostrich feather fan for a gay ball, a black lace fan for an evening at the opera, or a painted Oriental paper fan for a picnic in the country. Fans were manufactured in an endless array of materials and designs. There were fans of silk, lace, leather, paper, or feathers attached to sticks of wood, bamboo, celluloid, amber, bone, shell, or ivory. Some fans had blades made entirely from wood, ivory, or celluloid held together by silk ribbons. Many examples were hand painted or inlaid with mother-of-pearl.

During the latter part of the century a multitude of cheap paper fans were produced for use as advertising gimmicks. Imprinted with the names of products or firms, these fans are now sought by advertising collectors.

On today's market Victorian period fans can still be found easily in quantity; however, the collector should be aware that these fans have also been produced and reproduced throughout the twentieth century. The most recognizable Victorian fans—those made of silk, lace, and ivory—are also the most expensive. Prices of Victorian fans are based on size, style, materials used, applied or painted decorations (if any), and condition. High-quality early fans in near-mint condition often bring premium prices.

Price Ranges

Advertising fans: $20 to $500+.
Feather fans: $50 to $500+.
Lace fans: $35 to $300+.
Paper fans (nonadvertising): $15 to $45.
Silk fans: $50 to $500+.
Solid ivory fans: $500 to $2500+.
Solid wood fans: $35 to $100.

In all categories, prices more than three times the high range shown here have been paid for certain premium examples.

Suggested Reading

Armstrong, Nancy. *Collector's History of Fans.* New York: Crown Publishers, 1974.
Flory, M. A. *Book about Fans.* New York: Macmillan Publishing Company, 1985.

8-13 Silk fan with hand-painted flowers and teakwood blades.

Glove Boxes

While gloves were always necessary in a proper Victorian wardrobe, they were an obsession during the early part of the period. In the 1840s it was considered quite rude to touch someone, or even shake his or her hand, with an ungloved hand. Fashion magazines insisted that the proper lady wear gloves at all times (except meals) when in public. Gloves of kid leather were the most common, although gloves were produced in a variety of fine materials, such as silk or cotton. As with most of a lady's costume, different gloves were needed for different occasions, requiring a veritable wardrobe of gloves. While many of these were kept in drawers, those used most often were kept at the ready in a glove box atop a lady's dresser.

Like other boxes of the period, glove boxes were made of a variety of materials and decorated with a variety of embellishments. The glove box is identified by its long, narrow shape and lack of inner compartments. Probably the most recognized and collected glove boxes are those produced in celluloid near the turn of the century. These might be embossed with flowers, figures, or other designs, and are often painted in soft pastel colors.

Prices of glove boxes are based on materials used, applied decorations, and condition.

Price Range

Glove boxes: $35 to $150.

Suggested Reading

Little, Nina. *Neat and Tidy: Boxes.* New York: E. P. Dutton, 1980.

Hair Receivers

In the nineteenth century and before, hair was often thought of as somewhat of a commodity. In the poorer sections of London and New York, it was not uncommon for a lady to "harvest" her hair once or twice a year for sale to the wig factory. Even in the finest homes hair was used to make decorative wall hangings (see Chapter 2, The Front Parlor) and jewelry (see Jewelry, this chapter) by carefully interweaving individual strands. Hair was collected from brushes and combs and kept in a hair receiver until enough had been collected for a particular project. Hair receivers were small jars with a hole in the lid through which the tufts of hair were pushed.

Hair receivers were produced in glass (some with brass or silver tops), silver and silver plate, wood, celluloid, and, primarily, porcelain and ceramic. A variety of shapes, styles, and colors were designed, including some in the form of animals

8-14 Celluloid hair receiver showing braided hair. (Courtesy Georgia Fox, Foxes Den)

or other figures. Examples produced by some of the better porcelain manufacturers are now highly collectible (see Decorative Porcelain in Chapter 2, The Front Parlor).

Prices of Victorian hair receivers are based on material used, complexity of design, age, and condition. The lowest-priced examples are those made of celluloid or plastic; the highest prices are paid for famous-name porcelain. The average ceramic hair receiver sells for around $50 to $75.

Price Ranges

Celluloid hair receivers: $15 to $75.
Ceramic hair receivers: $25 to $125.
Fine porcelain hair receivers: $75 to $300+.
Glass hair receivers: $55 to $250+.

Hatpins and Holders

Until the Civil War, ladies generally wore bonnets or caps. Large brimmed hats slowly began working their way onto the fashion scene in the 1850s and received their first widespread use in the South by "bold ladies of fashion." In the North, the hat was reserved for picnics, rides, and beach outings.

8-15 Ceramic hatpin holder and assortment of Victorian hatpins. (Courtesy Georgia Fox, Foxes Den)

By the mid-to-late 1860s, caps and bonnets were considered frumpy. Hats were the rage, although a very wide brim still was considered a bit showy. By the 1880s, however, hats were full, wide brimmed, and highly decorated with flowers and feathers.

Keeping a hat on one's head was a problem at first. Some hats came equipped with a tie-scarf. On windy days, a separate scarf might be tied over the top of the hat. Large decorative hatpins were also available. By sticking the pin through the hat and under the hair, the hat could be held securely in place. These hatpins came with a variety of decorative tops made from ceramic, glass, silver and silver plate, crystal, enameled metal or wood, shell, and precious or semiprecious stones.

Most Victorian ladies owned a large number of hatpins, most of which were kept in drawers or boxes. Their favorites, however, probably would be kept standing in a hatpin holder on their dressing tables. These holders were also made in a variety of shapes and sizes and were primarily porcelain or glass.

Today hatpins and their holders are some of the most popular Victorian collectibles. There is even an international hatpin collector's club headquartered in Gardena, California. Because they were produced in such quantity and variety, they can be collected by type, such as Art Deco, Art Nouveau, crystal, porcelain, and so forth. Holders are collected primarily by porcelain manufacturer or glass type, for example, Belleek, Limoges, Doulton, carnival glass, cut-crystal, and so forth.

Prices of Victorian hatpins and hatpin holders are based on materials used, manufacturer (if known), elaborateness of design or decoration, and condition.

Price Ranges

Hatpins: $25 to $200+. Average: $35 to $65.
Hatpin holders: $35 to $500+. Average: $50 to $85.

Suggested Reading

Baker, Lillian. *Handbook for Hatpins and Hatpin Holders.* Paducah, Ky.: Collector Books, 1983.
Also see Suggested Reading for Decorative Objects in Chapter 2, The Front Parlor.

Jewelry

It is entirely appropriate that, in a era named for her, Britain's Queen Victoria had such a marked and widespread effect on fashion—especially jewelry fashions. After her marriage to Prince Albert in 1840 she began to adorn herself with gold and precious stones in celebration of her happy new life. The world followed suit. In 1861 her great love died an untimely death and Victoria wore only dark stones in simple settings. The world mourned with her. As time healed her

No. 710—$10.00.
Revolving Miniature Pin for Two Pictures.

8-16 Victorian period ad for brooch to hold photographs.

sadness she wore pale opals and moonstones. Later, as her grand Diamond Jubilee approached, diamond necklaces were found encircling nearly every slender Victorian neck. Trends have come and gone since Victoria's death in 1901, but the basic concepts of fashionable jewelry today are the same ones introduced during her reign.

Victorian jewelry included brooches, necklaces, earrings, bracelets, rings, lockets, and a variety of accessory pieces found in this chapter under other headings. While this category is far too extensive for the scope of this book, this section contains an overview of the definitive Victorian pieces.

Cameo brooches were extremely popular throughout the period. Cameos were produced from a variety of stones, but a classic cameo is made of shell. Produced primarily by Greek and Italian artisans, the cameo was made by carving away portions of the white surface of the shell to reveal the shiny pink or brown inner surface. The remaining white material became the cameo head in relief. While one thinks of a traditional cameo as a lady's head, cameos were produced picturing Christ and other religious themes, horses, Greek and Roman soldiers, characters from mythology, and Greek and Roman art works. Because cameos are handmade from specially selected shells, each one is unique. The most collectible pieces are those picturing novel subjects. A careful examination with a magnifying loop will reveal the fine quality of artisanship (or lack thereof). A high-quality example will also be quite thin, allowing light to pass through. (Modern plastic or composite replicas can be quite convincing but usually lack this transparency.)

Colorful enameled brooches were also quite popular throughout the period. These finely painted miniatures can be found in a variety of plain or elaborate settings. Subjects include portraits of family members or historical figures, flowers, animals, and scenes. When buying a brooch of any type, consider both the value of the

8-17 An assortment of cameo brooches showing the variety of subjects used.

stone and its setting. Some very ordinary stones have valuable settings, and vice versa.

Lockets were in vogue long before the Victorian era but have never seen such popularity before or since. These might contain a miniature painted portrait (1830s to 1840s), daguerreotype (1840s to 1850s), tintype (1850s to 1890s), or a lock of hair. Small lockets usually were worn high on the neck while larger pieces were worn on a long chain or cord and tucked into a waist pocket. Lockets were produced in nine-, twelve-, fifteen-, and eighteen-carat gold, rolled gold (a kind of early heavy gold plate), and electrogilt (a lightweight gold plate). Decorative designs were engraved, embossed, or acid-etched into the surface.

A number of Victorian jewelry items contained or were produced from human hair. Numerous items were made by taking a few small strands and interweaving them to produce a thread. These threads could then be interwoven to produce elaborate "hair chains" or other objects. When a certain amount of stiffness was required, a light coat of varnish was applied to the finished

8-18 Grape cluster pendant made from woven strands of human hair.

product. Lockets, bracelets, and rings containing woven hair may have been mourning jewelry, designed as a remembrance of a lost loved one. Other pieces may have contained the locks of a child or spouse worn simply for sentimental reasons. Regardless of their intended purpose, Victorian hair jewelry is now a unique and popular collectible. Values are determined primarily by the quality and complexity of the weaving and the setting.

Necklaces, bracelets, and earrings could be purchased, then as now, individually or as a set. Rubies and sapphires, with large quantities of small stones linked together in a simple silver setting, were popular in sets. The stones were often backed with shiny metal to increase their brilliance. Pearls were quite popular also and were frequently seen in long strands of large, perfectly round, and perfectly matched specimens. Diamonds were rare until the diamond boom of the 1880s; then they were seen in large quantities through the beginning of this century.

Although wristwatches were available in the 1850s, they did not become popular with Victorian ladies until the 1880s. Locket watches were worn on a long chain or cord about the neck and tucked into a small pocket in the skirt band. Like other lockets, watches were produced in a variety of gold and gold-filled cases. (For additional information on collecting Victorian watches, see Chapter 9, His Bedroom.)

Collecting jewelry intelligently, Victorian or otherwise, requires specialized knowledge of precious metals and gems. Collectors interested in this category should obtain a number of good books on the subject and familiarize themselves with all aspects of the field. Prices of Victorian jewelry are based on materials used, style and complexity of design, age, condition, and supply and demand.

Price Ranges

Cameo brooches: $35 to $500+. Average: $125 to $250

Enameled brooches: $50 to $750+. Average: $150 to $300.

Hair jewelry: $50 to $300+. Average: $100 to $150.

Ladies' locket watches: $75 to $500+. Average: $125 to $200.

Lockets: $25 to $500+. Average: $75 to $250.

Suggested Reading

Baker, Lillian. *Art Nouveau and Art Deco Jewelry.* Paducah, Ky.: Collector Books, 1983.

———. *100 Years of Collectible Jewelry.* Paducah, Ky.: Collector Books, 1986.

Goldenberg, Rose. *Antique Jewelry: A Practical and Passionate Guide.* New York: Crown Publishers, 1976.

Kaplan, Arthur. *The Official Price Guide to Antique Jewelry,* 5th ed. New York: Ballantine, 1985.

Snell, Doris. *Antique Jewelry.* Radnor, Pa.: Wallace-Homestead Book Company, 1981.

Jewelry Boxes and Dressing Cases

The familiar quote "A place for everything, and everything in its place" originated in a nineteenth-century magazine ad for a lady's dressing case. Organization was of primary importance to the Victorian lady—witness the wide array of chests, bureaus, and storage boxes found in a lady's bedroom. The dressing case was the ultimate in dresser-top organization. It contained drawers for mirrors, brushes, combs, button hooks, jewelry, a manicure set, writing implements, sewing equipment, and sometimes even a clock. The top of the case opened to reveal a mirror, which often folded out, and a compartment with jars for powders and creams, perfume bottles, a pincushion and pin tray, and various other fitted containers. Whether a lady left on a day trip, a weekend outing, or a European vacation, her securely locked dressing case went right along with her.

While a lady might keep her favorite baubles atop her dresser in a silver casket, keeping her other jewelry organized required a box with numerous compartments. Hundreds of various chests and cases were designed for the purpose, ranging from a shallow, compartmented box to massive multidrawered chests with padded linings. The exteriors of both dressing cases and jewelry boxes also ranged from the simple to the gaudy. Plain boxes in fine woods, possibly inlaid

8-20 Silver-plated jewelry casket of Art Nouveau design. (Courtesy Georgia Fox, Foxes Den)

8-19 Handmade early Victorian locking jewelry case.

with small bits of silver or mother-of-pearl, were favored by most, while those with more extravagant tastes might choose a case with an ebony finish and decorated with ornate silver mounts holding precious or semiprecious stones. The variety of sizes and styles was seemingly endless.

In today's market, Victorian jewelry boxes and dressing cases are not as easy to locate as one might imagine. Many examples are in poor condition or suffer from unskillful restoration attempts. Therefore, condition plays an important part in pricing these items. Prices are also affected by size, style, and materials used. Dressing cases with original fitted tools, jars, and bottles are most desirable and often bring premium prices.

Price Ranges

Jewelry boxes: $35 to $500+. Average: $150 to $200.
Ladies' dressing cases: $50 to $1000+. Average: $250 to $300.
Silver jewelry caskets: $75 to $225.
Silver-plated jewelry caskets: $15 to $125.

Suggested Reading

Coe, Brian. *Boxes.* San Mateo, Calif.: Pitman Publishing, 1976.

Manicure Sets

Ladies' manicure sets of the late nineteenth century are not much different from modern versions, except that the handles and cases are, of course, much more elegant. An example advertised in the 1890s consisted of nine pieces: two pairs of curved scissors, two cuticle tools, a buff pad, a file, two jars, and a tray. The jars were fine crystal with caps of plated silver. The tools and tray could be had in solid silver or silver plate, and as for the tool handles, one could choose either mother-of-pearl or ivory.

Manicure sets were also produced with handles and cases made of celluloid. These are quite common, and examples can be found in nearly every antiques and collectibles shop.

8-21 Example of silver-plated manicure set from a nineteenth-century catalog.

In today's market the prices of Victorian manicure sets are based on size and completeness of set and case, materials used, complexity of decorative design, and condition. Sets with missing pieces bring considerably less because the chance of locating replacements is extremely slim.

Price Ranges

Manicure sets (celluloid): $30 to $100+. Average: $65.
Manicure sets (silver, ivory, mother-of-pearl, and others): $75 to $500+. Average: $200 to $250.

Parasols and Umbrellas

When and where umbrellas were invented is unknown. We do know, from old figural chinaware and carvings, that sunshades were used in ancient times. Even so, the umbrella was not in general use in England until late in the eighteenth

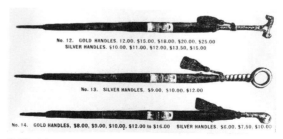

8-22 Advertisement for umbrellas with silver handles, circa 1880s.

century and only reached widespread popularity in Victorian times. At first it was considered effeminate for a gentleman to carry one, but in the second half of the century masculine styles with bold silver or gold handles were in wide use.

During the 1840s and 1850s ladies' parasols, or "sunshades" as they were then called, were usually small and quite dainty, with an abundance of frills and lace trim. After the Civil War they became larger and even more ornate. Better-quality examples have a central stick made of painted or varnished wood and a handle of silver, gold, or carved ivory or bone. The shade itself was made of silk, cotton, or alpaca, and the ribs supporting the material were made of whalebone and attached to a central metal ring that allowed the shade to be raised (opened) or lowered (closed). Cheap umbrellas had rattan ribs that frequently broke, especially on windy days.

By the 1870s nearly everyone owned one or more umbrellas or parasols. Of primary importance to the purchaser was the style of the handle, which, like those of canes, could be had in a variety of configurations—columns, loops, wings, balls, animals, and other figures—and materials—silver, gold, ivory, bone, gutta percha, plastic, and celluloid. On some examples the handles can be screwed off to reveal a hidden money compartment, whiskey flask, or dagger.

Today prices of Victorian parasols or umbrellas are based on size, style, materials used in various parts of the piece, and, above all, condition. Few examples have survived in mint or near-mint condition, and they now bring premium prices. Handles are often removed and sold separately (see Canes and Cane Handles in Chapter 9, His Bedroom).

Price Range

Parasols and umbrellas: $50 to $500+. Average: $200 to $250. Prices in excess of $1000 have been paid for elaborate examples in near-mint condition.

Suggested Reading

Gernsheim, Alison. *Victorian and Edwardian Fashion:* New York: Dover Publications, 1981.

Cranford, T.S. *History of the Umbrella.* New York: Taplinger Publishing Company, 1970.

Pelerines, Gloves, and Handkerchiefs

While it is beyond the scope of this book to give sufficient coverage to the collecting of Victorian clothing, there are several small accessories that are common in antiques shops and frequently collected by Victoriana afficionados.

During the early years of the Victorian era, neither ladies' nor gentlemen's shirts came with collars, which were considered a separate accessory (see also Collar Boxes in Chapter 9, His Bedroom). Ladies' collars, called pelerines, were made of linen, lace, or crochet work and ranged in size from a simple one- or two-inch collar to massive drapes measuring several feet in length. The needlework on these early pelerines is often so impressive that they are today highly sought by collectors as display pieces.

Two accessories the proper Victorian lady never would have been without were her gloves and her handkerchief. Gloves were made of cotton, wool, silk, lace, and a variety of types of

8-23 Small lace pelerine, circa 1860s.

leather, primarily kidskin. Specific colors and materials were deemed appropriate for particular activities or events. Handkerchiefs were made in cotton, silk, or lace and were carried in a lady's purse, sleeve, or skirt band. Again, the type of handkerchief carried depended not only on a lady's costume, but where she was going and what she would be doing there. For most occasions a few drops of the lady's favorite scent would be placed on the handkerchief, both for the benefit of those around her and for use by the lady herself, if she should become subjected to an offensive odor.

On today's collectibles market, the prices of these items are affected primarily by material, complexity of design, and condition. The personal taste of the collector is often a major determining factor in the purchase of this type of item. Collectors should be aware that the dating of clothing items and accessories is most difficult and requires a large degree of trust in the seller. Old fabrics often are quite fragile; therefore, a certain degree of care is required in handling and storing these items.

Price Ranges

Gloves: $10 to $250. Average: $35 to $60.
Handkerchiefs: $5 to $50. Average: $15 to $20.
Pelerines: $25 to $100+. Average: $45.

Perfume Bottles, Powder and Cream Jars

In the nineteenth century perfumes seldom came in attractive or elaborate bottles, as they do today. Instead the perfume and the bottle were purchased separately, according to a lady's taste, and there were normally a number of such bottles, as well as fancy jars to hold powders and creams, on her dresser.

All of these items were produced in the popular decorative glass and ceramic of the period, including cut-glass, pressed glass, ruby glass, amber glass, Amberina, Agata, Burmese, Pomona, Peachblow, Favrile, crystal, china, porcelain, parian, earthenware, and many others. (For more information on these various glass and ceramic variants, see Decorative Glass and Decorative Porcelain in Chapter 2, The Front Parlor).

Although sometimes difficult to determine, a bottle's use is indicated by its shape, size, and configuration. Both perfume and cologne bottles have stoppers that are often designed for use as applicators. Cologne bottles are usually larger than perfume bottles. Scent bottles were much smaller, made to take along in a purse or pocket (see also Vinaigrettes, Scent Bottles, and Chatelaines, this chapter). Atomizers have a spraying device, usually a rubber squeeze bulb, attached.

Cream and powder jars also vary in size, though not as widely. Jar tops may be made of the same material as the jar or of silver, silver plate, brass, plastic, or even gold. These held face powders, talcum, or beauty creams designed for application to a variety of body parts and for a variety of purposes. (Period catalogs and magazine advertisements indicate that Victorian ladies bought creams to remove freckles, flatten bulges, enlarge breasts, remove hair, grow hair, smooth wrinkles, strengthen fingernails, and cure a variety of real or imagined ailments.)

In today's collectibles market, perfume bottles and cosmetic jars are sought after by a wide array of collectors who often specialize in a particular type of glass or ceramic. Examples in ordinary glass may sell for as little as $5, while certain examples in rare glass or ceramic could bring several thousand dollars. Prices are affected by size, shape, decorative pattern, materials used, manufacturer (if known), and condition.

Price Ranges

Perfume and cologne bottles and atomizers: $5 to
  $500+. Average: $75 to $125.
Powder and cream jars: $5 to $200+ per set of two.
  Average: $30 to $75.

Suggested Reading

Jones-North, Jacquelyne. *Commercial Perfume Bottles.* West Chester, Pa.: Schiffer Publishing, 1987.
North, Jacquelyne. *Perfume, Cologne, and Scent Bottles.* West Chester, Pa.: Schiffer Publishing, 1987.
Sloan, Jean. *Perfume and Scent Bottle Collecting.* Radnor, Pa.: Wallace-Homestead Book Company, 1986.
  See also Decorative Glass and Decorative Porcelain
in Chapter 2, The Front Parlor, and Silver Service
Items in Chapter 3, The Dining Room.

Purses and Reticules

A variety of handbags, ranging from simple
hand-crocheted bags to jeweled eighteen-carat
gold mesh clutches, were used by Victorian ladies. Beaded reticules and silver or enameled
mesh purses were especially popular and are easily found at antiques shops and shows today.
Leather purses, common in modern times, were
relatively rare during the nineteenth century.

As the twentieth century approached, the development of celluloid plastics led to the manufacture of hard-cover purses and clutches, with
coverings made to resemble ivory, marble,
mother-of-pearl, and tortoise shell. This type of
purse was made well into the 1900s and can be
found in abundance in antiques shops, flea markets, and yard sales.

Prices of Victorian purses are based on style,
materials used, complexity of decoration, and
condition.

Price Ranges

Beaded purses: $25 to $100+. Average: $40 to $50.
Early celluloid purses: $15 to $100+. Average: $25.

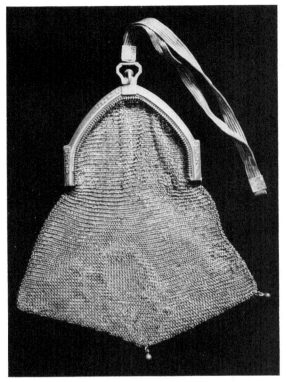

8-24 Silver chain-mail purse with sterling frame.

Enameled mesh purses: $25 to $500+. Average: $40 to
  $60.
Silver mesh purses: $35 to $255+. Average: $45 to
  $65.
  Prices well in excess of high end of range have been
paid for unique or highly ornate examples and/or those
manufactured of rare materials.

Suggested Reading

Haertig, Evelyn. *Antique Combs and Purses.* Carmel,
  Calif.: Gallery Graphics, 1983.
Holiner, Richard and Teresa. *Antique Purses.* Padu-
  cah, Ky.: Collector Books, 1987.

Quilts

It is interesting to note that quilts, among today's most valuable and valued collectibles, were originally produced because they were a thrifty way to produce bed coverings. During the seventeenth and eighteenth centuries cloth was considered precious by pioneer and farm families. Every scrap of material was saved—muslin from grain sacks and plain or patterned cloth from old shirts, curtains, and so forth. These scraps were cut into appropriate shapes, and pieced together to form a particular pattern for the top of the quilt. The finished top was then attached to a back piece by way of small stitched designs. These stitches, and the puffs of fabric they produce, are the actual quilting.

Over the centuries specific designs have become traditional and have been produced in some quantity. (Today, pattern books show the literally thousands of designs that are known to have been produced.) Some designs, however, are one of a kind. These various designs are formed by one of two methods: applying pieces of material to a larger piece (appliqué), or piecing together a large number of small pieces of material to form the entire top (patchwork).

Because of the enormous amount of work involved in their production, quilts have been protected and handed down from generation to generation as family heirlooms. In the antiques and collectibles market, their value is determined by design, materials used, accuracy of dating, quality of artisanship, condition, and overall beauty. Collectors search for particular designs and color combinations that appeal to their personal aesthetic tastes.

Price Range

Quilts: $300 to $2000+. Average: $700 to $1000. Prices in excess of $10,000 have been paid for certain rare or unique examples with documented origins.

Suggested Reading

American Quilter's Society. *Gallery of American Quilts, 1849–1988.* Paducah, Ky.: Collector Books, 1988.

Anderson, Suzy M. *Collector's Guide to Quilts.* Radnor, Pa.: Wallace-Homestead Book Company, 1991.

Burdick, Nancilu. *Legacy: The Story of Talula Gilbert Bottoms and Her Quilts.* Nashville: Rutledge Hill Press, 1988.

Florence, Cathy. *Collecting Quilts.* Paducah, Ky.: Collector Books, 1985.

Von Gwinner, Schnuppe. *History of the Patchwork Quilt.* West Chester, Pa.: Schiffer Publishing, 1988.

Towel Horses

Because bathing was usually done in the bedroom, towels were stored in one of the many chests of drawers or in the commode. For convenience, one or more towels would be left out on a towel rack attached to the commode or wall, or on a large standing rack with several rods called a "towel horse." These racks were produced in a variety of styles and sizes, some of which are adjustable.

Towel horses are a popular collectible, often used to display period clothing, quilts, or other textiles. Prices are determined by size, complexity of design, wood used, and condition.

Price Range

Towel horses: $75 to $250. Average: $125.

Suggested Reading

See Armoires, this chapter.

Trunks

A large variety of trunks were produced throughout the nineteenth century for use as a storage compartment or as luggage. They generally were made of wooden slats covered with leather, canvas, or pressed tin. Wooden strips often were added to the outside for strength and protection, and corners were protected with metal trimwork. Lids were held securely closed by one or more locks or latches. Trunk interiors frequently were decorated with wallpaper and often contained compartmented trays in the lid and in the upper half of the trunk itself.

One style of trunk especially popular with collectors today is called the "camelback," or "dome-top," because of its humpbacked lid. Both camelbacks and "flat-tops" were manufactured in large quantities from the 1870s into the twentieth century. Patent dates can often be found on hinges; however, the trunk itself may have been produced several years after the stated date. Many Victorian trunks can be found today stripped to their wooden skeletons and varnished or repainted for use as decorator pieces. Seldom does one find a truly restored trunk.

Antique trunk prices are based on size, design, materials used, completeness of interior compartments (if any), and condition. It is interesting that repainted trunks often sell for prices considerably higher than an original trunk in top condition. This is primarily because antique trunks are considered more as decorative items rather than nineteenth-century artifacts.

Price Range

Trunks: $50 to $500+. Average: $150.

8-25 Canvas trunk with leather trim, circa 1889.

Suggested Reading

Labuda, M. and M. *Price and Identification Guide to Antique Trunks.* Self-published, 1980.

Vinaigrettes, Scent Bottles, and Chatelaines

Sensitive Victorian ladies subject to fainting spells or greatly adverse to foul odors carried smelling salts and perfumes with them at all times. Vinaigrettes are small, decorative containers, usually made of silver or silver plate, that held smelling salts or scented vinegars formulated to revive the senses. These containers were manufactured in a variety of styles ranging from small decorative boxes to hinge-topped containers in the shapes of animals, flowers, books, eggs, and a variety of other objects.

No. 2837. $4.25.
Solid Silver
Vinaigrette.

8-26 Silver vinaigrette from a Victorian catalog.

8-27 Example of silver chatelaine from a nineteenth-century catalog.

Scent bottles are small perfume bottles, also produced in a variety of shapes from a variety of materials. Some were designed so that they could be attached to a chatelaine, which was a kind of brooch or waist pin, that had hooks or chains from which a variety of other items might be hung. (See Illustration 8-28 for examples.)

Prices of vinaigrettes and scent bottles are based on style, complexity of design, materials used, age, and condition. Prices of chatelaines are based on size, shape, complexity of design, metal used, condition, number of hooks or chains, and number and type of attached items (if any).

Price Ranges

Chatelaines: $100 to $2500+. Average: $250. Highest prices are paid for elaborate examples in precious metals with accessories attached.

Scent bottles: $50 to $1000+. Average: $150 to $200.

Vinaigrettes: $75 to $500. Average: $150 to $200.

Suggested Reading

Vinaigrettes and scent bottles: see Perfume Bottles, Powder and Cream Jars, this chapter. Chatelaines: see Jewelry, this chapter.

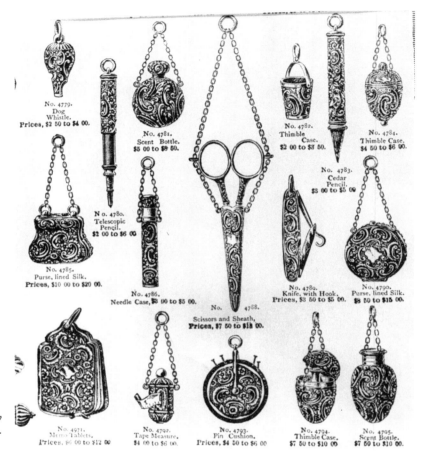

8-28 Advertisement for a variety of accessories designed for attachment to a chatelaine.

Washbowls, Water Pitchers, and Chamber Pots

Even when indoor plumbing became common after the turn of the century, most ladies still kept a pitcher and washbowl in the bedroom for freshening up. These items were not only functional but were often quite attractive decorative ceramic pieces as well. Today they are highly sought after for decoration.

Pitchers and bowls usually came as a set and were produced in a variety of styles and materials—primarily ceramic, but also in glass or silver. The set was usually kept atop a commode, which also may have contained a chamber pot in its cabinet base. Chamber pots also were produced in a number of ceramic variants and are collected

8-29 A simple ceramic chamber pot. (Courtesy Williams Antiques)

today primarily as conversation pieces or for use as planters.

All of these items are sought by collectors of specific types of ceramic or porcelain. (For various types, see Decorative Porcelain in Chapter 2, The Front Parlor, and Crockery, in Chapter 4, The Kitchen.) Prices are determined by complexity of design, materials used, decorative adornments (if any), and condition.

Price Ranges

Chamber pots (ceramic): $20 to $500+. Average: $60 to $75.

Pitcher and washbowl sets (ceramic): $125 to $1000+. Average: $200 to $250.

Highest prices in both categories are paid for certain examples in rare ceramic type. (See Chapter 2, The Front Parlor, and Chapter 4, The Kitchen.)

Suggested Reading

See Decorative Ceramics in Chapter 2, The Front Parlor, and Crockery in Chapter 4, The Kitchen.

CHAPTER 9

His Bedroom

The Victorian gentleman's bedroom contained many of the items discussed in the previous chapter. There was a bed with side tables, a commode, and a chest of drawers, but probably no a dresser, armoire, water pitcher, washbowl, chamber pot, towel racks, trunks, or quilts. The gentleman also kept a diary, used button hooks, and carried a calling card case. Instead of a fainting couch he may have had a large easy chair with a footstool, or possibly a basic settee.

One drawer of the commode would contain the various shaving tools and items of the male toilet: *mug, soap, brush, razor, strop* (for sharpening the razor), and a simple *comb.* He may have used cologne but probably thought it too feminine. In addition to the standard pitcher and bowl, a *shaving mirror* and *stand* may have sat atop the commode.

The master of the house probably spent as little time as possible in his bedroom. He slept, washed, and dressed there and probably thought of these activities as a necessary nuisance, although he probably took great pride in his appearance. (In the Victorian era there were many dandies who dressed in the latest styles, which could be quite extravagant.) Even if he planned to visit madam's boudoir, he first would undress and freshen up in his own room. If he expected

to wear his clothes again, he might place them on a *clothes tree* to allow some of the wrinkles to fall out. Items from his pockets—coin purse, *wallet, watch, pocket knife,* and so forth—would be placed on or in the bedside somnoe. Shirt *buttons* or *studs* and *stockpins* would be returned to their cases in a bureau drawer, and *canes* or *umbrellas* placed in the armoire. He would then dress in a night shirt, robe, and slippers before making the short walk across or down the hall. Madam would be waiting—also in night clothes—beneath the covers.

The primary interests of nineteenth-century gentlemen were gambling, smoking, drinking, hunting, fishing, politics, business, and nineteenth-century women. (If placed in order of importance, the latter subject might find itself first or last, depending on the gentleman's preoccupation with the other six.) Because he was sole provider for his family, his advancement in the business world was of primary importance. He probably spent at least ten hours a day at his job and may have made frequent business trips requiring long train rides. With the combined effects of alcohol, tobacco, stress, and nineteenth-century medicine, his chances of living past age forty-five were one in five. But, while he lived, he was master of his house.

Bags and Valises

On business trips the Victorian gentleman carried spare clothes, toilet items, and business papers in a small bag or valise. For the most part these were shaped much like a doctor's bag—wide at the bottom, narrow at the top—and they closed in the middle. These bags were made of a variety of materials, including silk, canvas, horsehair, tapestry (tapestry bags were called "carpet bags"), pony, and various types of leather. Many are found today with the material separating from the metal bail-type closure and with extensive wear on the corners. Early bags in good condition are rare and often bring premium prices.

In addition to condition, the value of a Victorian bag or valise is based on its size and the material from which it is made. Because of their durability, canvas and tapestry bags seem to have survived in better condition and therefore greater quantity.

Price Range

Bags or valises: $50 to $500+. Average: $250. Highest prices are paid for leather or pony bags in top condition.

Boot Jacks

Both shoes and boots were worn, but throughout the nineteenth century ladies and gentlemen alike preferred boots: They supported the ankles and protected the feet from rain and snow. They were, however, difficult to take off. Ladies' boots usually laced up the front for ease of removal, and in later years gentlemen's "spats" used buttons. But the most popular boot among gentlemen was the simple high-top black pull-on in a style we might call Western today. They went on fairly easily, but when filled with swollen appendages at day's end, it took a strong wife or a boot jack to get them off.

Boot jacks were made of wood, brass, or cast iron. They had a U-shaped end to grip the heel of the boot, and a flat, slanted section on which the other foot was placed for leverage. It was a simple device that saved many a strong wife or servant from flying across the room while removing the gentleman's boots.

On today's antiques market, wooden boot jacks (often handmade) can be found in quantity. Iron versions are less common, and original Victorian brass boot jacks are quite rare. Collectors are cautioned that boot jacks of all types have been reproduced throughout the twentieth century. Prices of Victorian boot jacks are based on material, complexity of design, accuracy of dating, and condition.

Price Ranges

Brass boot jacks: $100 to $500.
Cast-iron boot jacks: $50 to $250.
Wooden boot jacks: $25 to $50.

Suggested Reading

McNerney, Kathryn. *Antique Iron.* Paducah, Ky.: Collector Books, 1984.

Brushes and Combs

Hair-grooming items were basically the same for gentlemen as for ladies. (For complete details, see Chapter 8, Her Bedroom.) There were, however, a few exceptions. Gentlemen's brushes were much plainer in design and usually did not have a handle. From the 1870s on, vulcanized rubber combs were popular as pocket combs, or, if the gentleman preferred something a bit nicer, he might carry an ivory comb that folded into a silver case.

Prices of Victorian combs and brushes are based on complexity of design, material, and condition. Collectors are cautioned that many reproductions exist.

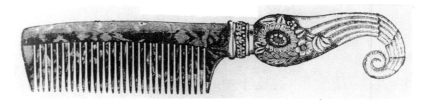

9-1 *Fancy comb that might have been used by a Victorian gentleman, from a catalog circa 1880s.*

Price Ranges

Gentlemen's brushes: $35 to $150.
Gentlemen's combs: $10 to $150.
    Highest prices are paid for items with silver settings or trimwork.

Canes and Cane Handles

Walking canes were an important part of the Victorian gentleman's wardrobe, especially when he attended formal occasions or evening events. The sticks were made primarily of wood, although novelty glass sticks were produced. A variety of woods and finishes were used, a rich black ebony finish being particularly popular. Some sticks were carved or incised; others may have been inlaid with bits of ivory or mother-of-pearl.

It was the handle of the cane, however, that provided the primary ornamentation. Gold, silver, brass, ivory, bone, gutta percha, celluloid, glass, porcelain, or hard rubber was carved, pressed, molded, or formed into a wide variety of shapes and figures for use as cane or umbrella handles. These are now often found (minus the stick in most cases) in antiques shops and shows and have become a collectible specialty. Collectors also look for canes with a secondary, often secret, purpose. Some have hidden compartments for money or papers; others contain daggers, swords, or even small derringers.

Even canes without hidden weapons were often used for self-defense or brandished against

CANES.

No. 1260. $60.00
A Magnificent Presentation Cane.
Flowers. Deer, etc., in Relief.

9-2 *A silver walking stick cap from a Victorian catalog.*

No. 1275.
Fine Gold Dog Head..... ....$32.00

9-3 A figural cane head from the same catalog (as 9-2).

an enemy. One famous example occurred on the floor of the U.S. Senate in 1856, when Senator Charles Sumner was severely beaten by a southern member of the House of Representatives over the admission of Kansas as a free state. This cane is frequently referred to in history books as having been made of gutta percha. More likely, only the handle was made of this highly brittle plastic substance. Contemporary drawings show that the weapon was not a cane, but a walking stick.

The two terms are often used interchangeably but, strictly speaking, a cane has a handle while a walking stick has only a cap or a knob at its top. Famous Western gambler Bat Masterson, known for his cane and derby hat, actually carried a walking stick with an ornate silver knob.

Prices of canes, cane handles, and walking sticks on today's collectibles market are based on age, condition, complexity of design, and type of materials used for the stick (if any) and the handle, knob, or cap.

Price Ranges

Cane handles: $35-500+. Average: $75 to $125.
Canes: $50 to $500+. Average: $100 to $150.
Walking sticks: $25 to $500+. Average: $50 to $75.

Highest prices in all categories are paid for examples with highly ornate or novel handles, or for those made of precious metals or inset or inlaid with precious or semiprecious stones.

Suggested Reading

Dike, Catherine. *Cane Curiosa.* Self-published, 1983.

Clothes Trees

The clothes tree, a sort of free-standing wooden hanger, was invented sometime late in the nineteenth century, so that one could hang an individual suit of clothing without going to the armoire. This item of great convenience allowed the businessman, tired from a long hard day, to quickly yet neatly hang his clothing en route to the bed, and allowed the well-prepared lady to lay out the next day's wardrobe in a tidy fashion. Clothes trees came in a variety of configurations; some provided places for pants, socks, shoes, and pocket change, and one even attached to the back of a chair.

Collectors are cautioned that clothes trees were produced in quantity during the mid-twentieth century, and relatively few Victorian examples are in existence. Even so, low demand has kept prices reasonable. Prices are based on style, materials, and condition.

Price Range

Clothes tree: $75 to $250+. Highest prices are paid for elaborate designs and chair varieties.

Coins and Currency

From 1837–1839, while Victoria was getting used to being Queen of England, Americans were trying to get used to the new look of their money. Since the first U.S. coins were produced in 1792, a bust portrait of Lady Liberty had graced the face of our coinage. Liberty was still on the new coins of 1837, but for the first time Americans saw her whole body as she sat on a throne holding a shield. Due to a complete reorganization of coinage regulations, some of the coins were also

9-4 *A modern penny seems dwarfed by the "large cent"
used during the first half of the nineteenth century.*

smaller and lighter in weight. At this time there
were seven coin denominations in circulation: a
half-cent, a cent (about the size of today's quarter), a half-dime (no one had even heard of a
nickel yet), a dime, a quarter, a half-dollar, and
a dollar. There were also gold coins in denominations of $2.50 (Quarter Eagle), $5 (Half Eagle),
$10 (Eagle), and $20 (Double Eagle).

The next major change came in 1857, when the
half-cent was discontinued and the "large cent"
was replaced by a one-cent coin about the same
size as it is today. Half-dimes were replaced by
nickel five-cent pieces in 1866. From 1849 to 1889
there were two one-dollar coins—one of silver

and one of gold. A variety of odd denomination
coins were produced at various times during the
Victorian period: a two-cent piece (1864–1873), a
three-cent piece (silver, 1851–1873 and nickel
1865–1889), a twenty-cent piece (1875–1878),
and a three-dollar gold piece (1854–1889).

Throughout history bank notes (representing
cash or coin on deposit) have been issued by various institutions and governments. These could be
used for trade or barter and exchanged at the
issuing bank for "hard money" (gold or silver).
During the Victorian period this type of paper
currency was issued by various banks and by the
U.S. government. Denominations followed that
of gold coinage—$1, $5, $10, and $20—but also
often included a two- and a three-dollar bill, as
well as larger denominations from fifty to one
million dollars. Paper script in amounts under
one dollar was also issued by some banks and by
the U.S. government during the Civil War.

Determining the value of an old coin has always been difficult. The age of a coin often has
very little to do with its value. The number of
pieces made, the condition (grade) of a coin, and
the current demand for a particular coin greatly
affect the price. The nature of coin collecting
(numismatics) has changed considerably during
the last quarter-century. Due primarily to the
fluctuating prices of gold and silver, coins are
now collected for investment purposes, and are

9-5 *Because of their large size,
nineteenth-century paper notes
were called "horse blankets."*

bought and sold without the owners ever actually seeing them.

Still, there are those who collect coins and paper currency for their history and for fun. Fortunately for them, individual pieces are still available through antiques shops and shows and through a few remaining neighborhood coin shops. To keep abreast of constantly changing prices, and to become familiar with coin-grading systems, collectors should invest in one or more of the many numismatic guide books and magazines.

Most nineteenth-century paper currency is quite rare and pricing is greatly affected by its condition. Civil War period script still can be found for reasonable prices.

Price Ranges

Victorian period coins in collectible condition can be had for as little as 75¢ each. The price ranges given here are for coins readily available to the average collector on a budget, and that grade very good to very fine on the established grading scale.

Coins: $1 to $35+. Prices in excess of $250,000 have been paid for certain rare coins.

Currency: $15 to 500+. Average price for "horse blanket" one-dollar bills from the turn of the century: $25. All others average: $75 to 125. Prices in excess of $100,000 have been paid for premium examples.

Suggested Reading

Beresiner, Yasha. *Collector's Guide to Paper Money.* Stein & Day, 1977.

Craig, W. D. *Coins of the World.* New York: Western Publishing Company, n.d.

Yeoman, R. S. *Guide Book of United States Coins.* New York: Western Publishing Company, published annually.

Collar Boxes

Many shirts produced during the nineteenth century came without collars, which were considered a separate accessory. Collars were often purchased by the dozen and kept atop a gentleman's dresser or bureau in a decorative box made of leather, velvet, wood, silver, celluloid, or plastic. These boxes were often quite ornate, with bits of inlaid ivory or mother-of-pearl, or with figures or scenes painted or pressed into the surface.

Prices of collar boxes are based on size, complexity of design, material, and condition. Some boxes still contain original collars, which are commonly available (average: $5 to $10 each) and used as conversation pieces.

Price Range

Collar Boxes: $20 to $125. Average: $35.

Liquor Flasks

As a general rule, the Victorian gentleman loved to drink. On outings where liquor would not be readily available, he might take along his

9-6 Nineteenth-century ad for liquor flasks.

own supply in a silver or silver-plated flask tucked inside a coat pocket.

Like all silver items, flasks could be as plain or ornate as the owner desired. Some versions have elaborately embossed or applied figures and designs; others are engraved with floral patterns, scrollwork, or initials. Silver and silver-plate flasks, especially popular during the Art Nouveau period near the turn of the century, were produced in the flowing styles of the day.

Liquor flasks were also produced in glass and examples can sometimes be found enclosed in protective covers of tin, leather, hemp, and canvas or other cloth.

Prices of Victorian liquor flasks are based on complexity of design, materials used, and condition.

Price Ranges

Glass flasks: $25 to $1000+. Average: $75 to $125.
Silver flasks: $250 to $2500+. Average: $350 to $400.
Silver-plated flasks: $35 to $125.

Pocketbooks, Card Cases, and Match Safes

A Victorian gentleman's coat pockets were filled with many of the same types of necessities that a lady carried in her purse. His pocketbook was quite large and filled with cards, business papers, and, of course, money. Wallets were made primarily of leather, although cloth and even rubber versions were produced. Few of these have survived the years in good condition, and even those that have are not particularly popular with collectors.

Gentlemen's calling card cases range from basic silver-plated covers to elaborate versions used by both men and women. (For additional information, see Calling Card Cases in Chapter 8, Her Bedroom.)

Cigarette lighters were not invented until late in the century and even then were not widely

9-7 A typically large wallet with multiple compartments, from an early catalog.

9-8 Clasp-type calling-card holder in embossed silver. (Courtesy Amador County Museum)

distributed. For several centuries matches had been carried in a silver or gold "match safe,"

9-9 Elaborately embossed silver match safe. (Courtesy Amador County Museum)

which looks very much like a small cigarette lighter case. These were usually embossed or engraved with artistic scenes, initials, or other decorations, and today are found, along with calling card cases, in the "smalls" cases at antiques shops.

Prices of wallets, card cases, and match safes are based on materials used, complexity of design and decoration, and condition.

Price Ranges

Leather wallets: $5 to $35. Average: $15.
Silver-plated calling card cases: $25 to $125. Average: $35.
Silver-plated match safes: $35 to $150. Average: $45.

Suggested Reading

Sullivan, Audrey G. *A History of Match Safes in the United States.* Self-published, 1978.

Pocket Knives

Folding knives of the Victorian period were very similar to those produced today, with a wide variety of blade combinations and handle materials. An 1896 catalog lists numerous styles, including the razor-blade jackknife, stag-handle chain knife, spear-point jack, carpenter's knife, Dick's Easy Opener, Texas stock knife, Sampson pruning knife, Western Chief, Texas Toothpick, Austrian Hunter, push-button knives, rack knives, and penknives, and a combination knife with nail file, scissors, and two sharp blades.

Combination pocketknives were particularly popular with soldiers during the Civil War. Some were mess knives containing knife, spoon, and fork. Others included files, drills, corkscrews, scissors, and other accessories. Among the numerous manufacturers of these combination knives were Norman Ely and Company; Thorpe, Neill, Hardie and Hayward; and American Knife Company.

Knife handles were produced in just about every material suitable for the purpose, including staghorn, bone, ivory, mother-of-pearl, gold, silver, and brass. They also were made in a variety of woods, especially ebony, rosewood, boxwood, and cocoa. Pocketknives by two of America's most familiar weapons makers of the period—Winchester and Remington—are sought after by collectors. Knife manufacturers of the period number in the hundreds. Those interested in collecting Victorian pocketknives should purchase one or more of the many detailed guide books in order to familiarize themselves with knife styles, blade shapes, and manufacturer codes.

Prices of nineteenth-century pocketknives are based on style, materials, age, manufacturer, model number (if any), and condition. Collectors usually seek mint-condition examples; damaged knives or those with missing pieces hold very little collectible value unless the item is particularly rare.

Price Ranges

Folding utensil knives: $75 to $1000+. Average: $325 to $400.

Pocket knives: $35 to $1500+. Average: $275.

Suggested Reading

Parker, James F., ed. The *Official Price Guide to Collector Pocket Knives.* New York: Ballantine, 1987.

Sargent, Jim. *Sargent's American Premium Guide to Pocket Knives.* Florence, Ala.: Books Americana, 1986.

Stewart and Richie. *Standard Knife Collector's Guide. Paducah, Ky.: Collector Books, 1986.*

Razors and Strops

The wealthy Victorian male seldom shaved himself. He instead included a trip to the barber as part of his daily routine. There he would receive a clean shave, have his hair trimmed or styled, get his shoes shined, and generally be pampered. His barber probably used a "seven-day set" of straight razors so that his clients were shaved with a fresh blade each day. These usually were made of fine Sheffield steel with fancy engravings, had elegant handles, and came in a fine wood- or leather-covered case with a slotted, velvet-lined interior.

Even if the gentleman shaved himself, he wanted a razor of the very best engraved steel with an elegant inlaid, carved, or molded handle. Handle materials include: bone, ivory, staghorn, tortoise shell, mother-of-pearl, ebony, silver, brass, hard rubber, and—after 1870—celluloid and other plastics. Blades were engraved with various designs; those with elaborate scenes are now sought by collectors. Before 1870 the best blades came from Sheffield, England. After 1870 commercially manufactured blades were produced in Switzerland, Germany, and the United States by various cutlery firms. An advertisement in an 1890s catalog reads "Let your beard be your guide to selecting a razor. A coarse, heavy beard requires a ¾-inch blade. A ⅝-inch blade fits an average beard. And a ½-inch blade is fine for a man with a light beard or who shaves every day. Our razors are suitable for either barbers or private use."

A comfortable shave with any razor requires the sharpest of blades, and straight razors were sharp. The straight razor was kept sharp by "stropping" it against canvas webbing and leather. Razor strops were produced in a variety

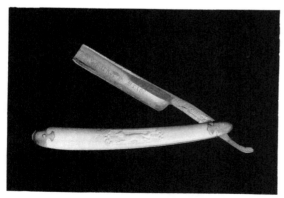

9-10 *Victorian straight razor with carved bone handle and engraved steel blade. (Courtesy Georgia Fox, Foxes Den)*

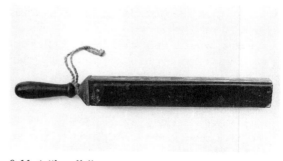

9-11 *A "handle" type razor strop.*

of designs, but there are two common configurations. One is a beltlike strap with leather on one side, webbing on the other, a hook on one end (for attaching to a wall, shaving stand, or barber's chair), and a leather grip at the other end. The other, a long wooden block with a handle, contains four separate sharpening surfaces around the block.

NOTE: Collectors are cautioned to use extreme care in examining antique razors. Some are so sharp that you will be unaware of the cut until it draws blood.

Straight razors maintained their popularity well into the twentieth century despite the introduction of the safety razor. These early versions of our modern razors were available in a variety of brands and styles at the turn of the century. They usually came in boxed sets containing a blade frame with detachable handle, a set of heavy steel blades, and some sort of mechanical sharpening device. The best sets came with seven blades so that a Victorian gentleman could have a fresh blade each day, then sit down and sharpen them all at once in his leisure time.

Like knife collectors, razor collectors look for fine-quality blades by well-known manufacturers and handles of quality materials and novel designs. Nearly every collector has a strop to display with his razors and, here as well, quality examples of novel designs are prized. Since early razors can be found in abundance, collectors should buy only mint or near-mint examples. Even slightly damaged pieces are worth considerably less.

Price Ranges

Razor strops: $15 to $35+.

Safety razor sets: $25 to $75+. The accompaniment of original boxes, advertising, or instructions adds to the value. Examples with missing pieces are worth considerably less.

Straight razor seven-day sets: $100 to $300+.

Straight razors (ivory, bone, shell, silver handles): $35 to $500+.

Straight razors (plastic, hard rubber, or celluloid handles): $7 to $45+. Highest prices are paid for fancy engraved blades.

Suggested Reading

Doyle, Robert. *Razor Collecting.* Paducah, Ky.: Collector Books, 1980.

Krumholz, Philip. *Value Guide for Barberiana and Shaving Collectibles.* Self-published, 1988.

Powell, Robert Blake. *Occupational and Fraternal Shaving Mugs of the United States.* Self-published, 1978.

Shaving Brushes and Mugs

In Victorian times shaving lather was produced by wetting a brush and swirling it around a cake of soap inside a mug. The brush was then used to apply the lather to the face. Soft bristles were inserted into plain or fancy handles made of silver, ivory, wood, porcelain, molded plastic, and other materials to produce a variety of brushes to suit the Victorian gentleman's tastes.

Victorian shaving mugs were produced in an enormous array of decorative designs, and there is an interesting bit of history that explains this

No. 9042.
Shaving Cup, $6.50
GOLD LINED.
Shaving Brush, $3.50

9-12 Ad for gold-lined shaving cup from a Victorian catalog.

abundance. Due to the spread of a skin disease called "barber's itch," barbers were required to use a separate mug for each individual. Since many clients were immigrants who could not speak or read English, barber supply houses began producing mugs decorated with fraternal symbols or scenes relating to certain occupations, such as watchmaker, butcher, baker, fireman, and so forth. Many of these mugs are one-of-a-kind custom pieces designed and manufactured for an individual client, whose name may also appear on the mug.

American supply houses imported many mugs from European porcelain factories, including blanks for custom work. Mugs were also produced in silver and silver plate, glass, copper, and tin. One type of shaving mug called a "skuttle" had a partition across the center so that water could be placed on one side and soap on the other. These were also produced in a variety of materials and decorative styles.

Prices of Victorian shaving mugs are based on style, decorative design, manufacturer (if known), material, age, and condition.

Price Ranges

Fraternal or occupational shaving
mugs: $35 to $1000+. Average: $185 to $250.
Other shaving mugs: $25 to $250. Average: $50 to $75.
Shaving brushes: $10 to $150. Average: $25.
Skuttles: $25 to $150. Average: $50 to $75.

Suggested Reading

See Razors and Strops, this chapter.

Shaving Cabinets, Stands, and Mirrors

A Victorian gentleman may have set his shaving mug atop the commode, alongside the pitcher and washbowl, and shaved himself in front of a large attached or hanging mirror. However, from the abundance of cabinets, mirrors, and stands designed for the purpose, we know that this was not always the case.

Small shaving stands designed to sit atop a table or commode were made of wood, silver plate, or bright metal. They consisted of a central swiveling mirror and some sort of storage area for brushes, razors, and mugs. Some provided a regular mirror on one side and a magnifying mirror on the other. Shaving mirrors of this type were also made to hang on the wall; one style was even attached to a folding bracket so that it could be pulled closer to the face.

Shaving stands were also produced in floor models, usually with a pedestal base, small table top, one or two drawers, and adjustable mirror. These units often were made of fine woods with marble tops and highly ornamented mirrors. Today these attractive pieces of furniture are in demand by period decorators.

Small shaving cabinets designed to hang on the wall provided a storage unit for shaving supplies as well as a convenient mirror. Some units had a small working surface that could be pushed back into the unit when not in use. Shaving cabinets were made in a wide array of sizes and configurations, including the popular styles of the period (French Revival, Renaissance Revival, and Eastlake). Small hanging mirrors with a single drawer or chest underneath were called "grooming mirrors" or "comb cases," and may have been used by either the gentleman or the lady, or simply as a decorative storage unit.

Prices of Victorian shaving stands, cabinets, and mirrors are based on complexity of design, materials used, age, and condition.

Price Ranges

Floor model shaving stands: $300 to $1000+. Average: $600.
Shaving cabinets, grooming mirrors, and comb cases: $50 to $300. Average: $175 to $225.
Shaving mirrors: $15 to $75.
Table-top shaving stands: $15 to $125.

Suggested Reading

McNerney; Kathryn. *Victorian Furniture: Our American Heritage.* Paducah, Ky.: Collector Books, 1988.

Swedberg, Robert and Harriett Swedberg. *Victorian Furniture,* vol. 3. Radnor, Pa.: Wallace-Homestead Book Company, 1985.

Studs, Buttons, and Stockpins

In Victorian times good-quality men's shirts had no buttons or collars, which were considered accessories and could be purchased separately in a style befitting a gentleman's taste, if not the latest style. During the first half of the nineteenth century, gentlemen wore large stiff collars called *"vatermoders,"* German for "father murderers."

9-13 Nineteenth-century advertisement showing a variety of buttons and studs.

The strange name was derived from the legend of a young man who wore a collar so stiff and sharp that, upon embracing his father, he accidently slit his throat.

Tall collars were covered almost completely with a cravat or "stock," a wide stiff scarf wrapped around the throat and carefully tied in front. The nickname "stock" came from the punishment device of the same name, in which a man is held motionless by a clamp across his neck. A properly tied cravat, however, was the mark of a true gentleman, and a jeweled stockpin was the icing on the cake. These pins were produced in a wide variety of styles ranging from a simple horseshoe or cloverleaf decoration in silver or gold, to elaborate examples with diamonds, rubies, or pearls. Among the more popular pieces were those in the shapes of swords, fraternal symbols, or golden wishbones.

As the century progressed tall *vatermoders* and stocks were replaced by turn-down collars and cravats, tied just as we tie them today. Stockpins became scarf pins as tie bars gradually took their place as a necessary part of the gentleman's wardrobe.

Modern shirts requiring cuff links are a throwback to Victorian times, when formal shirts had no buttons at all. Both the left and the right shirt plaques had buttonholes requiring a complete set of studs to close up the front of the shirt. The button portion of the stud was visible and may have been gold, silver, or silver plate, possibly inset with precious or semiprecious stones. Less-expensive versions were engraved or embossed with patterns, figures, or initials. Buttons or studs also were made of onyx, ivory, bone, wood, hard rubber, celluloid, and other materials.

As the twentieth century approached shirts were made with collars and buttons attached. Still, the well-dressed man continued to wear collar studs, cuff links, and occasionally a fancy tie pin.

Victorian period studs and stockpins are collected by those specializing in Victorian jewelry.

The prices of these items are affected by style, materials used, condition, completeness of set (if any), and supply and demand.

Price Ranges

Stockpins: $10 to $500+. Average: $50 to $150. Prices in excess of $10,000 have been paid for elaborate examples in rare or precious materials.

Stud sets: $50 to $500+. Average: $125 to $175.

Suggested Reading

Gernsheim, Alison. *Victorian and Edwardian Fashion.* New York: Dover Publications, 1981.

See also Suggested Reading for Jewelry, previous chapter.

Watches, Chains, and Pendants

In nearly every portrait of a gentleman taken during the nineteenth century, one can see a golden chain crossing from a vest button over to a small pocket that contains one of his most prized possessions: his pocket watch. Whether passed down from his father, received as a gift from his lady, won in a card game, or bought with his first big pay check, the watch almost always meant more to him than simply a way to tell time.

The pocket watch, invented sometime in the fifteenth or sixteenth century, had developed considerably by the 1900s. While wristwatches were manufactured as early as 1851, it was not until World War I that they came into wide use and, even then, the pocket watch continued to be the favorite portable timepiece. Several factors had to be taken into account when purchasing a pocket watch: the quality of the works (determined by the number of jewels), the type of dial, the type of metal used in the case, and the design of the case and cover (if any). Most jewelry catalogs of the late Victorian period show solid gold, solid silver, coin silver, gold-filled, silver-plated, Alaska silver (not real silver, but a combination of metals made to look like silver), and nickel-

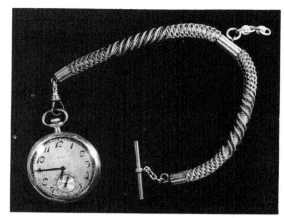

9-14 Gold pocket watch with chain woven from human hair.

plated watches. A nickel-plated watch without jeweled movement could be had for $.94; a seven-jewel watch with an Alaska silver case was $2.40; and an eighteen-carat-gold, fifteen-jewel-watch with an embossed train (and diamond headlight) on the cover was $190 in an 1896 catalog.

A watch was just a watch without a chain attached to it. These also came in a variety of weights, styles, and metals to match the watch. The best chain in the aforementioned catalog was a heavy fourteen-carat-gold version that sold for $120. Albert vest chains (named for Victoria's prince consort) contained a separate ring for a pendant. Pendants were available in an almost endless array of shapes, sizes, stones, and metals, but the most popular were those representing the gentleman's profession or fraternal affiliation.

In today's antiques market, watch collecting is a popular but somewhat formidable specialty. A thorough knowledge of the subject is required to avoid costly mistakes. Watches are collected primarily by manufacturer and type of works, with the case style being of only secondary importance. Even so, the size of the case (represented by the numbers 18/0 through 20), the number of

9-15 Sampling of watch chain ornaments from a period catalog.

jewels (tiny gems used as bearings in the watch), the type of case, and the metal from which it is made all play a part in determining a watch's value.

Price Ranges

Pocket watches: $35 to $1500+. Average: $150 to $250.

Watch chains: $15 to $1000+. Average gold-filled watch chain: $80.

Watch chain pendants: $15 to $1000+. Average gold fraternal or occupational pendant: $125 to $175.

Suggested Reading

Ehrhardt, Roy. *American Pocket Watches. Vol. 1, Encyclopedia and Price Guide.* Kansas City, Mo.: Heart of America Press, 1982.

Guappone, Carmen. *Antique Chains.* Self-published, 1978.

———. *Antique Watches.* Self-published, 1978.

Meis, Reinhard. *Pocket Watches: From the Pendant Watch to the Tourbillon.* West Chester, Pa.: Schiffer Publishing, 1987.

Shugart, Cooksey and Tom Engle. *The Official Price Guide to Watches.* New York: Ballantine, 1990.

Smith, Alan. *Clocks and Watches: Antique Collector's Guide.* New York: Outlet Book Company, 1989.

CHAPTER 10

The Children's Room

The young Victorian madam put great effort into preparations for her first-born. The right wall coverings and furniture were chosen; the best cradle, crib, blankets, nursing bottles, rattles, and perambulators were purchased; and she looked forward to the big day with great anticipation. Just as she probably was unprepared for her wedding night, she just as likely was unprepared for the pain and drain of childbirth. The average Victorian woman would repeat parturition five to seven more times. If more than half of her offspring survived childhood diseases and accidents, they would have beaten the odds, for throughout the nineteenth century child mortality remained very high.

The first and second children may have shared the room with the infant third, but by the time the fourth came along it was time for the older children to have a room of their own. If the couple was blessed with children of both sexes there would be a boys' room and a girls' room, and woe be it to the sibling that ventured into the other room.

In wealthier homes the children may have had child-sized furniture during their younger years. This furniture, along with other outgrown items, would be passed down for use by younger siblings and replaced at the appropriate time with full-sized pieces. In the boys' room, the walls would be hung with pictures of horses and dogs, a fishing rod or two, and in their teen years, probably a squirrel rifle. Among the books on the shelves one might find a jar containing a spider, garter snake, or frog, and perhaps a metal *bank* with almost enough pennies inside to buy that new slingshot. Beneath the bed there might be a well-worn *sled* awaiting the winter's first snow, and next to it a *toy chest,* whose contents are likely scattered elsewhere. In the corner a *rocking horse,* now deserted for the real thing, awaits the next little cowpoke.

The girls' room is a castle of lace and frills. A variety of old perfume bottles sits atop the dresser, their contents long since replaced with colored water. *Dolls,* parts of dolls, and doll clothing are found nearly everywhere in the room. One doll lies in a black *perambulator* with a silk hood—at least until mother needs the carriage to take the new baby for a walk. In one corner of the room a miniature tea table might be spread with toy cups and dishes, or maybe an unfinished jigsaw puzzle. Already preparing for her predetermined role, the young lady sits before a *doll house* and pretends to cook, clean, care for babies, and give teas, but when she reaches adulthood she instead may find herself organizing political rallies, holding a job, and marching for women's rights. As the twentieth century approached the role of children remained much the same but the role of women did not.

Banks

If in 1870 a Victorian gentleman opened a new banking account and was known to have children, he probably came home with a metal coin bank stamped with the institution's name. Throughout the second half of the century, cast-iron coin banks were frequently given away by banks and other businesses as a form of advertising. Today there is a large group of collectors who specialize in this category, making nineteenth-century cast-iron banks a highly sought-after and valuable collectible.

Even more valuable are those mechanical banks produced from the end of the Civil War until the turn of the century. These were manufactured in a seemingly endless array of characters and configurations, all of which are activated by the placement of a coin. Some perform when the coin is inserted in a slot; others actually carry or flip the coin into the bank's interior.

A large number of mechanical banks were produced by J. and E. Stevens in Cromwell, Connecticut, including "Three Clowns on a Tub," "Paddy with His Pig and Elephant," "Big Frog, Little Frog," "The Chinamen," and "The Kicking Mule." To operate the Kicking Mule, a coin was placed between his rear legs and a lever was pressed, causing a small dog to jump out of his house, in turn causing the mule to kick the coin into a nearby barn. The mechanics of many of these banks were often quite elaborate, incorporating two or more separate sets of movements.

No one knows when the first piggy bank was produced, but pigs were always considered a symbol of good luck, and banks were given to Victorian infants as a wish of good fortune (or at least the accumulation of a fortune). A variety of banks in these and other shapes were produced in glass and ceramic, as well as wood, brass, pewter, lead, and tin.

The price range of Victorian coin banks is as wide as any collectible on the market. Prices in excess of $20,000 have been paid for certain rare mechanical versions. Values are based on shape, materials, mechanical function (if any), and condition. Prices are greatly affected by local or international supply and demand. Examples with completely original parts and paint are most desirable. Seriously interested collectors should purchase and study one or more of the many authoritative books on the subject. Collectors are warned that modern and early modern reproductions were produced.

Price Ranges

Cast-iron advertising banks: $100 to $300+.
Mechanical banks: $100 to $1000+. Average: $350.
Other banks: $25 to $500+.

Suggested Reading

Meyer, John. *Old Penny Banks.* Watkins Glen, N.Y.: Century House Publishing, 1960.
Moore, Andy and Susan Moore. *Penny Bank Book.* West Chester, Pa.: Schiffer Publishing, 1984.
Norman, Bill. *The Bank Book.* San Diego, Calif.: Collector's Showcase, 1984.

Bicycles and Tricycles

Along with baseball, vulcanized rubber, and photography, the bicycle was born at about the same time as the Victorian era, in 1839. The invention of Kirkpatrick McMillan of Scotland was

10-1 Early magazine ad for Monarch bicycles of Chicago.

not manufactured in any quantity until Pierre Michaux of France opened his factory in 1867. The very next year a bicycle race held at the Parc de St. Cloud in Paris received worldwide coverage. Even so, it was 1878 before A. A. Pope manufactured the first American-made bicycle. Interestingly, that same year a motorized tricycle was built in Germany. Invented by Karl Benz (note the familiar last name), it attained speeds in excess of five miles per hour.

In 1885 the first ladies' bicycle was introduced. Because ladies still wore only skirts and dresses, it was nearly impossible for them to delicately mount the standard-style bicycle, which had a straight bar running from the seat support to the handlebar neck. This cross-bar was lowered considerably on the ladies' version, so that the foot need only be lifted about twelve inches off the ground when mounting.

By the turn of the century a variety of bicycles were available in both mens' and womens' versions. A number of accessories were also made available, including gas (carbide) lamps, warning bells and whistles, camera carriers, and even a device that allowed a bicycle to be ridden on railroad tracks.

The tricycle was originally a three-wheeled version of the bicycle and designed to be ridden by adults. Some of these were impressively large, of the types seen today in parades and circuses.

Because tricycles are so easily balanced, smaller versions called "velocipedes" were designed for children and remain popular to this day.

It is interesting to note that many nineteenth-century bicycles and velocipedes were made by gun manufacturers. Remington made several fine bicycles, as did Ivers and Johnsons Arms and Bycycle Works. Other early bicycle manufacturers of note included Columbia, Mercury, Kenwood, and Edgemere, among others.

Prices of Victorian bicycles and tricycles are based on age, style, manufacturer, and condition.

Price Ranges

Bicycles: $250 to $5000+. Average: $1500.
Tricycles: $150 to $2500+. Average: $750.

Children's Books

Who was born in the Victorian era? Oliver Twist (1838), Handy Andy (1842), Moby Dick (1851), Alice in Wonderland (1865), Hans Brinker (1865), Tom Sawyer (1875), Uncle Remus (1880), Huckleberry Finn (1885), Little Lord Fauntleroy (1886), and Hansel and Gretel

(1893)—not to mention all the characters in Louis Carroll's *Through the Looking Glass* and Rudyard Kipling's *Jungle Book*. This, of course, only touches on the wonderful literature of the period written for children and young adults.

Also popular were small, colorful books with predominant illustrations accompanying simple rhymes, jingles, or prose. During the latter part of the century, many of these contained bright chromolithographic scenes that unfolded and popped out when the page was turned.

Today nineteenth-century children's books are collected by those interested in rare or first-edition literature, as well as by those who simply feel connected to children of another time and place. On the collectibles market value is based on size, style, quality, number of illustrations, author, and condition.

Price Range

Children's books: $10 to $1000+. Average: $35 to $75.

Suggested Reading

Bader, Barbara. *American Picture Books from Noah's Ark to The Beast Within.* New York: Macmillan Publishing Company, 1976.

Collecting Children's Books. Watkins Glen, N.Y.: American Life Foundation; 1968.

Cribs and Children's Furniture

As the baby began to grow from infant to toddler, it was transferred from the cradle in its mother's room to a crib in the nursery. Cribs were produced in a variety of styles and configurations, including the popular styles of the period (French Revival, Renaissance Revival, and Eastlake). During the last quarter of the century folding cribs were produced to facilitate storage until the next infant came along. These cribs often had a metal frame base with cross-springs to support a mattress and were extremely sturdy. Others may have had wooden slats or a solid wood base.

A style of crib sometimes called a "swinging crib" or "platform cradle" was attached via a pivot or spring to a solid base. By removing a locking pin, the child could be rocked gently to sleep without being removed from its bed.

After outgrowing the crib a child might graduate directly to a full-sized bed and accessories. In wealthier households, however, the parents may have purchased child-sized furniture in single pieces, or a complete set with bed, dresser, chair, commode, chest of drawers, and armoire, all in one-third size. Except for the miniature armoires, these items can be found on today's antiques market without too much difficulty.

Prices of Victorian cribs and child's furniture are based on style, woods used, manufacturer (if known), and condition.

Price Ranges

Children's beds: $150 to $750.
Children's chairs: $75 to $400.
Children's dressers, chest of drawers, and commodes: $150 to $1500+.

In all categories the lowest prices are paid for Country and basic spindle pieces; highest prices are paid for ornate duplicates of full-sized pieces in the styles of the period.

Cribs: $250 to $475.
Rocking cribs: $350 to $650+.

Highest prices in both categories paid for ornate cribs in the styles of the period.

10-2 Child-sized chair shown with a variety of doll furniture. (Courtesy Amador County Museum)

Suggested Reading

Swedberg, Robert W. and Harriett Swedberg. *Victorian Furniture,* vols. 1–3. Radnor, Pa.: Wallace-Homestead Book Company, 1984–1985.
Knopf Collectors' Guides to American Antiques. Vol. 1, *Furniture.* New York: Chanticleer Press, 1987.

Doll Houses

The first miniature model houses were produced for adults by artisans in Germany (complete houses) and Holland (individual rooms). These were decorative pieces, designed to show off high-quality, hand-crafted miniature furniture and accessories. It was no doubt difficult to keep small hands away from these displays, and eventually artisans began to produce miniatures for children.

Wealthy children in the United States were presented with fine European crafted doll houses, while those less fortunate received homemade versions or, from the 1880s on, American-made lithographed doll houses. The invention of the chromolithographic process in midcentury allowed manufacturers to simulate a variety of objects in bright, natural colors. The basic shape of the house was formed in wood, and printed representations of clapboard, latticework, and brick were pasted to the outside.

Individual rooms and commercial shops were produced in miniature as well. Some of the "store front" miniatures were actually commissioned by store owners for display in their windows. As these are one-of-a-kind or limited-edition pieces, they are highly sought by collectors and often bring premium prices. Many store front miniatures were quite elaborate: butcher shops with miniature hams and chickens hanging from the ceilings, dry goods shops with numerous tiny bolts of cloth, and grocery stores with miniature pickle barrels, jars, and bottles.

Also popular with Victorian children (and twentieth-century collectors) were the miniaturized "tin kitchens." Walls, floors, stoves, hearths, and kitchen tools and accessories were reproduced with amazing accuracy in formed or pressed tin. Tin workshops with working machinery also were produced around the turn of the century and are now becoming quite rare. The most impressive examples came from German artisans, but a number of good-quality versions were produced in the United States as well.

Doll house furniture is collected both individually and to accessorize a house. These tiny handcrafted pieces often are so accurately reproduced that they are impossible to tell from the real thing when seen in close-up photographs. Miniature furniture was produced in fine-quality woods with metal or gilded trim, as well as wicker and wrought iron. Nearly every piece of furniture discussed in this book, as well as lamps, chandeliers, vases, and even wallpaper, was reproduced in miniature for doll houses.

The first major manufacturer of doll houses in the United States was R. Bliss Manufacturing. Other American makers included Morton Converse, McLoughlin, Schoenhut, Field and Francis, Bergmann, Althof, and Stevens and Brown. Collectors should remember, however, that although all of these manufacturers produced Victorian doll houses, their period of greatest production came after the turn of the century. Prices of Victorian doll houses are based on size, complexity of style and construction, materials used, manufacturer (if known), and condition. Artisanship and accuracy of reproduction are primary factors. Serious collectors should purchase one or more of the comprehensive guides and familiarize themselves with the various styles and manufacturers so that they will be able to recognize valuable examples.

Price Ranges

Doll house furniture: $10 to $150 each. $25 to $500 set.
Early European wood doll houses: $1500 to $5000+.
Handmade doll houses: $50 to $1000+. Average: $125.

Lithographic doll houses: $100 to $1500+. Average: $200.
Miniature workshops: $100 to $1000+. Average: $200.
Store front doll houses: $100 to $1000+. Average: $500.
Tin kitchens: $50 to $1000+. Average: $200 to $250.

Suggested Reading

McClinton, Kathryn. *Antiques of American Childhood.* New York: Clarkson Potter, 1970.
Mitchell, Donald and Helene Mitchell. *Doll Houses, Past and Present.* Paducah, Ky.: Collector Books, 1980.
Stille, Eva. *Doll Kitchens, Eighteen Hundred to Nineteen Eighty.* West Chester, Pa.: Schiffer Publishing, 1988.
Whitton, Blair. *Bliss Toys and Doll Houses.* New York: Dover Publications, 1979.
Also, most extensive books on antique toys have a section on doll houses.

Dolls

Is there a house anywhere in the world, with or without children, that does not contain at least one doll of some sort? Dolls have been around as long as there have been children. Prehistoric people carved wooden dolls for their little ones, and dolls have since been produced in a variety of materials including cloth, wax, porcelain, glass, and plastic. Today doll collecting is one of the largest areas of the antiques trade, especially among women. There are a number of large doll museums, collector's clubs, magazines, and conventions.

Probably the most recognizable Victorian dolls are those called "fashion dolls." These were produced primarily in France starting in the 1840s to display miniature versions of the latest fashions. Like most dolls from the early Victorian period, they were made in the form of an adult. The heads, arms, and feet were usually formed in fine china with a high-gloss finish. These were at-

10-3 Early wax-type fashion doll with original clothing. (Courtesy Jensen's Antiques)

As the century progressed a variety of dolls were made from a number of substances, including wax, wood, metal, porcelain, bisque, cloth, celluloid, and others. Two of the materials used—composition and stockinet—were unique to doll making. Composition is exactly what its name implies: a combination of numerous ingredients, primarily glue, tree sap, or varnish mixed with sawdust, flour, cloth fibers, or other materials. This compound not only was used for heads but also for bodies and limbs, which were sometimes jointed and moveable. Most of the least-expensive collectible dolls are made of this material. Stockinet was a combination of a sheer, stockinglike cloth that was soaked in a composition substance and then molded into the shape of a head. Stockinet dolls produced by Izannah Walker (patent 1873) have brought more than $15,000 at auc-

tached to a body of cloth or kid leather. Fashion dolls with both china and bisque heads remained popular well into the next century. They were produced in quantity by German manufacturers as well, although these non-French versions are usually called "china heads" or "shoulder heads." Fashion dolls by certain manufacturers from the 1870s and before now frequently bring in excess of $10,000 at auction. Basic German china head dolls can be found in nearly every antiques shop and usually sell for an average of $100 to $200, depending on size and condition.

In 1851, an award-winning display of dolls at the Great Exhibition in London received widespread attention. Among the dolls shown were several infant dolls, and in the months that followed "baby dolls" were in great demand. The head and extremities on most early versions were made of wax, with real hair and glass eyes. Bodies were made of cloth or leather.

10-4 Close-up of early fashion doll with individually attached human hairs. (Courtesy Jensen's Antiques)

tion. Some stockinet dolls, manufactured in greater quantities by Martha Chase starting in the late 1880s, can be purchased for under $500.

Among the most popular dolls of the Victorian era are those produced by Armand Marseille and J. D. Kestner of Germany. Marseille produced beautiful bisque-head dolls in a variety of styles and sizes from the 1880s into the twentieth century. Kestner began doll making in 1816, but most of the dolls bearing his name date from 1880 to the 1920s. His, too, had bisque heads with composition or kid-leather bodies. Kestner dolls range in size from four to forty-two inches in length.

Prices of Victorian period dolls on today's collectibles market are affected by a wide variety of factors.

Form—Whether baby, child, adult, male, female, character, and so forth, form is important.

Size—Dolls almost always increase in value as they increase in size.

Materials used—Various combinations were used for head, body, and limbs.

Style and condition of clothing—Original clothing in good condition adds considerably to the value of a doll.

Manufacturer—Many dolls are marked with the manufacturer's name or symbol at the base of the neck. Collectors should obtain one of the many books identifying manufacturers' marks and numbers.

Age—Marked dolls often can be accurately dated by the symbol or number. Other dolls must be dated by comparison to similar dolls with established dates. Collectors should use caution when buying unidentified dolls that appear to be old. Dolls of early style and construction have been produced throughout the twentieth century.

Condition—Most dolls with cracks, holes, missing pieces, and so forth are worth considerably less than near-mint examples. Dolls with stained or dirty faces can be cleaned; however,

this should be done only by an experienced professional.

Supply and demand—Dolls are an investment, and as such their value is susceptible to market fluctuations. Serious collectors should join one of the many doll-collecting clubs and subscribe to a doll-collecting magazine or newsletter to keep abreast of changing trends.

Price Ranges

All-composition dolls: $50 to $1000+. Average: $150 to $250.

Bisque-head and all-bisque dolls: $50 to $20,000+. Average: $175 to $325. This category is the largest in collectible dolls and therefore has an extremely wide range of prices, affected primarily by manufacturer and size.

China-head dolls: $100 to $5000+. Average: $275 to $325.

Composition-head dolls (no manufacturer's identification): $75 to $500+. Average: $175 to $200.

French fashion dolls: $500 to $10,000+. Average: $1200 to $1500.

Suggested Reading

Bach, Jean. *Collecting German Dolls.* New York: Carol Publishing Group, 1983.

Cieslik, Jurgen and Marianne Cieslik. *German Doll Encyclopedia.* Cumberland, Mich.: Hobby House Press, 1985.

Coleman, Dorothy. *Collector's Encyclopedia of Dolls,* vol 2. New York: Crown Publishers, 1986.

Foulke, Jan. *Blue Book Dolls and Values.* (Various volumes and editions.) Cumberland, Md.: Hobby House Press.

Herron, R. Lane. *Herron's Price Guide to Dolls.* Radnor, Pa.: Wallace-Homestead Book Company, 1990.

Knopf Collectors' Guides to American Antiques: Dolls. New York: Alfred A. Knopf, 1983.

Miller, Robert. *Wallace-Homestead Guide to Dolls.* Radnor, Pa.: Wallace-Homestead Book Company, 1986.

Roeder, Ronny. *Antique Dolls and Toys for Collectors.* International Specialities, 1985.

Marbles

Among the precious items found in a young Victorian boy's pocket, one might find a rabbit's foot, a jackknife, a hand-carved wooden whistle, a train-flattened penny, and his prized "shooter." The shooter is a marble chosen as the best of his collection, and would be used in the game of marbles that would inevitably occur sometime in his busy day. The game began by drawing a circle within which each boy would place a marble. The shooter was fired by flicking it with the thumb, with the purpose of knocking an opponent's piece out of the circle and thereby capturing it. If the game was particularly heated—and the boys daring enough—it might be suggested that they "play for shooters," and the young man's prized possession would be put at risk.

Today, we associate the word "marbles" with the familiar spheres of clear glass containing bits of color inside, still sold in toy stores. But when they were first introduced in Roman times, they actually were made of marble. During the Victorian era, marbles were made of wood, earthen-ware and other ceramics, steel, onyx, and, primarily, glazed clay. Glass marbles were imported from Germany where they were made by hand. Clear "sulfide" marbles containing clay figures of birds and other animals are highly prized by today's collectors. "Swirl" marbles, produced by melting colored glass rods into clear molten glass, are collected by pattern, each of which has been given a descriptive name (for example, Indian Swirl, Candy Swirl, Latticinio, Onion Swirl, and so forth).

The value of Victorian marbles is based on size, material, decorative pattern (if any), and condition. Minor scratches and nicks are expected, but obvious chips or cracks considerably lessen the value. Serious collectors should purchase one or more of the specialized guides on antique marbles to familiarize themselves with their appearance.

Price Ranges

Clay marbles: $1 to $25. Average: $5.
Steelies (steel marbles): $1 to $15.
Sulfides: $75 to $1000+. Average: $150.
Swirl marbles: $25 to $250+. Average: $45.

Suggested Reading

Baumann, Paul. *Collecting Antique Marbles*. Radnor, Pa.: Wallace-Homestead Book Company, 1991.
Grist, Everett. *Antique Marble Price Guide,* second ed. Paducah, Ky.: Collector Books, 1988.
Randall, Mark E., and Dennis Webb. *Greenberg's Guide to Marbles.* Greenberg Publishing Company, 1988.

10-5 Early marble with typical "swirl" pattern.

Perambulators

Although the custom was far more prevalent in England, it was not unusual, on a pleasant morning in any U.S. city, to see a number of women sitting on a park bench, gently rocking a fancy

10-6 An elaborate woven rattan baby carriage and a typical child's carriage. (Courtesy Amador County Museum)

baby carriage. Whether they were governesses, nannies, or young mothers, they met to discuss the weather and the latest fashions—and to show off their babies.

Essential to this morning perambulation (stroll) was an impressive carriage (also called a buggie or stroller) and these were produced in a large number of sizes and styles. Their frames were made of wood, rattan, or wrought iron; they were upholstered in silk or leather; and most included a hood or a parasol with ruffles, ribbons, and lace. A turn-of-the-century catalog describes their "very finest carriage" as follows:

> This carriage is without equal and is the finest manufactured today. The upholstery is extra quality silk damask with a satin back lining and silk cords and tassels. The reed work is the most artistic, fully shellacked and finished with a beautiful French roll at the top and sides, and a full French roll dash to correspond. It comes with the highest grade Walker gear, the finest steel axles

and springs, and the Kinley automatic brake. The parasol is of the finest quality silk satin, fully lined, and having three flounced ruffles and puffing.

> Our special price. $19.63
> Rubber Tires, 55 cents extra.

Carriages of this type usually wore well and saw use through several infants—with additional use by puppy dogs and dolls in between. This latter use could be avoided by purchasing "pretend mommies," a smaller version of the perambulator called a "doll carriage." These were also manufactured in a wide variety, some resembling the real thing, others incorporating the shapes of animals in their designs or in other ways decorated so as to appeal to youthful tastes.

Few of these early carriages have survived in good shape. Collectors watch for examples in near-mint condition or those that have been adeptly restored. Prices are based on size, complexity of design, materials used, age, manufacturer (if known), and condition. Highest prices are paid for quality wooden examples in the styles of the period (French or Renaissance Revival, Eastlake) and elaborate pieces with plush upholstery.

Price Ranges

Baby carriages: $250 to $1000+. Average: $350 to $400. Examples in average worn condition or worse are often found marked in this price range. In most cases, they are worth considerably less.

Doll carriages: $100 to $500+. Average: $150.

Rattles

Baby rattles were made of glass, ceramic, metal, and celluloid and ranged from simple bulbs with handles to elaborate toys incorporating whistles, bells, and other amusements. Most

173

10-7 An assortment of silver baby rattles with whistles and teething handles of pearl, ivory, and coral. (Courtesy Jensen's Antiques)

that survive in today's antiques market are either made with some amount of silver or other precious materials, or they are celluloid examples from around the turn of the century. Due to their endearing, emotional appeal, all items related to babies and motherhood are widely collected and therefore often difficult to locate.

Prices of Victorian baby rattles are based on material, complexity of design, condition, and emotional appeal. Both rare and common examples can be found in all styles and materials at a wide range of prices.

Price Range

Baby rattles: $20 to $1000+. Average celluloid rattle: $35. Average sterling silver rattle: $75 to $100.

Rocking Horses

The primary mode of transportation in the nineteenth century was the horse, and just as children today like to play with toy cars, Victorian children liked toy horses. The closest they could get to the real thing was the rocking horse.

Rocking horses have been around for many centuries. Even the gallant knights of medieval times rode and trained on large rocking horses in their youth. Those produced for children during the nineteenth century were often quite realistic and artistic. Many examples were carved from a single piece of wood, then hand painted in bright colors. Even mass-produced examples exhibit a certain quality of artisanship.

Some rocking horses were simply a carved horse's head attached to an open bentwood or iron-frame rocker; others had two one-dimensional horses on either side supporting an upholstered seat that hung in between. This latter version, called the "Shoofly," was intended for younger children who might fall from a straddled horse.

Elaborate rocking horses may have been covered entirely in ponyhide with a real horsehair mane and tail. In the latter part of the century "swinging rockers" were introduced. These sat on stationary platforms and rocked by means of springs and pivots.

Because most Victorian rocking horses were made of wood, and because they often received a high degree of use and abuse by their owners, few have survived in good condition. Protruding features such as ears, tails, legs, and rockers were easily broken, and surviving examples may have had these pieces repaired or replaced. Rocking horses with original features and reasonably well-preserved paint are prized by collectors of folk art or Country antiques, and they often bring premium prices.

Prices of Victorian rocking horses are based on size, materials, complexity of design and applied paint or adornments, manufacturer (if known), and condition.

Price Range

Rocking horses: $250 to $1000+. Average: $475. Repaired, repainted, or otherwise altered examples should sell for considerably less, although this is usually not the case.

Sleds

Winter: To Victorian adults it meant cold floors, heavy clothes, visits by the doctor, and a lot of mud to look forward to next spring. To Victorian children it meant snowmen, snowball fights, hot chocolate, and sled rides. Even before the first snow fell the trusty wooden vehicles were pulled down from the shed rafters or out from beneath the bed, and were dusted and waxed in preparation of the big event. Early versions had solid sides ending in bow-shaped runners, while later versions had bentwood or metal slats attached to the platform by supports. These platforms were painted with representations of animals or other figures, and bold letters spelling out names like "Go Devil," "Snow Flake," and "American Racer."

Like all wooden Victorian toys few sleds have survived in top condition, and those that have usually bring premium prices. Sleds with novel shapes or carved figureheads are prized by collectors, as are those with high-quality painted designs in mint or near-mint condition. Prices of Victorian sleds are based on size, complexity of design and painted or applied ornamentation, manufacturer (if known), and condition.

Price Range

Sleds: $125 to $1000+. Average: $275 to $325.

Repaired or repainted examples should sell for considerably less, although this is not always the case.

Toys

Generally speaking, toys from the early part of the Victorian era were one-of-a-kind, individually manufactured pieces. Most often they were made of wood, but as the century progressed more and more examples were made of metal or at least had some metal parts. A large number of toys were imported from Europe, especially Germany. Produced by the cottage industry, these toys were made by individual cabinetmakers and wood carvers in their homes or local shops and distributed to U.S. toy stores by German exporters. During the latter part of the century, tinplate toys from Germany took up a large portion of the U.S. toy market. (Made by covering a thin sheet of iron or steel with tin, Tinplate was used for a variety of mechanical and "visual" toys. See tin kitchens under the heading Doll Houses, this chapter.)

Victorian toys basically can be broken down into four categories: educational, mechanical, representative, and mobile. A particular toy may fit into one or more or even all of these categories.

Educational toys were meant to teach the child. The message presented by a particular toy may have been religious, scholarly, or even political. Some were designed to improve dexterity and mechanical skills. Perhaps the most common and recognized educational toys are alphabet blocks. These small wooden blocks have been produced in various forms since the 1600s. While building and stacking the child was became familiar with

10-8 A variety of miniature enamelware for children. (Courtesy Amador County Museum)

the shapes of the various letters of the alphabet painted on the sides of the blocks. Building blocks have also been popular for many centuries. Some Victorian sets were quite elaborate and architecturally accurate, and included columns, pedestals, and pediments. "Log cabin" sets were introduced in the mid–nineteenth century and are still popular today. Other educational toys included sewing, knitting, and weaving kits for girls; and woodworking, steam engine, and chemistry kits for boys.

Mechanical toys were produced in Egypt as early as 1000 B.C. The invention of the clock in the thirteenth century popularized the use of gear-driven mechanics, which after a number of improvements over the centuries, would become the basis for nineteenth-century mechanical tinplate toys. The first of these to be patented in the United States was a walking doll called Autoperipatetikos, introduced by E. R. Morrison in 1862 and produced in several styles by Martin and Runyon of New York. (Examples of these can now bring in more than $1500 on today's antique toy market.) The largest manufacturer of clockwork toys was Ives, Blakeslee, and Company of Bridgeport, Connecticut. Included among their large stock of mechanicals was a child on a swing, a dancing couple, a lady churning butter, a crawling baby, and various walking dolls (including one representing General B. F. Butler that is currently selling for $1000 to $2500, depending on condition).

Representative toys are usually miniaturized versions of people, places, and things found in the adult world—dolls and stuffed animals being the most popular among girls, and toy guns and toy soldiers among boys. (Of course many mechanical and mobile toys also fit into this category.) Stuffed toys were produced in the nineteenth century but few have survived. This type of toy was not made in quantity until the twentieth century, when it was popularized by the teddy bear, named for President Theodore Roosevelt. Rag dolls were quite popular throughout the Victorian era and both home-made and manufactured versions have survived, although usually not in very good condition. (Most commercially produced rag dolls found in today's antiques market date from the period following the introduction of Raggedy Ann and Andy in 1915.) Toy soldiers have been produced for centuries in a variety of materials, including wood, papier-maché, cardboard, ceramic, and metal. Again, most of the recognized examples and manufacturers date from the early twentieth century, and verifiable Victorian pieces are quite uncommon. Toy guns, mostly in carved wood or cast iron, were produced throughout the nineteenth century. Cast-iron cap pistols were introduced in the 1870s (primarily by J. and E. Stevens) and are today among the most popular of collectible toys. Especially sought after are pistols cast in highly ornamental shapes (animals, trains, Indians, and even racial or political figures).

Mobile toys included sleds, bicycles, carriages (see individual headings, this chapter) and a large variety of wheeled pieces. Miniaturized

10-9 Mechanical wind-up toy carriage in tinplate. (Courtesy Jensen's Antiques)

10-10 Figural cap pistols: anti-Chinese theme (left) and popular puppet characters Punch and Judy (right). (Courtesy Jensen's Antiques)

versions of Victorian carts, carriages, trains, circus wagons, military apparatus, fire equipment, and other vehicles were produced in wood, cast iron, tinplate, and other materials. Some were equipped with pull strings; others were spring driven; some simply needed a gentle (or not so gentle) shove to propel them across a floor. Victorian mobile toys are highly prized by collectors who look for examples in the best possible condition—especially examples with extensive original paint.

Prices of all Victorian period toys are greatly affected by the condition the pieces. Other factors include materials, complexity of design or mechanics, manufacturer (if known), and supply and demand. Various toys produced during the Victorian era have been manufactured in similar or identical forms well into the twentieth century, and many fakes and replicas abound. The existence of an original box or container adds considerably to a toy's value and helps to verify its date and origin.

Price Ranges

Alphabet blocks: $150 to $1000. Average: $250 to $300.

Building blocks: $75 to $500+. Average: $175 to $200.
Cap pistols: $75 to $1000+. Average: $150 to $200.
Clockwork toys: $500 to $5000+. Average: $1000.
Log cabin sets: $200 to $500+. Average: $250 to $300.
Miniature steam engines: $100 to $500+. Average: $200 to $250.
Pull toys: $75 to $5000+. Average: $400 to $500.
Toy soldiers: $15 to $100+ each. Average: $50 each. Prices in excess of $10,000 have been paid for complete sets of military miniatures used by actual military personnel in the planning of battles.

Suggested Reading

Most of the books listed below cover all of the items listed in this chapter.

Bagdade, Susan and Al Bagdade. *Collector's Guide to American Toy Trains.* Radnor, Pa.: Wallace-Homestead Book Company, 1989.

Fintel, Fred and Marilyn Fintel. *Yesterday's Toys with Today's Prices.* Radnor, Pa.: Wallace-Homestead Book Company, 1985.

Gardiner and Morris. *Illustrated Encyclopedia of Metal Toys.* New York: Harmony Books, 1984.

Longest, David. *Character Toys and Collectibles.* Paducah, Ky.: Collector Books, 1985; 2nd ed. 1987.

O'Brian, Richard. *Collecting Toys.* Florence, Ala.: Books Americana, 1985.

Rinker, Harry L. *Collector's Guide to Toys, Games, and Puzzles.* Radnor, Pa.: Wallace-Homestead Book Company, 1990.

Whitton, Blair. *American Clockwork Toys.* West Chester, Pa.: Schiffer Publishing, 1981.

———. *Knopf Collectors' Guides to American Antiques: Toys.* 1984. New York: Alfred A. Knopf.

Wagons

Most toy wagons produced during the nineteenth century were made of wood; some even had wooden axles and wheels. The first metal

wagons were made in cast iron, and painted tin wagons of the familiar modern style came along just prior to the turn of the century. All toy wagons of the Victorian period are prized by toy collectors, who look for examples in the best possible condition and with original paint.

Other factors affecting price include size, style, materials used, manufacturer, and decorations (if any).

Price Ranges

Toy wagons: $125 to $1000+. Average: $225.

10-11 A nineteenth-century photograph shows a young boy and his wooden wagon with large spoked wheels.

CHAPTER 11

Miscellaneous Victorian Collectibles

Advertising

While the Victorians were blessed with not having to listen to an endless stream of radio and television ads, they did receive their share of promotional influences. These often took the form of functional "giveaways"—items such as ashtrays, pencils, ink pens and blotters, storage bins, doorstops, coin banks, bookmarks, calendars, clocks, fans, pocket mirrors, paperweights, tape measures, and shoe horns. Most general stores had windows filled with a variety of metal or cardboard signs touting the various brand name products they carried. Screen doors were often painted in the package colors of a bread, cigarette, or soda company, the company name colorfully printed on the door push. While newspapers of the Victorian era did not rely heavily on advertising profits, a small advertising section usually was included on the last two or three pages. Printed advertisements most often took the form of giveaway almanacs, handbills posted on walls and fences, or colorful "trade cards" handed out in stores.

Today's advertising collector looks for anything—signs, cards, trays, clocks, poster, or tins—that has the name of a product or service imprinted on its surface. Condition is of primary

11-1 Magazine ad (circa 1880s) for Macy's department store.

179

11-2 Small pocket mirror with advertising on back.

importance, with mint or near-mint examples often bringing premium prices. Other factors in determining value include type of item; size, shape, and purpose; materials; age; manufacturer or imprint; and supply and demand.

Price Ranges

Calendar: $35 to $250. Average: $75.
Door push: $25 to $150+. Average: $45 to $50.
Ink blotter: $10 to $50. Average: $25.
Pocket mirror: $15 to $100+. Average: $45.
Sign: $50 to $5000+. Average: $150 to $225.
Tins: see Chapter 4, The Kitchen, and Store-Related Items, this chapter.
Trade cards: $2 to $50+. Average: $10.

Suggested Reading

Klug, Ray. *Antique Advertising Encyclopedia,* vol. 2. West Chester, Pa.: Schiffer Publishing, 1988.
Kovel, Ralph and Terry Kovel. *Kovel's Advertising Collectibles Price List.* New York: Crown Publishers, 1986.
See also Suggested Reading under Store-Related Items, this chapter.

Architectural Antiques

A variety of items that were once part of Victorian houses, business establishments, and other structures are now sold on the antiques market. Most of these items will be used in restorations or

11-3 Fancy brass doorknob and keyhole. (Courtesy McHenry Mansion)

neo-Victorian buildings; others will be used simply as decorative or conversation pieces. Such pieces include stained-glass windows, fireplace mantels, street lights and lampposts, hitching posts, bathtubs, post office boxes, doorknobs, door hinges, door knockers, and weather vanes, among others. Made mostly of metal, these items have usually survived in good condition or can be easily restored. While it is sad that their original locations could not be preserved and protected, it is fortuitous that these items have been spared to be used and appreciated again.

Doorknobs, door knockers, and door hinges were produced primarily in brass and often had elaborate embossed or engraved ornamentation. Doorknobs also often were inset or inlaid with ivory, bone, celluloid, crystal, porcelain, or enameled metal. Ornate Victorian doorknobs are a collectible specialty, with collectors searching for unusual examples in top condition.

Weather vanes are also a collectible specialty. They were produced in wood, brass, copper, cast iron, and tin, shaped into the silhouettes of farm animals (frequently roosters) or some sort of ornate arrow. When the wind caught its flat surface, the ornament rotated on a pivot so that the object faced the wind, indicating the direction of its source. Collectors look for unusual shapes and styles and are attracted by the colorful patina and oxides that form on the vanes as a result of weathering.

Price Ranges

Bathtubs: $75 to $1000+.

Door hinges (ornate): $15 to $1500+ set. Average: $50 to $75. per set. Prices in excess of $5000 have been paid for a pair of hinges from a famous building or house.

Door knobs: $10 to $500+. Average: $35.

Door knockers: $25 to $1000+. Average: $65 to $75.

Lampposts: $35 to $1000+.

Post office boxes: $150 to $1500+. Average four-to-six-box set: $200.

Weather vanes: $25 to $5000+. Average: $250 to $300.

Suggested Reading

Eastwood, Maud. *The Antique Doorknob.* Self-published, 1976.

Robertson, Alan. *Architectural Antiques.* San Francisco: Chronicle Books, 1987.

Robertson, Graeme. *Castiron Decoration.* New York: Whitney Library of Design, 1977.

Cameras

It is interesting to note that cameras were in use long before the invention of photography. A type of camera was used in 1544 to view the solar eclipse, and a large projection box called the "camera obscura" was used by artists in the seventeenth and eighteenth centuries. Scientists were experimenting with this type of camera, basically just a box with a lens attached, when they discovered the photographic process in the early nineteenth century.

11-4 Eastman view camera and tripod, circa 1890s.

The two earliest commercially produced photographic cameras were designed to take daguerreotypes (on silver-coated copper plates) and calotypes (on salted paper). These cameras are now quite rare and can sell for in excess of $100,-000. Wet-plate cameras dating from the late 1850s until the turn of the century are also highly sought and seldom bring in less than $1500.

The introduction of dry plates and gelatin films in the 1880s brought photography into the hands of the general public, and cameras were mass produced in a large variety of configurations, from simple to elaborate. The two general types of collectible cameras from this period are view cameras and the smaller box-type cameras. George Eastman introduced the Kodak in 1888, and over the next two decades he produced over fifty variants and improved examples.

Cameras made before 1900 are not difficult to find but usually bring higher prices than their early-twentieth-century equivalents. Collectors are cautioned that patent dates, usually marked somewhere on the camera body, are not an accurate dating method since the camera was probably manufactured for many years after it was patented. Serious collectors should invest in one or more of the camera catalogs that show the various models and their dates of production. Prices are based on style, size, manufacturer, and especially condition.

Price Ranges

Other box cameras: $10 to $100+. Average: $25.
Pre-1900 Kodaks: $25–1000+. Average: $125. Certain examples bring in more than $5000.
View cameras: $50 to $500+. Average: $250.
Wet-plate cameras: $1500–5000+. Average: $2200.

Suggested Reading

McKeown, Jim, and Joan McKeown. *Price Guide to Antique and Classic Still Cameras,* seventh ed. Self-published, 1989.
Schneider, Jason. *Camera Collecting,* vol. 2. Radnor, Pa.: Wallace-Homestead Book Company, 1985.

Wolf, Myron. *Blue Book Illustrated Price Guide to Collectible and Useable Cameras.* Lexington, Mass.: Photographic Memorabilia, published annually.

Civil War Artifacts

From 1861 to 1865, the United States fought its bloodiest war. It has been variously called the War Between the States, the War for the Union, the War of Rebellion, and, most commonly, the Civil War. Even though the war began a third of the way into the Victorian era, one seldom sees the terms "Victorian" and "Civil War" in the same sentence. The word "Victorian" has become synonymous with romance, charm, style, and good times. The Civil War had few of these qualities. Even so, artifacts associated with the war are from the Victorian period and are prized historical collectibles.

Probably the smallest and most abundant Civil War collectibles are bullets. The well-equipped Union soldier was given a measured amount of ammunition (commonly .58 caliber minie ball lead bullets enclosed in a paper wrap containing explosive powder). The soldier filled his ammunitions box with these, placed a few backups in his

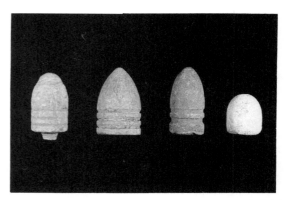

11-5 Selection of bullets from a Civil War battlefield shows the variety of ammunition types used by both sides.

pocket, and stored the rest in his knapsack or bedroll. Loaded down with his gun, bayonet, ammunitions box, bedroll, knapsack, mess gear, and personal items, the average foot soldier carried over forty-five pounds into the field. When the weight became too much, the heaviest item—the excess ammunition—was dumped. It can only be speculated that the soldier assumed he would be able to get more ammunition when the need arose. In any case, this accounts for the large number of unfired bullets located with metal detectors in and around large battlefields. These bullets usually sell for around $3 to $5 each in antiques and military shops. The grey-white oxide on the surface of these artifacts is desirable and should not be cleaned or polished away.

Probably the second most common Civil War collectibles are belts and buckles. Union buckles are fairly common and comparatively low in price ($25 to $75). Confederate buckles are prized by collectors and can bring more than $1000 each. Original belts add considerably to the value. Collectors are cautioned that Civil War buckles have been widely reproduced and fakes abound.

Other collectible accoutrements include cartridge belts and boxes, cap boxes (designed to hold the explosive caps required by percussion

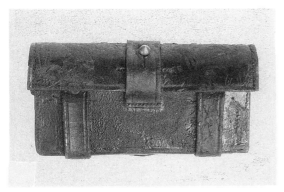

11-6 Civil War period cartridge box with embossed decorations.

firearms), bayonet scabbards, haversacks, and various specialized pouches.

Civil War weapons are varied and numerous. New soldiers frequently carried their personal hunting rifles or sidearms. Confederate forces used whatever weapons they could get their hands on. The official arms for the Union generally were the .58-caliber rifle-musket (produced primarily by government armories in Springfield, Massachusetts, and Harper's Ferry, Virginia); the .52-caliber carbine (produced by private gunmakers—primarily Henry, Sharps, and Spencer); the .36-caliber Colt Navy revolver; and the .44-caliber Remington army revolver. The collector should have no trouble locating any of the above in good condition and at a reasonable price. Serious gun collectors should purchase one or more of the extensive guides to antique weapons to familiarize themselves with the wide variety of types and manufacturers. (See also Guns and Weapons in Chapter 7, The Library)

Other items relating to the Civil War are generally quite uncommon and are becoming increasingly so as time passes. Many items are properly finding their way into museums, and battlefield parks are strongly enforcing relic-hunting restrictions. Anyone who discovers an important Civil War artifact at an estate sale or flea market is lucky indeed. The collector generally must deal with long-established dealers who, in most cases, can name their own price.

Prices of Civil War artifacts and relics are based on type of item, materials, identification of user or military unit, condition, and, primarily, supply and demand factors. Collectors are cautioned that highly accurate replicas of Civil War artifacts have been produced continuously throughout the twentieth century. Large quantities of uniforms, weapons, and accoutrements were manufactured for use in Civil War films— sometimes as early as 1915. These would, of course, exhibit the apparent age and wear of authentic examples. Before paying a large amount of money for a Civil War artifact, be sure of the seller and, if possible, have the piece authenticated by an expert.

Price Ranges

Belt and buckle (Confederate): $150 to $2500+. Highest prices are paid for officers' "wreath" buckles.

Belt and buckle (Union): $50 to $500+. Highest prices are paid for officers' "eagle" buckles.

Cartridge pouch (United States): $75 to $500+. Average: $250.

Sword (United States officer): $125 to $500+. Average: $225.

Uniform (United States): $350 to $1000+. Average: $500 to $600.

Weapons: See Chapter 7, Guns and Weapons.

Suggested Reading

Elting, John R., ed. *Military Uniforms in America: Long Endure, The Civil War Period 1852–1867.* Company of Military Historians. Novato, Calif.: Presidio Press, 1976.

Hogg, Ivan V. *Weapons of the Civil War.* New York: Crown Publishers, 1987.

Lord, Francis. *Civil War Collector's Encyclopedia.* Memphis: Castle Books, 1965 (out of print).

Schuyler, Hartley and Graham. *Illustrated Catalog of Civil War Military Goods.* New York: Dover Publications, 1985.

Coin-Operated Machines

Although coin-operated vending apparatus have been around for centuries, vending machines and coin-operated amusements became common only in the late nineteenth century. Among the first of these was a viewing device that simulated the action of motion pictures by flipping rapidly through a sequence of individual scenes. The phenakistoscope, as it was called, was the forerunner of the motion picture, first shown in another coin-operated viewer designed by Thomas Edison.

Edison's Kinetoscope was introduced in New York City in 1894. A loop of 35mm positive film was exposed in a rapid exposure camera at the rate of sixteen or more frames per second. The developed film, viewed in the Kinetoscope at exactly the same speed, showed the subject in true-to-life action. Improvements were made by numerous other manufacturers, and the motion picture business was born.

Called "peep shows" because they often showed scantily clad dancers, Kinetoscopes and phenakistoscopes formed the basis for the penny arcades popular from the turn of the century. These arcades also included player pianos, coin-operated music boxes and calliopes, and a variety of machines dispensing everything from chocolate and cigars to fortunes.

Coin-operated machines that can positively be dated to the period prior to 1900 are rare and extremely valuable. Prices are based on size and function, age, manufacturer, and condition.

Price Range

Coin-operated machines: $1000 to $10,000+. Average: $3500.

Suggested Reading

Ayliffe, Jerry. *American Premium Guide to Jukeboxes and Slot Machines, Gumballs, Trade Stimulators, Arcade.* Florence, Ala.: Books Americana Inc., 1985.

Costa, Nicholas. *Automatic Pleasures: The History of the Coin Machine.* Cincinnati: Seven Hills, 1988.

Holiday-Related Items

Many of the customs related to Christmas and other holidays were traditionalized during Victorian times, although their roots are much deeper and more ancient. Prince Albert brought the tradition of the Christmas tree from Germany to Britain with his marriage to Victoria. American artists such as Thomas Nast helped to keep alive the traditional Santa Claus through their wonderful Christmas prints in *Leslie's, Harper's,* and

11-7 Victorian folding "pop-up" valentine.

Godey's magazines. The elflike Father Christmas took form in little figures of wood, ceramic, or papier-mâché called *Belsnikles.*

Christmas trees were decked with a variety of manufactured or homemade ornaments. Wonderful little carved miniatures of rocking horses, toy soldiers, and other toys were imported from the German cottage-trade woodworkers. European and American glass and ceramic factories turned out a variety of ornaments ranging from simple glass balls to elaborate hand-painted ceramic houses and scenes. A variety of ornaments were made of lead, cast iron, silver, and other metals as well. The first electric lights were used on Victorian Christmas trees in the 1880s. Inter-

estingly, trees previously were lit with burning candles—in a time when fire was the biggest destroyer of homes and even of entire towns. Clip-on candle holders provided some degree of protection, but often the decorator simply set the candle in wax dripped from the candle onto the end of a branch.

The color-printing process called chromolithography provided hundreds of cheap ornaments and decorations, not only for Christmas, but for Easter, New Year's, and, especially, Valentine's Day. Although the sending of greeting cards is pretty much a Victorian idea, the custom of exchanging valentines dates back to Roman times, when it was actually a form of lottery used in determining a mate. The church, unable to extirpate this pagan ceremony, changed its form: on February 14 unmarried church members of both sexes would place in a bowl anonymous notes of affection to selected members of the opposite sex—the fun was in trying to determine the identity of the unknown valentine. The valentine tradition developed into its present form during Victorian times, and card printers such as Howland, Whitney, Meek, and Ward produced hundreds of thousands of cards throughout the latter part of the century. Today's collector looks for elaborate versions with lace trimwork, colorful embossed scenes, or die-cut stand-ups.

Prices of holiday-related items are based on novelty or complexity of design, size, purpose, materials, age, manufacturer (if known), and condition. The collector is cautioned that Victorian-style Christmas cards and ornaments, as well as valentines, have been reproduced throughout the twentieth century.

Price Ranges

Celluloid Christmas ornaments: $25 to $100+. Average: $35

Chromolithographic Christmas ornaments: $10 to $150+. Average: $20 to $25.

Glass or ceramic Christmas ornaments: $30 to $500+. Average: $45. Highest prices paid for rare glass or ceramic forms and those with imprints of quality manufacturers.

Valentines: $3 to $100+. Average: $8 to $10. Prices in excess of $500 have been paid for certain rare and elaborate examples.

Suggested Reading

Brenner, Robert. *Christmas Past.* West Chester, Pa.: Schiffer Publishing, 1986.

Johnson, George. *Christmas Ornaments and Decorations.* Paducah, Ky.: Collector Books, 1986.

Kersch, Francine. *Christmas Collectibles.* Radnor, Pa.: Wallace-Homestead Book Company, 1985.

Schiffer, Margaret. *Holiday Toys and Decorations.* West Chester, Pa.: Schiffer Publishing, 1985.

Medical, Dental, and Apothecary Items

Although there were constant improvements throughout the century, Victorian medicine often verged on barbarism. Until late in the century the two primary methods of treating internal ills were bleeding and voiding. It was thought that by removing poisoned blood or stomach and bowel contents, the patient could be cured. Few were. Those who survived did so purely out of a will to live, for the treatment often was far more devastating to the patient's health than the illness. Civil War physicians often used mercury and laudanum (an addictive opiate) as general treatment for a variety of ills. Fortunately, one of the drugs used, quinine, did help to save the lives of many soldiers struck with malaria.

Alcohol in one form or another was used both as an anesthetic (local and general) and an antiseptic. Chloroform began to see wider acceptance after Queen Victoria allowed herself to be anesthetized during the birth of her seventh child in 1853. Ether was first used as a general anesthesia by a surgeon in 1842 and later by a dentist in 1846. Both anesthetics required the use of ex-

11-8 Alligator skin doctor's bag, circa 1870s. (Courtesy Amador County Museum)

treme caution in their administration, as they are highly volatile and flammable and it is easy to give an overdose. To avoid its inhalation by others in the room, a measured amount of the liquid was dropped onto a piece of cloth inside a brass or silver mask, then quickly placed over the patient's mouth and nose.

Patent medicines and quack treatments were advertised and sold without regulation of any sort. Medicine shows frequented small towns, especially in the West, dispensing concocted potions made up primarily of cheap whiskey. Catalogs contained large sections advertising tobacco and liquor cures, obesity powders, nerve and brain pills, arsenic complexion wafers, breast developers, hair restorers, and a variety of cure-all tonics. One of the most common quack cures was the battery-powered electric belt, which delivered a constant low-voltage electric shock to the back, stomach, and sexual organs. A turn of the century ad says this device will "promote digestion, relieve constipation, tone up the liver, cure impotency, and even arrest that terrible disease, cancer of the stomach." The device "can be worn by women (without the suspensory attachment), and is invaluable for all cases of female weakness peculiar to their sex."

Early medical and dental tools were often quite ornate, with mother-of-pearl or ivory handles and

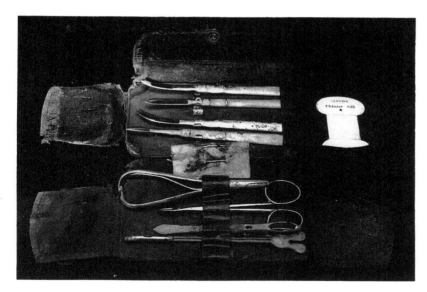

11-9 Doctor's portable tool kit includes several types of scalpels, forceps, needles and thread. (Courtesy Amador County Museum)

silver or gold plate. (One can only assume that the owner hoped to impress his patients by his good taste if not his ability.) Surgeon's kits contained a variety of knives, probes, forceps, and, of course, a drill and a saw. His bag would contain a stethoscope, several syringe and needle combinations, and a variety of medicine bottles. On drugstore shelves and in the doctor's office, quantities of medicines and powders were kept in large apothecary jars and tins. Medicine bottles and jars can be found in the familiar blue or amber glass of the period and are often embossed with the name of the medicine or patent elixir they contained. Drugstore tins come in a variety of shapes and sizes and are usually printed with a colorful scenic or descriptive label.

In many towns dentistry was performed by the town barber. For his purposes, all that was really needed was a pair of strong pliers, some whiskey, and some clove oil. Treatment began with applications of the latter two, and usually terminated within a few days with the use of the former. Early dental drills operated by a foot-action pump and were little better than attacking the tooth with a pick and hammer. The advent of

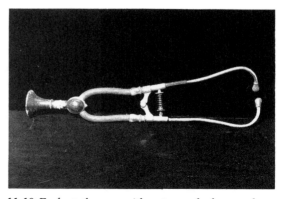

11-10 Early stethoscope with gutta percha horn and earpieces. (Courtesy Amador County Museum)

electrical power late in the century improved this device considerably.

On today's collectibles market, all items relating to the early years of medicine are in high demand. Prices are determined by type and purpose of item, complexity of design or decoration, age, manufacturer (if known), condition, and supply and demand. Serious collectors should purchase one or more of the extensive books on the subject to familiarize themselves with the styles and manufacturers of Victorian medical and apothecary items.

Price Ranges

Apothecary jars (with labels or identification): $65 to $500+. Average: $175 to $250. Highest prices are paid for ornately decorated examples.

Bleeding vessels or cups: $50 to $500. Average: $75 to $100. Highest prices are paid for elaborate silver or silver-plated examples.

Dental cabinets: $250 to $2500+. Average: $1500. Prices are affected by quality of wood and design, size, and number of drawers.

Dentist drills (foot pedal operated): $75 to $500+. Average: $175 to $250.

Drug store tins: $5 to $1000+. Average: $10 to $35. Prices are greatly affected by supply and demand.

Doctors' bags (empty): $35 to $150+. Condition is of primary importance.

Electric belts: $150 to $500. Average: $250 to $275.

Ether masks: $50 to $250. Average: $75 to $100.

Medical or dental tool sets: $350 to $1000+. Average: $500. Highest prices are paid for sets with fancy handles and complete sets in fitted compartments.

Medicine bottles (with patented brands or other identification): $10 to $500+. Average: $35.

Suggested Reading

Baldwin, Joseph K. *Collector's Guide to Patent and Proprietary Medicine Bottles of the 19th Century.* Nashville: Thomas Nelson Publishing, 1973.

Bennion, Elisabeth. *Antique Dental instruments.* New York: Sotheby Publications, 1986.

Bergevin, Al. *Drug Store Tins and Their Prices.* Radnor, Pa.: Wallace-Homestead Book Company, 1990.

Carter, William. *Catalog of Dental Collectibles.* Bethany, Okla.: Dental Folklore, 1984.

Fredgant, Don. *Medical, Dental, and Pharmaceutical Collectibles.* Florence, Ala.: Books Americana, 1981.

Wilbur, Keith. *Antique Medical Instruments.* West Chester, Pa.: Schiffer Publishing, 1987.

Nautical Items

In the Victorian era intercontinental transportation was by ship. The first steam-powered vessel crossed the Atlantic Ocean in 1818, and by 1840 there were a number of large steamships making scheduled crossings. The *Great Western,* fastest of the trans-Atlantic steamers, would make the trip from Bristol, England, to New York in slightly over sixteen days. By the turn of the century the trip would take less than a week.

Life aboard ship was uncomfortable and generally unpleasant. The primary purpose of marine vessels was to transport goods or protect the coastal waters. The comfort of passengers and crew was secondary. To stay on schedule or beat a record, ships' captains often pressed their crews beyond endurance. Those who did not desert often became alcoholics or, even worse, mutineers and pirates.

Despite the hardships, the many who sailed the seas were proud of and dedicated to their chosen profession. The romance and lure of the sea, generally propagated by writers who had never set foot on a gangplank, brought many a young man in search of employment in the ports of New York, Boston, and San Francisco. If he could get used to the sailor's life, he would see far-off lands about which others could only dream. He would learn to use the compass and sextant to chart the ship's course, and he would scan the horizon with a heavy spyglass or brass telescope. (Spyglasses are small telescopes, usually single-draw, where larger telescopes may draw as many as six to eight sections extending five or more feet in length. Telescopes are found with a variety of coverings ranging from cardboard and rope to brass and silver.) In his spare time, the sailor might learn macrame (the art of making decorative and functional items from knotted rope) or scrimshaw (artistic carving of ivory or whalebone). He would keep his personal items in a sea chest and a small, ornate ditty box.

Today the mystery of the sea still calls to many, and some relive the golden years of sailing by collecting the various artifacts associated with that period. In addition to the items mentioned previously, they search for log books, bell clocks, speaking trumpets, harpoons, maps, whistles, and a variety of instruments and furniture associated with ships and navigation.

Prices of nautical antiques and collectibles are based on design and purpose, materials, complexity of decoration (if any), manufacturer (if known), age, and condition. Serious collectors should obtain one or more of the many guides to historical nautical items to familiarize themselves with the appearance and function of such items produced and used during the Victorian era.

Price Ranges

Compasses: $75 to $500+. Average: $250. Highest prices are paid for large examples with fitted wooden boxes.

Ditty boxes: $100 to $1500+. Average: $175 to $200. Highest prices are paid for highly decorated or inlaid pieces.

Sea chests: $100 to $5000+. Average: $175 to $250.

Sextants: $250 to $1000+. Average: $450 to $500.

Ship's wheels: $500 to $2500+. Average: $900 to $1000. Highest prices are paid for wheels positively identified as belonging to a specific ship.

Ship's whistles: $100 to $1500+. Average: $600 to $750. Prices are based primarily on complexity of design, age, and manufacturer.

Telescopes and spyglasses: $75 to $5000+. Average: $250.

Suggested Reading

Major, Alan P. *Maritime Antiques*. San Diego: A.S. Barnes and Company, 1981.

Randier, Jean. *Nautical Antiques*. New York: Doubleday and Company, 1977.

11-11 Fireman's speaking horn from a Victorian catalog.

Police and Firefighting Artifacts

In the United States the provisions for the repression of crime and the detection and arrest of criminals were copied from those of Great Britain. Each county had a sheriff and deputies and, where there were town organizations, there were town constables. Justices of the peace, of whom there were a considerable number in each county, were elected by the people of the town or county and had absolute jurisdiction in petty civil and criminal cases. In 1857 the municipal legislature of New York passed an act establishing a metropolitan police force, which was quickly copied by other large cities such as Philadelphia, Boston, and New Orleans. In 1860 the average annual salary for a New York foot patrolman was $800, or about $15 per week. Policemen in the United States, unlike their British counterparts, were equipped with pistols in addition to the standard night stick and whistle. They wore standardized blue uniforms and a badge designating their city, district, rank, and identification number.

Informal fire departments were organized as soon as a town became big enough to provide volunteers. Even well-organized "bucket brigades" seldom won out over an established blaze, and most towns, with or without fire departments, were completely or partially destroyed by fire at some time during the nineteenth century. The standard firefighting equipment for modernized fire departments was the fire engine—horse-drawn wagons carrying some sort of water pump. Early versions were human powered; later versions used steam engines to propel the water through a "water cannon," or canvas hose fitted with a brass nozzle. The cone shape of this nozzle resulted in a marked increase in water pressure, allowing the firemen to spray water on the fire from a safe distance.

Speaking trumpets, an early form of loudspeaker, allowed the fire chief to shout directions to his crew over the roar of the fire. Most surviving trumpets are presentation pieces, given as awards for heroism or long-term service. These are, therefore, one-of-a-kind examples that often bring premium prices.

Items related to nineteenth-century law enforcement and firefighting hold a strong fascination for many modern-day collectors. Badges alone represent one of the most popular collectible items on the market. Prices of police and firefighting collectibles are based on design and purpose of item, materials, size, age, manufacturer (if known), city or department identification, condition, and supply and demand.

Price Ranges

Badges: $25 to $500+. Average: $50 to $75. Prices are greatly affected by supply and demand.
Brass fire hose nozzles: $45 to $250. Average: $75.
Speaking trumpets: $300 to $1500+. Average: $1200.

Suggested Reading

Piatti, Mary Jane, and James Piatti. *Firehouse Collectibles.* Engine House, 1979.
Virgines, George E. *Police Relics.* Paducah, Ky.: Collector Books, 1982.

11-12 Typical railroad lantern. (Courtesy Williams Antiques)

Railroad Artifacts

The first steam-powered wagon was patented in 1782 by Oliver Evans of Philadelphia, and carts were designed to run on wooden rails long before that. But the steam train as we know it was not introduced in the United States until 1829, when it connected the cities of Charleston and Hamburg in South Carolina. The first major railroad was the Baltimore and Ohio, which commenced operation in 1830 and transported over eighty-thousand passengers during its first full year of operation. By 1840 there were 1,843 miles of railroad in the United States; by 1860 there were over thirty-thousand miles of track.

The vast network of railways in the North was instrumental in the victory of Union forces in the Civil War and the exploration and development of the West. The idea of connecting the full width of the United States by rail was seriously considered as early as the 1830s, but the dream was not realized until May 10, 1869, when the east and west links were combined with the driving of a final spike in Promontory, Utah. During the last half of the century, railroads were a primary factor in the growth and industrialization of the United States, as they not only transported passengers and freight but also ideas and technology as well. Railways provided a pathway and repair service for the telegraph, and carried mail and newspapers to a people once starved for information.

It is a sad fact that today's railroads are quickly dying out. Collectors are for this reason quickly snatching up anything related to those early years. Across the United States there are several organizations for railroad enthusiasts dedicated to preserving the history and dignity of the locomotive and its associated elements. Collectors are interested in old ticket stubs, engineer and conductor hats and badges, lanterns, watches, and the variety of imprinted tableware used in their often-luxurious dining cars.

Prices of railroad collectibles are based on style and purpose of object; materials; manufacturer; imprint, identification, or line; condition; and supply and demand.

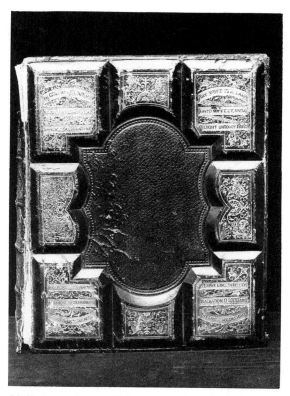

11-13 Large family Bible with deeply embossed papier-mâché cover.

Joyce, James. *Railroad Spikes: A Collector's Guide.* Lititz, Pa.: Sutter House, 1985.

Price Ranges

Hat and badge combination: $50 to $500+. Average: $125.
Lantern: $50 to $500+. Average: $200 to $250.
Railroad plates: $35 to $1000+. Average: $65 to $125. Prices of plates and other dinnerware are greatly affected by supply and demand.

Suggested Reading

Baker, Stanley. *Railroad Collectibles.* Paducah, Ky.: Collector Books, 1985.

Religious Items

It is obvious, upon studying the diaries, letters, and autograph albums of the period, that the Victorians generally had a strong belief in God, heaven, and the afterlife. While they were not necessarily devoutly religious, there generally were few agnostics and atheists in nineteenth-century America. In a time when one out of ten women did not survive childbirth; when children often did not make it to their teenage years; and when men seldom made it to retirement age—there was great comfort in the thought that a better place lay beyond death's door.

Freedom of religion was and is one of the building blocks of American liberty. In the nineteenth century there was scarcely a church or religious sect without representation. The primary churches were Congregationalist, Unitarian, Presbyterian, Episcopalian, Methodist, Universalist, Roman Catholic, Calvinist, and Lutheran. Hebrew synagogues also dotted the landscape. During the final third of the century the largest group, made up primarily of working-class people, was Baptist.

There are generally two categories of religious antiques: personal items such as Bibles, rosaries, prayer books, mezuzoth, Seder plates and trays, and hymnals; and church artifacts such as crucifixes, icons, altars, reliquaries, Torah finials and pointers, and shofars. There is some controversy as to whether items in the latter category should be sold to the general public or be returned to an appropriate church, synagogue, or religious museum.

Prices of religious artifacts and collectibles are based on style and purpose, materials, complexity of design or decoration, age, affiliation (if known), and condition.

Price Ranges

Family Bibles: $15 to $150+. Average: $35 to $50. Highest prices are paid for large, highly decorated examples with extensive geneology or photo album pages.

Icons: $350 to $2000+. Average: $750 to $850.

Mezuzoth (reprints produced in the nineteenth century): $500 to $1000+. Average: $750.

Prayer books: $15 to $100+. Average: $25 to $30. Highest prices are paid for examples with mother-of-pearl or carved ivory covers.

Seder plates and trays: $500 to $2500+. Average: $1000 to $1200.

Torah finials and pointers: $500 to $5000+.

11-14 Typical nineteenth-century wooden card file.

Store-Related Items

In small towns or big cities, there was almost always a general store nearby that could provide you with all the necessities, and even a few luxuries. The store owner was very likely the clerk, cashier, accountant, and janitor, although other family members might have helped. Because of the wide variety of merchandise they carried, most general stores were very neat and organized. Once again, that Victorian axiom "A place for everything, and everything in its place" was put to use.

A variety of wonderful wood-and-glass cabinets and bins held groceries, candy and gum, sewing notions, tools, seeds, and hardware. The thread or spool cabinets are extremely popular with today's collectors, as they have a number of shallow drawers that are convenient for storing spools or other small collectibles. Seed and hardware cabinets often contain large numbers of drawers in a variety of sizes and configurations. Nut and candy bins have framed glass lids or fitted glass jars. Most of this cabinetry was made of durable, high-quality woods, and cabinets have survived in excellent condition. Attached labels and advertisements, if in good condition, add considerably to the value of a store display or cabinet. Other factors affecting prices of store

11-15 Rolling Record cash register.

cabinets and bins include size, purpose, number of compartments, construction materials, complexity of adornments or decoration (if any), and condition.

Several devices were available to the store owner to keep track of the day's receipts. A register provided a secure drawer for cash and coin, a receipt for the customer, and a record of sales that could be matched with the money in the till at the end of the day. One of the earliest registers was the "Rolling Recorder," basically a long wooden box that contained a cash drawer, a long roll of paper stretched between two spools, and a bell. The amount of a sale was written on the paper through a small slot in the top of the box. When the money drawer was opened, the bell rang and the paper advanced to a clean area, ready for the next sale.

The familiar crank-style cash registers were produced from the 1890s well into the twentieth century, primarily by National Cash Register (NCR). (Today NCR produces multiterminal computerized systems for many of the world's major department store chains.) Because of their ornate brass, copper, and nickel adornments, these early registers are widely collected as decorative antiques. Cash register prices are based on size, style, construction materials, manufacturer,

type and complexity of decorations, condition, and supply and demand.

Price Ranges

Gum and candy counter cabinets: $50 to $300+.
Hardware, candy, or seed bins: $150 to $1000+. Average: $450 to $500. Prices depend on size and number of bins.
Ornate cash registers (pre-1900): $500 to $5000+. Average: $800 to $1000.
Rolling Recorder type registers: $35 to $250+. Average: $100.
Spool cabinets: $75 to $500+. Average: $150 to $175. Primary price factors are size and condition.
Wooden card files: $25 to $100 (single or double); $75 to $500+ (larger sizes).
Wooden file cabinets: $125 to $500+. Average: $225 to $250.

Suggested Reading

Congdon-Martin, Douglas. *Country Store Collectibles.* West Chester, Pa.: Schiffer Publishing, 1990.
Hothem, Larry. *Country Store Antiques.* Florence, Ala.: Books Americana, 1982.

Telephones, Telegraphs, and Electrical Items

With apologies to conventional U.S. history, Samuel Morse did not invent the telegraph, and Alexander Graham Bell did not invent the telephone. What these two brilliant scientists did do was to make considerable improvements upon established ideas, resulting in the first practical and commercially viable communications apparatus.

The first practical telegraph began operation between Washington, D.C., and Baltimore on May 27, 1844. By 1860 there were over fifty thousand miles of telegraph lines connecting various cities in the United States. The vast West was spanned by a St. Louis to San Francisco telegraph that began operation in October

11-16 Telegraph transmitter and key. (Courtesy Amador County Museum)

1861 and required only a few minutes to send and receive a signal. Mail by Pony Express took ten to fourteen days. Prior to 1860 communications from the West Coast took an average of four to six months.

The first telephone was demonstrated in Germany in 1860 but received little recognition and was thought to be only a clever toy. Bell's version exhibited at Philadelphia's Centennial Exhibition in 1876 also received little notice. But through the young entrepreneur's persistence and salesmanship, the importance of this new invention was soon realized and the first private phones were installed in 1877.

The inventions of both Morse and Bell relied heavily on the principles and actions of electricity. Experiments in electricity had been taking place for many centuries, but electricity only came into the control of humankind with the invention of the cell battery in 1800. The first electric light bulb was invented in France in 1854, but practical lighting did not come into being until

improvements were made by Thomas Edison and J. W. Swann in 1880. Production of Ediswan electric lamps began in 1887.

Items relating to the earliest years of three of the world's most important inventions are, of course, quite valuable and highly collectible. Early telegraph keys seldom sell for less than $400 to $500. Early telephones, marked "Charles Williams," "American Bell," "National Bell," or "Bell-Blake," usually bring $1200 to $1500 and up. Early switchboards similarly marked bring $2000 and up.

Probably the most recognizable and affordable collectibles in this category are the porcelain and glass insulators by which telegraph, telephone, and electrical wires were attached to each pole. Highly sought by collectors are insulators without threaded interiors, which date from 1850 to 1870. Collectors should be aware that the design of many insulators made during the nineteenth century remained unchanged well into the twentieth century.

Price Ranges

Insulators: $35 to $250. Average: $50 to $75. Twentieth-century models are worth considerably less.

Telegraph instruments (post-1880): $45 to $250. Average: $125 to $150.

Telephones (common turn-of-the-century styles): $250 to $1000+. Average: $500 to $700. Pre-1898 models are worth considerably more.

Suggested Reading

Cranfill, Gary G., and Greg A. Kareofelas. *The Glass Insulator: A Comprehensive Reference.* Self-published, 1973.

Knappen, R. H. *History and Identification of Old Telephones,* 2 vols. Self-published, 1978.

————*Old Telephones Price Guide and Picture Index to History of Old Telephones.* Self-published, 1981.

Milholland, M. and E. Milholland. *Milholland's Final and Complete Glass Insulator Reference Book.* Self-published, 1971.

Woodward, N.R. *The Glass Insulator in America.* Self-published, 1973.

Tools

The Victorian period, the "age of invention," saw the birth of literally thousands of useful and useless tools and devices. A number of excellent tool collector's guide books only touch on the wide variety of items manufactured during the nineteenth century, suggesting that it might be beyond the scope of this book to do justice to this category. Even so, a number of definitively Victorian tools highly sought by collectors are worth noting.

Anvil—An anvil is a large, heavy piece of iron used as a solid base for hammering, pounding, and shaping. Anvils were used by jewelers, shoemakers, and, most commonly, blacksmiths. Dating anvils is difficult, although some marked with the name of a manufacturer can be traced to a particular time period. Size and novelty of shape are primary price factors.

Adze—An axlike tool with a flat arching blade, an adze is used primarily in the building of log cabins to flatten the tops and bottoms of logs, remove bark and knots, and notch the ends. Dating is difficult. Condition is the primary price factor.

Axe—Used for clearing land, chopping logs for homes, and splitting wood for fires, an axe occasionally was used also as a weapon. Collectors are especially drawn to broadaxes by known makers. Size and manufacturer are important in determining price.

Calipers—These were used whenever a small but precise measurement was required, calipers consist of two metal arms riveted together at one end. Those with arms curving outward were designed to measure inside diameters; those curving inward, outside diameters. Value is based on metal used (brass, copper, or steel) and size.

Drills and augers—Augers are basically large drill bits for boring holes in wood. The earliest examples have wooden handles and are screwed into the wood by hand. Two types of drills were used in the nineteenth century; the common crank-type, usually made of iron with wooden handles; and the eggbeater style, often made of brass. Prices are affected by size, materials, and condition.

Jacks—Even though wagon wheels never went flat, they did break, and changing them was no easy matter. The wagon or buggy jack was basically a well-braced, heavy metal lever. Many are marked with the date of manufacture. Original paint in good condition adds considerably to the value.

Levels—Early levels were made of wood with brass trim, and the leveling tubes made of clear glass with clear bubbles in a colored liquid. Collectors look for fine woods such as rosewood or ebony. Manufacturer and condition are also important price factors.

Planes—Used to smooth and shape the surface of wood, the plane was the Victorian cabinetmaker's primary tool. A wide variety of styles were produced with blades and configurations designed for specific woodworking functions. Prices are affected by style, manufacturer, type of wood and other materials used, and condition.

Saws—The bucksaw is a framed saw meant for use on logs or wood supported by sawhorses. A bow saw is similar but has a less-complicated, bow-shaped frame. Large trees were felled with a large flexible saw, called simply a "two-man saw," with wooden handles at each end. Saws with manufacturers' identification are sought. Condition is also a primary factor.

Spoke shave—A spoke shave is a sharp blade with a wooden handle at both ends used to carve and shape the wood spokes of wagon wheels. Manufacturer identification, shape, and condition are price factors.

Surveyor's transit—A high-quality telescopic instrument, with markings for angle and elevation, the surveyor's transit is used to survey and plot tracts of land. It usually is kept in a fitted wooden case. Prices are based primarily on materials used, manufacturer, and condition.

Wrenches—A wrench is a tool designed to tighten nuts and bolts. Early versions usually were designed to be used on a particular machine or device. Prices are based on size, style, and purpose, as well as type of metal, manufacturer, and condition.

Price Ranges

Adzes: $25 to $75. Average: $40.
Anvils: $35 to $100+. Average: $50.
Broad axes: $50 to $250+. Average: $75.
Calipers: $15 to $100+. Average: $85.
Levels: $20 to $250+. Average: $45 to $75.

Planes: $25 to $1500+. Average: $65 to $150. Prices in excess of $5000 have been paid for certain elaborate examples.
Saws: $25 to $250+. Average: $45.
Wagon Jacks: $75 to $250+. Average: $100 to $125.
Wrenches: $15 to $150. Average: $25 to $30.

Suggested Reading

Barlow, Ronald. *Antique Tool Collector's Guide*. El Cajon, Calif.: Windmill Publishing Company, 1987.

McNerney, Kathryn. *Antique Tools: Our American Heritage*. Paducah, Ky.: Collector Books, 1979.

Salaman, R. A. *Dictionary of Tools*. New York: Charles Scribner's Sons, 1974.

Washboards and Washing Machines

In America's pioneer years, women met at a local creek on wash day to engage in gossip while pounding their laundry between two rocks. While wash-day gossip came to an end with the invention of the washboard and tub, clothes were no doubt much cleaner. The washboard is basically a wooden frame surrounding a rippled surface made of glass, ceramic, or metal. Metal washboards were made in enamelware, graniteware, brass, tin, and zinc. The washboard saw continued use well into the twentieth century, despite the introduction of mechanical washers in the 1870s.

Washboards are widely collected by afficionados of Country antiques and folk art. Collectors are especially attracted to glass and porcelain examples and those with painted wooden frames. Prices are determined by size, style, materials used, manufacturer, and condition.

By the turn of the century most homes had some sort of washing machine. Most were simply wooden, tin, or enamelware tubs or boxes containing a set of wooden paddles attached to a hand crank. A variety of configurations were designed and manufactured by firms, who advertised "the latest and as we believe the best invention in washing machines yet made." Attached to or standing near the washer would be a wringer plus two wooden or rubber-coated rollers designed to squeeze excess water from clothing between washing and rinsing and before taking them to the line for drying.

Even though few washing machines from the nineteenth century have survived in good condition, prices are not terribly high due to low demand. Valuable examples are usually unusual configurations or first models from well-known manufacturers. Other price factors include materials used and condition of both finish and mechanics.

Price Ranges

Washboards: $10 to $125+. Average: $18 to $25.
Washing machines: $150 to $1500. Average: $285 to $325.

CHAPTER 12

Guide to Restoration, Preservation, and Storage

Restoration does not mean repair, although repair is part of the restoration process. To restore something is to make it look and act as it did during the initial period of its use. A camel-backed trunk that has been painted gold and black on the outside and wallpapered on the inside may look very nice, but it is even further from restoration than it was when it was just rusty metal and dirty wood. In order to restore something, you must first know what the item looked like when it was manufactured, then you must replicate that manufacturing process using modern methods and materials. It often is an arduous task, and sometimes it is even impossible. If you are not completely confident that you or the person you have retained to perform a restoration is capable of perfection in the task, it would be in the best interest of the artifact to simply protect it from further abuse and leave it as is.

In the real world, of course, cleaning and repairs are attempted by nonprofessionals every day. This chapter has been included for just those people, to help them do the best they can. It familiarizes the reader with the types of materials used in nineteenth-century furniture and artifacts. It explains what may have caused damage to an item, how the damage can be arrested or

reversed, and how to protect the item from future damage or abuse. The best advice to any prospective restorationist probably is *don't rush*. Many wonderful antiques have been ruined by a quickie repair or refinishing.

Wood

Types

Apple, ash, birch, box, cedar, ebony, elm, mahogany, maple, oak, olive, pine, satinwood, sycamore, walnut, and exotic imports.

Finishes

Bird's-eye—Circle pattern formed by cutting through knots in the wood, especially maple.

Ebonized—Darkly stained to resemble ebony wood.

Marquetry—Inlays of contrasting veneered woods set into patterns.

Oiled—Woods with an oil finish are usually quite soft.

Painted—Pigmented applications cover the natural grain of the wood and may bleed into the pores on its surface, making it difficult if not impossible to completely remove.

Parquet—Geometric patterns of inlaid wood.

Varnish—Woods with shellacked or varnished finishes usually exhibit some degree of gloss and may yellow with age.

Veneer—Thin sheets of finished wood glued to the surface.

Waxed—Woods with a waxed finish generally retain the natural appearance of unfinished wood.

Enemies

Excessive moisture, excessive dryness, insects, fungus, fire, and mistreatment or vandalism.

Repairs

Scratches and nicks in wood can sometimes be made to swell back to the original level of the surface by the application of steam; however, the side effects can be disastrous. Putty and crayon fillers never look natural and seldom are permanent. Some light blemishes can be made less apparent by the careful application of an appropriately colored shoe wax.

Rings and "foggy" spots were caused by moisture on the surface of the object. If you can't live with the blemish, it can only be removed by altering or refinishing the surface. Once you have made that decision first try an application of denatured alcohol, rubbing the area gently to blend it with the surrounding finish. If these results are not satisfactory, then a complete refinishing of the surface is required.

Loose joints may be reglued, but make sure the old glue is removed completely, and use only a high-quality glue designed specifically for wood. Hold the joint together with a clamp or clamps and check it periodically throughout the drying process to make sure it hasn't slipped. Protect the wood from indentations by placing a small piece of acrylic plastic between the clamp and the surface. Use only a bead of glue—do not allow it to squeeze out onto the finish.

Refinishing

Refinishing consists of removing old paint or varnish and replacing it with a modern finish of similar appearance. Before undertaking the refinishing of a piece of antique furniture or other wooden artifact, you should be aware of certain factors: first, the history etched into the object's surface will be lost forever; second, paint and varnish strippers can cause the wood to deteriorate, blanch, or permanently discolor; third, they are highly toxic and dangerous; and finally, making a new finish look old-fashioned requires a thorough knowledge of materials and methods and patient, painstaking hand labor.

Cleaning and Protecting

Before cleaning any piece of furniture or wooden artifact, take a lightly dampened cloth and carefully test a small area to see how the finish reacts to water and how much of the finish is removed by the cleaning. If the result seems acceptable, the entire object may be wiped down with a clean white cotton cloth and plain water. Be careful not to overwet the surface, and use a dry cloth to remove residual moisture immediately. If the results of this cleaning are not satisfactory, a small amount of nondetergent soap may be added to the water. (Do not use commercial furniture cleaners containing oil or petroleum distillates, as these may damage or even remove the original finish.) If results are still not satisfactory, try a cloth lightly dampened with denatured alcohol—but remember that this will likely remove a small amount of the finish as well. After cleaning, reapply a clean cloth dampened with clear water followed by a dry cloth.

Paint, varnish, shellac, and wax are protective finishes; oil is not. Oil penetrates the pores once filled with water and thereby softens the wood. If you wish to give additional protection to an antique wooden surface, a good-quality beeswax, carnauba, or microcrystalline wax is the best choice. Apply the wax to a cloth first, then apply the cloth to the wood. For items receiving daily use apply several coats of wax, buffing thoroughly between applications. Colored shoe waxes can take the place of a stain and varnish combination, providing natural-looking color and protection in one step. Be aware that the colors obtained from one particular can of wax will vary widely, depending on the surface to which it is applied. Test first.

Storage

Wood reacts adversely to extremes in moisture or dryness, resulting in warping or rot. Therefore, wooden antiques should be stored in an area with a reasonable amount of humidity control. Items to be stored should be wrapped in breatheable cloth—definitely not in plastic or nylon. They should be kept safe from jostling and wood-boring insects; however, do not allow insecticides to contact the surface of the wood.

Metal

Types

Iron, steel, copper, nickel, tin, lead, pewter, gold, silver, platinum, and a variety of base or combination metals.

Finishes

Blued—Used primarily for guns and other weapons, bluing is a somewhat protective finish created by the application of heat and/or acids to steel and resulting in a blue- or brown-colored finish.

Enameled—Sturdy, baked-on enamel finishes were used on kitchen items and other functional pieces.

Painted—A wide variety of decorative painted finishes were used, including the artistic hand application of scenes and patterns.

Plated—The invention of electroplating early in the nineteenth century introduced the ability to apply a coating of one metal to another through electrolysis. Common types are silver plate, gold plate, brass plate, and galvanized zinc.

Polished—Many metal objects were given a simple and natural polished finish, which allows the natural beauty of the metal to show. Some of these metals develop a discoloration known as "patina," which some collectors find attractive.

Varnished—Metals that are highly susceptible to tarnishing or discoloration were often given a protective coat of clear varnish.

Enemies

Except for gold, all the metals discussed in this section are to some degree susceptible to the following: excessive moisture, acids (from fingers, wrappings, and so forth), oxides (from wrappings and polluted air), salts (from fingers, wrappings, and sea air), and dents and abrasions.

Repairs

Probably the most common repair undertaken on metal objects is the replacement of broken hinges, latches, rings, or mechanical parts. In some cases modern replicas of these parts are available (trunk hardware, jewelry catches, furniture knobs and handles, and others). In other cases someone will have to produce the piece from raw materials. This person should, of course, possess a high degree of aptitude and skill so that the replicated piece looks and acts exactly like the original piece.

Breaks and tears in metal only can be repaired by the application of extreme heat or solders and welds. The use of these methods may improve the function of a piece but seldom improve its appearance. There are those with the patience and ability to finish a soldered or welded piece so that the repair is virtually unnoticeable. However, repairs by these persons are usually appropriately expensive.

Refinishing, Cleaning, and Protection

Metal objects without painted or applied finishes can be washed in soap and water, but items made of iron, steel, and tin must be quickly and thoroughly dried to avoid the formation of rust. Cleaned metal should be given some sort of protective coating immediately. Almost all metal objects (except for gold and silver) benefit from a protective coating of light oil. A good-quality carnauba or microcrystalline wax lasts longer and is less messy than oil but is more difficult to remove, should the need arise.

Two of the most common cleaning problems are rust on iron, steel, and tin; and tarnish on brass, silver, and copper. Rust can be avoided by keeping the metal object away from moisture, but once it starts it is difficult to stop. Removing rust usually requires the use of chemicals or abrasives that also remove the natural tone or patina of old metal. Commercial rust removers are often highly acidic and toxic. Also, removal of deep-seated rust by chemical action often leaves the metal heavily pitted. It is sometimes best just to leave the rust alone and arrest its spread by applying oils or waxes. Never paint over rust. If the object requires repainting, all rust must be completely removed first.

The beauty of natural patinas on silver, brass, and copper are in the eye of the beholder. Natural tarnish generally gives character to a piece: it makes an antique item *look* antique. However, here is a case where restoration is quite simple. All of these metals if uncoated usually can be cleaned by a simple polishing. Do not use commercial cleaners containing acids, chlorides, or harsh abrasives. Especially avoid dip-type cleaners. The safest polishes are simply made of alcohol and precipitated chalk, talc, or diatomaceous earth. These should be applied with a plain cotton ball or pad. Keep in mind that each time a metal object is polished, some degree of metal is removed. If the object is plated you can easily polish the surface metal away in a very short time.

Storage

All metal objects should be stored in a dry environment. Wrappings should be free of acids, salts, or other corrosives. (Acid-free archival paper is best.)

Paper

Types

Tissue, stationery, newspapers, books, magazines, documents, photographs, and papier-maché.

Enemies

Excessive moisture or dryness, light, insects, stains, tears, adhesives, skin salts and acids, metal fasteners, mold, and the internal properties of the paper itself.

Cleaning and Repairs

Most old papers are extremely fragile and require the highest degree of care and attention. Documents that have survived for hundreds of years have been destroyed in seconds by careless handling. Hands should be thoroughly washed, and clean white cotton gloves should be worn. Loose surface dirt should be gently removed with a soft brush or cotton ball. Be careful not to abrade the surface of the paper. Removal of stains should be attempted only by a professional conservator, and even he or she will probably recommend that it be left alone.

Two of the most detrimental things to old paper are tape and glue. They contain acids that stain paper and cause irreparable damage to its structure. If the paper is fragile there is very little that can be done. One method that can be used on strong surfaces is heating the tape carefully with a hair dryer, then slowly peeling it away.

201

However, excessive heat can discolor paper and there is always the danger of fire. Careful practice and testing is recommended first. Tape residue and difficult spots of dirt may be removed with a soft artist's eraser but, again, use caution and test first.

Tears should be left alone if possible. If the care and appreciation of the item requires repair, specific types of archival tapes or adhesives can be used. These are available through archival supply houses such as those listed at the end of this chapter. Book repairs should be left to the professional. Most major cities have bookbinders who specialize in rebinding old books.

Storage

All folded letters and documents should be unfolded and placed in archival folders or boxes with acid-free interleaving tissue between each item. All staples or metal clips must be removed. Documents that may see extensive handling should be placed in clear Mylar sleeves for protection, but they must be continuously checked for condensation or mold growth. Letters and documents should always be stored flat, never on end.

A framed document should be mounted onto an archival mounting board with a hinged mat to provide a protective space between the document and the glass. Glass or acrylic sheets designed to filter ultraviolet rays will help keep documents from fading and avoid other problems caused by continuous exposure to light.

Rare books should be handled as seldom as possible, and then only with clean hands and the utmost care. The greatest damage to old books occurs when they are removed from the shelf and opened. Never pull an old book from the shelf by the top of its spine. When opening a book support the spine with one hand and don't open it flat. Always keep the front and back of the book at an angle to the spine.

Glass and Ceramics

Types

Blown glass, pressed glass, cut glass, leaded glass, earthenware, stoneware, redware, yellowware, ironstone, and porcelain.

Forms

Bottles, jugs, crocks, cups, plates, drinking vessels, bowls, vases, statuary, lamps, and a variety of other decorative and functional pieces.

Enemies

Thermal shock (quick changes of temperature), fragmentization (crazing or breakage).

Repairs

Proper repair of a glass or ceramic item requires that all pieces, even the tiniest fragments, be carefully collected and kept safe until reconstruction begins. Several sizes of tweezers and clamps should be used, but the most important tool is the adhesive. While new adhesives are constantly being developed, the consensus is that nothing yet is better for repairing glass and ceramics than epoxy glue.

Epoxy comes in two parts: a resin and a hardener. Once the glue is mixed the user must complete the repairs within a designated "pot life"— the amount of time between mixing and setting. If the work is not complete, a new batch of epoxy must be mixed.

Of primary importance in repairing glass or ceramic objects is patience. The proper piece must be located, a very thin layer of glue applied, then the piece must be held in place until the next part of the puzzle is added. It must be right the first time, because epoxies are permanent. Tools, fingers, and the inside and outside surfaces of the object must be kept free from glue residue throughout the process. To hold the object in place during repair, use a cardboard box or dish-pan filled with sand.

Cleaning

Clean glass and sealed ceramics with plain soap and water. Use a plastic bucket or dishpan so that there is less chance of breakage if you slip. Glass containers with dried deposits on the inside should be allowed to soak overnight in a mixture of fabric softener and dishwashing detergent. The next day place a few metal BBs in with the mixture and gently roll them around over the coated area. Do not use the BB method on thin or exceptionally fragile glass. Always make sure glass or ceramic objects are completely dry before storing them or placing them on display.

Storage

Glass and ceramic objects can be given maximum protection from breakage by wrapping them first in archival tissue, then in bubble wrap or multiple layers of newspaper. Do not place newspaper directly on glass and ceramic items, as they will then require rewashing and unnecessary handling. Additional protection for stored breakables can be given by placing each object in its own compartment, made by taping cardboard dividers into a storage box. Mark all containers in large red letters: FRAGILE—DO NOT DROP OR CRUSH! Written warnings usually receive more attention than preprinted labels.

Leather

Types

Buckskin, suede, split, patent, rawhide, chamois, deerskin, pigskin, russet, and moroccan.

Enemies

Moisture, mold and mildew, excessive heat and dryness, insects, salts, acids, oils (except oil-tanned leathers), tape, and rough handling.

Repairs

Torn leather can be repaired only by attaching it to a reinforcement piece or by sewing it together. Neither remedy will restore the original appearance of the piece. Some faded, stained; or scuffed leathers benefit from treatment with an appropriately colored wax-type shoe polish. However, areas of the leather that are highly polished, glued, or treated will not accept the color.

Cleaning and Protection

Hard-surfaced leathers can be cleaned with a mild solution of common saddlesoap and water. Avoid overwetting and apply an appropriate leather dressing as soon as the object is dry. Mink oil, the favorite leather treatment for centuries, may be beneficial to some leathers but detrimental to others. Conservators now recommend the newly developed microcrystalline waxes preceded by a treatment with LNO dressing to loosen stiff leather and protect it.

Storage

Leather items not in use or on display should be treated, waxed, and wrapped in archival tissue. Items should be stored in an acid-free box away from any moisture or excessive heat.

Archival Supply Sources

For archival wrapping tissue, interleaving papers, mounting boards, glues, tapes, Mylar sleeves, microcrystalline waxes, boxes, desiccant, and so forth, contact:
Light Impressions Corporation
439 Monroe Ave.
Rochester, NY 14607-3717.
Conservation Materials, Ltd.
340 Freeport Blvd.
Box 2884
Sparks, NV 89431.

Appendix

Museums

This partial listing is provided to give the collector an idea of the wide variety of museums throughout the United States that present historical displays relating to the Victorian era. Although this list was comprised from numerous sources, it only touches on the large number of museums that can be visited in each state, including many privately owned Victorian homes that are open to the public. A more thorough listing is available from the individual state chambers of commerce.

Alabama
Museums of the City of Mobile, Mobile

Alaska
Alaska State Museum, Juneau
Anchorage Museum of History and Art, Anchorage

Arizona
Arizona Historical Society, Tucson and Phoenix
Rosson House, Phoenix

Arkansas
Arkansas Museum of Art and History, Little Rock
Old Fort Museum, Fort Smith

California
Amador County Museum, Jackson
Bernhard Museum, Auburn
California Museum of Photography, Riverside
California State Railroad Museum, Sacramento
Civic Center Museum, San Francisco
Gamble House, Pasadena
General Phineas Banning Residence, Wilmington
Haas-Lilienthal House, San Francisco
Hollyhock House, Los Angeles
J. Paul Getty Museum, Malibu
Lace Museum, Mountain View
McHenry Mansion, Modesto
Museum of Vintage Fashion, Lafayette
National Maritime Museum, San Francisco
Oakland Museum, Oakland
San Diego Historical Society Museum, San Diego
San Jose Historical Museum, San Jose
Whittier Mansion, San Francisco

Colorado
Colorado Historical Museum, Denver
Rosemount House Museum, Pueblo

Connecticut
American Clock and Watch Museum, Bristol
Connecticut Historical Society, Hartford
Lockwood-Mathews Mansion, Norwalk
Mark Twain House, Hartford

Mystic Seaport Museum, Mystic
Scott-Fanton Museum, Danbury
Stamford Historical Society, Stamford
Tobacco Museum, Greenwich
Wadsworth Atheneum, Hartford
Winchester Center Kerosene Lamp Museum, Winchester Center

Delaware
Delaware State Museum, Dover
Rookwood Museum, Wilmington

District of Columbia
Smithsonian Institute National Museum of American History, Washington
Washington Dolls House and Toy Museum, Washington

Florida
Historical Museum of South Florida, Miami
Museum of Florida History, Tallahassee
Pensacola Historical Museum, Pensacola

Georgia
Atlanta Historical Society Museum, Atlanta
Augusta County Museum, Augusta
Columbus Museum, Columbus
Museum of Georgia Folk Culture, Atlanta
Toy Museum of Atlanta, Atlanta

Hawaii
Hawaii Bottle Museum, Honolulu
Mission Houses Museum, Honolulu
The Sterling Collection, Bardstown

Idaho
Idaho State Historical Museum, Boise
Museum of Northern Idaho, Coeur d'Alene

Illinois
Austin Village, Chicago
Chicago Historical Society, Chicago
Illinois State Museum, Springfield
Museum of Science and Industry, Chicago
Wilmette Historical House, Wilmette

Indiana
Ball Corporation Museum, Muncie
Indiana State Museum, Indianapolis
Spring Mill State Park, Mitchell

Iowa
Sioux City Public Museum, Sioux City
State Historical Museum, Des Moines
State Historical Society, Iowa City

Kansas
Boot Hill Museum, Dodge City
Kansas Museum of History, Topeka
Santa Fe Trail Center, Larned

Kentucky
Appalachian Museum, Berea
Barton Museum of Whiskey History, Bardstown
Kentucky Museum, Bowling Green
Museum of History and Science, Louisville

Louisiana
Gallier House Museum, New Orleans
Historical Pharmacy Museum, New Orleans
Historic New Orleans Collection, New Orleans
Lafayette Museum, Lafayette
Louisiana State Museum, New Orleans and Shreveport
R.W. Norton Art Gallery, Shreveport

Maine
Colonel Black Mansion, Ellsworth
Maine State Museum, Augusta
Old Gaol Museum, York
Reddington Museum, Waterville
Ruggles House, Columbia Falls
The Shaker Museum, New Gloucester
Victoria Mansion, Portland

Maryland
Baltimore Museum of Industry, Baltimore
B & O Railroad Museum, Baltimore
Carroll County Farm Museum, Westminster
Maryland Historical Society, Baltimore

Massachusetts
Hancock Shaker Village, Hancock
Historic Deerfield, Deerfield
Kendall Whaling Museum, Sharon
Longfellow House, Cambridge
Museum of Transportation, Boston
Old Sturbridge Village, Sturbridge
Salem Children's Museum, Salem
Sandwich Glass Museum, Sandwich
Society for the Preservation of New England Antiquities, Boston
Wenham Historical Museum, Wenham
Yesteryear's Museum, Sandwich

Michigan
Detroit Historical Museum, Detroit
Henry Ford Museum, Dearborn
Manistee County Museum, Manistee
Monroe County Museum, Monroe

Minnesota
Gibbs Farm Museum, St. Paul
Lake Superior Museum of Transportation, Duluth

Missouri
Doheny Museum, Perryville
Kansas City Museum, Kansas City
Museum of History, St. Louis
National Museum of Transportation, St. Louis
Phelps County Museum, Rolla
Pony Express Museum, St. Joseph
St. Louis Medical Museum, St. Louis

Montana
Museum of the Rockies, Boreman
World Museum of Mining, Butte

Nebraska
Nebraska State Historical Society, Lincoln
Stuhr Museum of the Prairie Pioneer, Grand Island
Western Heritage Museum, St. Joseph

Nevada
Clark County Heritage Museum, Las Vegas
Churchill County Museum, Fallon
Nevada State Museum, Carson City
Northeast Nevada Museum, Elko

New Hampshire
Franklin Pierce Homestead, Hillsboro
Goodwin Mansion, Portsmouth
New Hampshire Historical Society, Concord
St. Gaudens House, Cornish Mills
Thomas Bailey Aldrich House, Portsmouth

New Jersey
Burlington County Historical Society, Burlington
Newark Museum, Newark
New Jersey State Museum, Trenton
Raggedy Ann Antique Toy and Doll Museum, Flemington
Thomas Edison Home, West Orange
Wheaton Museum of American Glass, Millville

New Mexico
Albuquerque Museum, Albuquerque
Los Alamos Historical Museum, Los Alamos
Museum of New Mexico, Santa Fe

New York
Albany Institute of History and Art, Albany
American Numismatic Museum, New York City
Carriage Museum, Stony Brook
Cooper-Hewitt Museum, New York City
Corning Museum of Glass, Corning
George Eastman House, Rochester
Huntington Historical Society, Huntington
International Museum of Photography, Rochester
Jefferson County Historical Museum, Watertown
Margaret Woodbury Strong Museum, Rochester
Mills Mansion, Staatsburg
Museum of American Folk Art, New York City
Museum of the City of New York, New York City
National Bottle Museum, Ballston Spa
New York State Historical Society, Cooperstown
Seneca Falls Historical Society, Seneca Falls
Shaker Museum, Chatham
Suffolk County Historical Museum, Riverhead

North Carolina
Greensboro Historical Museum, Greensboro
Mint Museum of History, Charlotte
North Carolina State Museum, Raleigh

North Dakota
State Historical Society, Bismarck

Ohio
Blair Museum of Lithopanes, Toledo
Dittrick Museum of Medical History, Cleveland
East Liverpool Historical Society, East Liverpool
Ohio Historical Society, Columbus
Warren County Historical Society, Lebanon
Western Reserve Historical Society, Cleveland

Oklahoma
Eliza Cruce Hall Doll Museum, Denver
Museum of Pioneer History, Chandler
State Museum, Oklahoma City

Oregon
Columbia River Maritime Museum, Astoria
Klamath County Museum, Klamath Falls
Oregon Historical Society, Portland
Tillamook County Pioneer Museum, Tillamook

Pennsylvania
Bucks County Historical Society, Doylestown
Chester County Historical Society, West Chester
Fairmount Park Historic Houses, Philadelphia
Gettysburg Visitors Center, Gettysburg
History Museum of Philadelphia, Philadelphia
Landis Valley Museum, Lancaster
Mary Merritt Doll and Toy Museum, Douglassville
Perelman Antique Toy Museum, Philadelphia
State Museum, Harrisburg
Toy Train Museum, Strasburg

Rhode Island
Blithewold Gardens and Arboretum, Bristol
Newport Historical Society, Newport
Rhode Island Historical Society, Providence

South Carolina
Historic Charleston, Charleston
State Museum, Columbia

South Dakota
Overstate Western Heritage Museum, Vermillion
Shrine to Music Museum, Vermillion

Tennessee
Museum of Tobacco Art and History, Nashville
National Knife Museum, Chattanooga
State Museum, Nashville

Texas
Bayou Bend Collection, Museum of Fine Arts; Houston
Carter Amon Museum, Fort Worth
Panhandle Plains Historical Museum, Canyon

Vermont
Bennington Museum, Bennington
Shelburne Museum, Shelburne
Vermont Museum, Montpelier

Virginia
Chrysler Museum, Norfolk
Mariner's Museum, Newport News
Museum of the Confederacy, Richmond
National Tobacco and Textile Museum, Danville
Stabler-Leadbeater Apothecary Shop, Alexandria
Valentine Museum, Richmond

Washington
Museum of History and Industry, Seattle
Washington State Historical Society, Tacoma
Washington State Museum, Olympia

West Virginia
West Virginia State Museum, Charleston

Wisconsin
Bergstrom-Mahler Museum, Neenah
Cochrane-Nelson House, Westfield
Milwaukee Public Museum, Milwaukee
State Historical Society, Madison
Swarthout Memorial Museum, LaCrosse

Wyoming
Buffalo Bill History Center, Cody
Fremont County Pioneer Museum, Lander
Old Fort Laramie, Fort Laramie
State Museum, Cheyenne
Sweetwater County Historical Museum, Green River

Collector's Clubs

This partial listing is provided to give the reader an idea of the wide variety of clubs and organizations throughout the United States that provide interaction with fellow collectors and help to keep one abreast of recent finds and developments in a chosen specialty. Although this list was comprised from numerous sources, it only touches on the large number of clubs that have been established. Our apologies to those who have been missed.

The collector should be aware that clubs are constantly being formed and disbanded. A listing here does not necessarily mean that the organization still exists or has not moved. It is suggested that a self-addressed, stamped envelope be included with any inquiry to help ensure an answer.

American Bell Association
    Route 1, Box 286, Natronia Heights, PA 15065
American Cut Glass Association
    23570 Letchworth Rd., Beachwood, OH 44122
American Game Collectors Association
    4628 Barlow Dr., Bartlesville, OK 74006
American Graniteware Collectors Association
    525 Hawthorn Pl. #1201, Chicago, IL 60657
American Historical Print Collectors
    555 Fifth Ave. #504, New York, NY 10017
American Lock Collectors
    14010 Cardwell St., Livonia, MI 48154
American Musical Instrument Society
    USD Box 194, Vermillion, SD 57069
American Numismatic Association (coins)
    P.O. Box 2366, Colorado Springs, CO 80901
American Philatelic Association (stamps)
    P.O. Box 800, State College, PA 16801
American Photographic Historical Society
    520 West 44th St., New York, NY 10036
Antique and Historic Glass Foundation
    P.O. Box 7413, Toledo, OH 43615
Antique Phonograph Collectors Club
    502 E. 17th St., Brooklyn, NY 11226
Antique Valentines Association
    P.O. Box 178, Marlboro, NJ 07746

Association for Recorded Sound Collectors
    P.O. Box 1643, Manassas, VA 22110
Association of American Military Uniform Collectors
    446 Berkshire Rd., Elyria, OH 44035
Collector's Circle (thimbles)
    1313 S. Killian Dr., Lake Park, FL 33403
Company of Military Historians
    North Main St., Westbrook, CT 06498
Daguerreian Society (daguerreotypes)
    203 W. Clarence, Lake Charles, LA 70601
Doll Collectors of America
    14 Chestnut Rd., Westford, MA 01886
Early American Industries Association (tools)
    P.O. Box 2128, Empire State Plaza Station, Albany, NY 12220
East Bay Fan Guild
    P.O. Box 1054, El Cerrito, CA 94530
Ephemera Society
    124 Elm St., Bennington, VT 05201
Federation of Historical Bottle Clubs
    10118 Schuessler St., St. Louis, MO 63128
Happy Hours Brotherhood (paper Americana)
    87 School St., Fall River, MA 02720
International Club for Collectors of
Hatpins and Holders
    15237 Chanera Ave., Gardenia, CA 90249
International Postcard Collector's Association
    6380 Wilshire #907, Los Angeles, CA 90048
International Society of Bible Collectors
    P.O. Box 2485, El Cajon, CA 92021
International Stamp Collectors Society
    6253 Hollywood Blvd., Hollywood, CA 90028
Lewis Carroll Society
    617 Rockford Rd., Silver Springs, MD 20902
Lithophane Collectors Club
    2032 Robinwood Ave., Toledo, OH 43620
Manuscript Society
    P.O. Box 27, Alhambra, CA 91802
Marble Collector's Society
    P.O. Box 222, Trumbull, CT 06611
Mechanical Bank Collectors
    P.O. Box 189, Beverly, NJ 08010
Music Box Society
    P.O. Box 202 Route 3, Morgantown, IN 46160
National Association of Paper and Advertising
Collectors
    P.O. Box 471, Columbia, PA 17512

National Association of Watch and Clock Collectors
P.O. Box 33, Columbia, PA 17512
National Button Society
2722 Juno Pl., Akron, OH 44313
National Insulator Association
126 N.W. 144th St., Miami, FL 33150
National Knife Collectors Association
P.O. Box 21070, Chattanooga, TN 37421
National Sheet Music Society
P.O. Box 2901, Pasadena, CA 91125
National Valentine Collectors Association
111 E. Cubbon St., Santa Ana, CA 92701
Paperweight Collectors Association
761 Chestnut St., Santa Cruz, CA 95060
Pewter Collectors Club of America
15 Indian Trail, Woodbridge, CT 06515
Pipe Collectors International
P.O. Box 22085, 6172 Airways Blvd., Chattanooga, TN 73422
Postcard History Association
P.O. Box 3610, Baltimore, MD 21214
Railroad Enthusiasts
456 Main St., West Townsend, MA 01474
Railroadiana Collectors Association
3363 Riviera West Dr., Kelseyville, CA 95451
Sadiron Collectors Club
500 Adventureland Dr., Altoona, IA 50009
Society of Inkwell Collectors
5136 Thomas Ave. So., Minneapolis, MN 55410
Society of Philatelic Americans
P.O. Box 34, Skokie, IL 60076
Society of Philatelists and Numismatists
1929 Millis St., Montebello, CA 90640
Steamship History Society
170 Westminster #1103, Providence, RI 02903
Telephone Collectors International
P.O. Box 700165, San Antonio, TX 78270
Thimble Collectors International
P.O. Box 2311, Des Moines, IA 50310
Thimble Collectors International
P.O. Box 143, Intervale, NH 03845
Tin Container Collectors Association
11650 Riverside Dr., North Hollywood, CA 91602
United Federation of Doll Clubs
2814 Herron Ln., Glenshaw, PA 15116
Universal Autograph Collectors Club
P.O. Box 467, Rockville Center, NY 11571

Victorian Society of America
East Washington Square, Philadelphia, PA 19106
Western Photographica Collectors Association
P.O. Box 4294, Whittier, CA 90607

Periodicals

This partial listing is provided to give the reader an idea of the variety of antique-, collectible-, and Victorian-related magazines and newsletters that currently are being published in the United States. Although this list was current at the time of this writing, the collector should be aware that new magazines are constantly coming on the scene and old ones occasionally fall by the wayside. Our apologies to any publications that were missed in this listing.

American Collector
P.O. Drawer C, Kermit, TX 79745
American Philatelist
P.O. Box 800, State College, PA 16801
Americana
381 W. Center St., Marion, OH 43302
Antique and Auction News
Box B, Murietta, PA 17547
Antique and Collector's Mart
15100 W. Kellogg, Wichita, KS 67235
Antique Review
P.O. Box 538, Worthington, OH 43085
Antique Toy World
4419 Irving Park Ave., Chicago, IL 60641
Antique Trader
P.O. Box 1050, Dubuque, IA 52001
Antique Trader Weekly
P.O. Box 1050, Dubuque, IA 52001
Antiques
551 5th Ave., New York, NY 10017
Antiques and Collecting Hobbies
1006 S. Michigan Ave., Chicago, IL 60605
Antiques Journal
4 Church St., Ware, MA 01082
Antiques World
P.O. Box 900, Farmingdale, NY 11737
California Collector
P.O. Box 812, Carmichael, CA 95608

Clockwise
   1236 E. Main, Ventura, CA 93001
Coin World
   P.O. Box 150, Sidney, OH 45367
Collector News
   P.O. Box 156, Grundy Center, IA 50638
Collector's Showcase
   P.O. Box 837, Tulsa, OK 74101
MidAtlantic Antiques Magazine
   P.O. Box 908, Henderson, NC 27536
National Glass and Pottery Journal
   P.O. Box 3121, Wescosville, PA 18106
Paper Americana
   736 N. Frazier St., Baldwin Park, CA 91706

Southern Antiques
   P.O. Box 1550, Lake City, FL 32055
Spinning Wheel
   Fame Ave., Hanover, PA 17331
Victoria
   P.O. Box 7115, Red Oak, IA 51591
Victorian Accents
   P.O. Box 508, Mt. Morris, IL 61054
Victorian Homes
   P.O. Box 61, Millers Falls, MA 01349
Victorian Sampler
   P.O. Box 546, St. Charles, IL 60174
West Coast Peddler
   P.O. Box 5134, Whittier, CA 90607

Index